First book of [illegible]'s Kitchen collection :)

the complete book of italian cooking

the complete book of italian cooking

Explore the authentic taste of Italy in over 200 fabulous recipes shown step-by-step in more than 800 stunning photographs

Carla Capalbo

HH
HERMES
HOUSE

Publisher: Joanna Lorenz
Project Editor: Lindsay Porter
Designers: Patrick McLeavey and Jo Brewer
Photographer: Amanda Heywood
Assistant Home Economists: Marilyn Forbes, Beverly Le Blanc, Wallace Heim

PUBLISHER'S NOTE
Although the advice and information in this book are believed to be accurate and true at the time of going to press, neither the authors nor the publisher can accept any legal responsibility or liability for any errors or omissions that may be made nor for any inaccuracies nor for any harm or injury that comes about from following instructions or advice in this book.

Previously published as *Italian*.

This edition is published by Hermes House, an imprint of Anness Publishing Ltd, Hermes House, 88–89 Blackfriars Road, London SE1 8HA;
tel. 020 7401 2077; fax 020 7633 9499

www.hermeshouse.com; www.annesspublishing.com

If you like the images in this book and would like to investigate using them for publishing, promotions or advertising, please visit our website www.practicalpictures.com for more information.

ETHICAL TRADING POLICY
Because of our ongoing ecological investment programme, you, as our customer, can have the pleasure and reassurance of knowing that a tree is being cultivated on your behalf to naturally replace the materials used to make the book you are holding. For further information about this scheme, go to www.annesspublishing.com/trees

ETHICAL TRADING POLICY
Because of our ongoing ecological investment programme, you, as our customer, can have the pleasure and reassurance of knowing that a tree is being cultivated on your behalf to naturally replace the materials used to make the book you are holding. For further information about this scheme, go to www.annesspublishing.com/trees

NOTES
For all recipes, quantities are given in both metric and imperial measures and, where appropriate, measures are also given in standard cups and spoons. Follow one set, but not a mixture, because they are not interchangeable.

Standard spoon and cup measures are level.
1 tsp = 5ml, 1 tbsp = 15ml, 1 cup = 250ml/8fl oz
Australian standard tablespoons are 20ml. Australian readers should use 3 tsp in place of 1 tbsp for measuring small quantities of gelatine, cornflour, salt, etc.

Medium eggs are used unless otherwise stated.

Contents

Introduction 6

Antipasti and Soups 14

Vegetables 42

Pasta 76

Rice, Polenta, Eggs and Cheese 122

Pizzas, Pastries and Bread 152

Fish and Shellfish 180

Meat, Poultry and Game 200

Desserts 232

Index 253

Introduction

Italy is a country of great diversity. Its long Mediterranean coastline encloses a landscape of fertile plains, forest-covered mountains and arid rocks. From the hot, dry south to the cool Alpine foothills, the climate varies markedly. So do the local crops: rice, maize and ham are northern staples, while olives, durum wheat and tomatoes thrive in the southern heat.

Italy's many kingdoms, states and duchies were unified as a nation in 1861. Each region had distinct linguistic and cultural differences, still present in the culinary practices today. Despite the advent of industrialization and mass-marketing, traditional foods are still central to the cultural identity of each region. This is partly due to the way in which recipes are learned: orally passed from generation to generation, and rarely written down in cookbooks, they survive in families for years with little or no change made to them.

A great deal of Italian food comes from this *contadino*, or peasant, heritage. The best combines fresh ingredients with simple cooking techniques. Meats, fish and vegetables are flavoured with herbs and olive oil, and often grilled or baked. Aromatic sauces can often be assembled in the time it takes pasta to boil. Many of these recipes can be prepared quickly and economically.

The Italian diet, which is high in vegetables and carbohydrates and low in animal fat, is a healthy one. It also tastes exceptionally good.

Fresh Produce

Italian cooking is based on the creative use of fresh, seasonal ingredients. Vegetables and herbs play central roles in almost every aspect of the menu. In the markets, there is a sense of anticipation at the beginning of each new season, heralded by the arrival, on the beautifully displayed stalls, of the year's first artichokes, olives, chestnuts or wild mushrooms. Seasonal recipes come to the fore and make the most of available produce.

Many of the vegetables once considered exotically Mediterranean are now readily available in the markets and supermarkets of most countries. Fennel and aubergine, peppers, courgettes and radicchio are now increasingly present in pasta sauces, soups and pizzas, as well as wonderful accents to meat and fish.

Wherever you shop, look for the freshest possible fruits and vegetables. Choose unblemished, firm, sun-ripened produce, preferably locally or organically grown. Fresh herbs like basil, parsley and sage are easy to cultivate in window boxes and gardens and have an infinitely finer flavor than their dried counterparts. Italian cuisine is not a complicated or sophisticated style of cooking, but your recipes will benefit immeasurably by starting with the best quality ingredients you can find.

Below: *Italian cuisine does not rely on unusual produce, but it must be as fresh as possible.*

Store Cupboard Ingredients

Perhaps the single most important ingredient in a modern Italian kitchen is olive oil. The fruity flavour of a fine extra-virgin olive oil perfumes any dish it is used in, from pesto sauce to the simplest salad dressing. Buy the best olive oil you can afford: one bottle goes a long way and makes a huge difference to any recipe.

Balsamic vinegar has only recently become widely available outside of Italy. Made by the slow wood-aging process of wine vinegar, the finest varieties are deliciously mellow and fragrant. The taste is quite sweet and concentrated, so only a little is needed.

Porcini mushrooms are found in the woods in various parts of Europe in autumn. They can be eaten cooked fresh, or sliced thinly and dried in the sun or in special ovens. A few dried porcini soaked in water adds a deliciously woodsy flavour.

Olives are one of Italy's most wonderful native ingredients. Unfortunately, freshly cured olives do not travel very well, and many of the most delicious varieties are not available outside the Mediterranean. Sample canned or bottled olives before adding them to sauces as they sometimes acquire an unpleasant metallic taste that could spoil the flavor of the dish.

A typical Italian store cupboard also contains a supply of dried, natural ingredients. Dried beans, lentils and grains are stored in air-tight dispensers for use in soups and stews. Polenta, the coarsely ground yellow maize, is a staple of the northern Italian diet, as is the rice used to make risotto. Of the special varieties grown in the area for this purpose, the best known are Arborio, Vialone Nano and Carnaroli.

Capers, pine nuts, sun-dried tomatoes, dried chillies, juniper berries and fennel seeds are some of the other ingredients commonly used to give Italian dishes their characteristic flavours, and are good basics to keep in the store cupboard.

Above: *An Italian kitchen might have a selection of dried beans, pulses and rice; olives, olive oil and good quality vinegar; as well as dried spices and other flavourings.*

Meats and Cheeses

Antipasti do not always entail large amounts of preparation, and are often simply composed of the ingredients typical of the region. A popular antipasto consists of a plate of mixed prepared meats and sausages. Salamis, pancetta, air-dried bresaola, coppa and mortadella sausages are some of the meats most commonly used in Italy, often served with an accompaniment of crusty bread and butter. Prosciutto crudo, raw Parma ham, is the most prized of all meats, and is delicious served thinly sliced with ripe melon or fresh figs.

An Italian meal is more likely to end with a selection of cheeses and fruit than a sweet dessert. Among the huge variety of cheeses, the following are some of the best known:

Gorgonzola is made in Lombardy and is a creamy blue cheese. It has a mild flavor when young, which becomes stronger with maturity.

Mascarpone is a rich, triple-cream cheese with a mild flavour. It is often used in desserts as a substitute for whipped cream.

Mozzarella is a fresh, white cheese made from water buffalo's or, more commonly, cow's milk. The texture is soft and chewy and the taste mild.

Parmesan is a long-aged, full-flavoured cheese with a hard rind, used for both grating and eating in slivers. The large wheels are aged from 18–36 months. Fresh Parmesan is superb, and is incomparably better than the ready-grated varieties sold pre-packaged.

Pecorino is made from ewe's milk, and comes in two main types, Pecorino Romano and Pecorino Toscano. This salted, sharp-flavoured cheese is widely used for dessert eating, and for grating when mature.

Scamorza is made from cow's milk. Its distinctive shape is due to being hung from a string during aging.

Below: *A typical Italian meal might include cured meat as an antipasto, and finish with cheese instead of a sweet dessert.*

Equipment

1 *Earthenware pot*. Excellent for slow-cooking stews, soups or sauces. Can be used either in the oven or on top of the stove with a metal heat diffuser under it to discourage cracking. Many shapes and sizes are available. To season an earthenware pot before using it for the first time, immerse in cold water overnight. Remove from the water and rub the unglazed bottom with garlic. Fill with water and bring slowly to a boil. Discard the water. Repeat, changing the water, until the "earth" taste disappears.

2 *Pasta rolling pin*. A length of dowelling of 5 cm/2 in diameter can also be used. Smooth with sandpaper before using for the first time.

3 *Pestle and mortar*. For hand-grinding spices, pepper, herbs and breadcrumbs.

4 *Hand food mill*. Excellent for soups, sauces and tomato "passata": the pulp passes through the holes leaving the seeds and skin behind.

5 *Colander*. Indispensable for draining hot pasta and vegetables.

6 *Parmesan cheese knife*. In Italy Parmesan is not cut with a conventional knife, but broken off the large cheese wheels using this kind of wedge. Insert the point and apply pressure.

7 *Pizza cutting wheel*. Useful for cutting slices, although a sharp knife may also be used.

8 *Spatula*. Very useful for spreading and smoothing.

9 *Spaghetti spoon*. The wooden "teeth" catch the spaghetti strands as they boil.

10 *Meat hammer*. For pounding escalopes. Also useful for crushing nuts and spices.

11 *Pasta machine*. Many are available, including electric and industrial models. Most have an adjustable roller width and thin and wide noodle cutters.

12 *Icing nozzles*. For piping decorations, garnishes, etc. Use with a nylon or paper pastry bag.

13 *Wide vegetable peeler*. Very easy to use for all sizes of vegetable.

14 *Italian gelato scoop*. Good for soft ices that are not too solid.

15 *Ice cream scoop*. Better for firm and well-frozen ice creams.

16 *Olive pitter*. Can also be used for pitting cherries.

17 *Whisk*. Excellent for smoothing sauces, beating egg whites.

18 *Fluted pastry cutter*. For cutting fresh pasta or pastry.

19 *Cookie cutter*. Also used for cutting fresh pasta shapes.

Pasta

Pasta in its many forms is a staple of Italian cuisine. These are just some of the varieties available.

1 *Alfabeto*. Small alphabet pasta for soups.

2 *Anellini*. Little rings used in soups and broth.

3 *Canneroni*. Pasta rings for thick vegetable soups.

4 *Capellini*. Very fine "angel hair" pasta, can be broken up and used in broths.

5 *Chifferi piccoli lisci*. Smooth, macaroni-like pasta used in baked dishes.

6 *Chifferi piccoli rigati*. Ridged version of the above.

7 *Conchigliette*. Small shells used in soups.

8 *Conchigliette rigati*. Small, ridged shells used in thick soups.

9 *Conchiglioni rigati*. Large, ridged shells used for stuffing and baking.

10 *Ditali*. Used in soups, traditionally with dried beans.

11 *Ditalini*. Soup pasta, smaller than ditali.

12 *Ditalini lisci*. Smooth ditalini, also used in soups.

13 *Elicoidali*. Good for baked dishes, or those with chunky sauces.

14 *Fagiolini*. "String beans" used in soups.

15 *Farfalle*. Butterflies or bows. Excellent with prawns and peas and in cold pasta salads.

16 *Fusilli*. These spirals are ideal with tomato and vegetable sauces.

17 *Fusilli integrali*. Whole wheat spirals. Good hot or cold with thick vegetable sauces.

18 *Fusillata casareccia*. The twisted shape is good with tomato sauce.

19 *Gnocchi*. Shells for chunky vegetable or meat sauces. Gnocchi tricolori (19a) is flavoured with tomato and spinach.

20 *Gnocchi integrali*. Whole wheat shells popular in vegetarian dishes, hot or cold.

21 *Gnocchetti sardi*. Sardinian shells. Good with lamb or fish sauces.

22 *Lasagne doppia riccia*. Frilly-edged lasagne. This is a dry version of the popular egg pasta, used for stuffed and baked dishes.

23 *Lasagne verdi*. Spinach gives this lasagne its green colour.

24 *Lingue di passero, Bavette*. Traditionally paired with the classic pesto sauce.

25 *Linguine, Bavettine*. This finer version of lingue de passoro is good with fish sauces.

26 *Lumache rigate grandi*. These large, ridged "snails" are suitable for thick sauces with strong flavours such as olives and capers. Also good for pasta salads.

27 *Macaroni*. This is the English version of Italian maccherone, most popular baked with cheese.

28 *Mafaldine*. This is often eaten with sauces made from soft cheeses, such as ricotta.

29 *Mezze penne rigate tricolori*. The pasta is tinted with tomato and spinach to produce Italy's favourite colours.

30 *Orecchiette*. Dry version of the traditionally hand-made pasta popular in the south of Italy. Cooked with green vegetables.

31 *Penne lisce*. Quills or pens. Cut diagonally to catch more sauce.

32 *Penne rigate*. Ridged quills, a favourite shape in Italy. Great with tomato sauces.

33 *Pennoni rigati*. Large ridged quills. Good for baked dishes.

34 *Peperini*. Little pasta dots to add to broth or soups.

35 *Perciatellini*. This is a hollow spaghetti. Can be used with any of the usual spaghetti sauces.

36 *Pipe rigate*. "Ridged pipes". Good for thick, chunky sauces with peas or lentils.

37 *Puntalette*. For adding to soups and broths.

38 *Rigatoni*. Often baked with meat sauces and cheeses. Mezza rigatoni (38a) are smaller in size.

39 *Ruote*. Pasta wheels, always popular with children.

40 *Spaghetti integrali*. Wholewheat version of spaghetti (40a), more popular abroad than in Italy.

41 *Spaghettini*. Finer version of spaghetti, good with delicate sauces.

42 *Stelline*. Little stars, another small soup pasta.

43 *Tagliatelle*. Dried egg noodles, good with creamy sauces.

44 *Tagliatelle verdi*. Dried spinach-flavoured egg noodles.

45 *Tomato spirals*. Specially made tomato-flavoured pasta.

46 *Tortellini*. Small dumplings, often cooked and eaten in broth.

47 *Tortelloni*. Pasta dumplings stuffed with meats or cheeses.

48 *Zite*. A long hollow pasta often used with fish or tomato sauces.

23
26
19a
16
17
44
36
9
19
39
45
6
20
38
33
43
5
21
38a
13
32
15
18
3
27
29
10
14
8
4
11
37
7
31
30
34
1
2
42
46
47

ANTIPASTI AND SOUPS

Hot or cold antipasti are the perfect start to any meal, and are also great for parties. Hearty vegetable soups with grains and pasta make warming first courses and nutritious light meals.

Raw Vegetables with Olive Oil Dip

Pinzimonio

Use a combination of any fresh seasonal vegetables for this colourful antipasto from Rome, where the dip usually consists only of olive oil and salt. The vegetables should be raw or lightly blanched, and the olive oil of the best quality available.

Ingredients
3 large carrots, peeled
2 fennel bulbs
6 tender stalks celery
1 pepper
12 radishes, trimmed of roots
2 large tomatoes, or 12 cherry tomatoes
8 spring onions
12 small cauliflower florets

For the dip
125 ml/4 fl oz/½ cup extra-virgin olive oil
salt and freshly ground black pepper
45 ml/3 tbsp fresh lemon juice (optional)
4 leaves fresh basil, torn into small pieces (optional)

serves 6–8

1 Prepare the vegetables by slicing the carrots, fennel, celery and pepper into small sticks.

2 ▲ Cut the large tomatoes into sections if using. Trim the roots and dark green leaves from the spring onions. Arrange the vegetables on a large platter, leaving a space in the centre for the dip.

3 ▲ Make the dip by pouring the olive oil into a small bowl. Add salt and pepper. Stir in the lemon juice and basil, if using. Place the bowl in the centre of the vegetable platter.

Celery Stuffed with Gorgonzola

Sedano ripieno di Gorgonzola

These celery sticks are very easy to make. Serve them with drinks, or take them to a picnic.

Ingredients
12 crisp sticks celery, leaves left on
75 g/3 oz/½ cup Gorgonzola
75 g/3 oz/½ cup cream cheese
fresh chives, to garnish

serves 4–6

1 ▲ Wash and dry the celery sticks, and trim the root ends.

2 ▲ In a small bowl, mash the cheeses together until smooth.

3 ▲ Fill the celery sticks with the cheese mixture, using a spatula to smooth the filling. Chill before serving. Garnish with chopped chives.

Crostini with Cheese

Crostini con formaggio

Crostini are small pieces of toasted bread. They can be made with various toppings, and are served hot or cold with drinks. This cheese-topped version is always popular.

Ingredients

4–6 slices day-old white or brown bread
75 g/3 oz/$^3/_4$ cup thinly sliced cheese (fontina, Cheddar or gruyère)
anchovy fillets
strips of grilled red pepper
freshly ground black pepper
serves 6

1 ▲ Cut the bread into small shapes (triangle, circle, oval etc). Preheat the oven to 190°C/375°F/gas 5.

2 ▲ Place a thin slice of cheese on each piece of bread, cutting it to fit.

~ VARIATION ~

For a colourful addition use strips of green or yellow pepper.

3 ▲ Cut the anchovy fillets and strips of pepper into small decorative shapes and place on top of the cheese. Grind a little pepper on each.

4 ▲ Butter a baking sheet. Place the crostini on it, and bake for 10 minutes, or until the cheese has melted. Serve straight from the oven, or allow to cool before serving.

Crostini with Mussels or Clams

Crostini con cozze o vongole

Each of these seafood crostini is topped with a mussel or clam, and then baked. This recipe comes from Genoa. Use fresh seafood whenever possible.

Ingredients
16 large mussels or clams, in their shells
4 large slices bread, 2.5 cm/1 in thick
40 g/1$^{1}/_{2}$ oz/3 tbsp butter
30 ml/2 tbsp chopped fresh parsley
1 shallot, very finely chopped
olive oil, for brushing
lemon sections, to serve
makes 16

1 ▲ Wash the mussels or clams well in several changes of water. Cut the "beards" off the mussels. Place the shellfish in a pan with a cupful of water, and heat until the shells open. (Discard any that do not open.) As soon as they open, lift the molluscs out of the pan. Spoon out of their shells, and set aside. Preheat the oven to 190°C/375°F/gas 5.

2 ▲ Cut the crusts off the bread. Cut each slice into quarters. Scoop out a hollow from the top of each piece large enough to hold a mussel or clam. Do not cut through to the bottom.

3 ▲ Break the scooped-out bread into crumbs, and reserve. In a small frying pan, heat the butter. Cook the parsley with the shallot and the breadcrumbs until the shallot softens.

4 ▲ Brush each piece of bread with olive oil. Place one mussel or clam in each hollow. Spoon a small amount of the parsley and shallot mixture onto each mollusc. Place on an oiled baking sheet. Bake for 10 minutes. Serve at once, while still hot, with the lemon sections.

Mixed Seafood Salad

Insalata di frutti di mare

All along Italy's coasts versions of this salad appear. Use fresh seafood that is in season, or use a combination of fresh and frozen.

Ingredients
350 g/12oz small squid
1 small onion, cut into quarters
1 bay leaf
200 g/7oz prawns, in their shells
750 g/$1^1/_2$lb fresh mussels, in their shells
450 g/1lb fresh small clams
175 ml/6 fl oz $^3/_4$ cup white wine
1 fennel bulb

For the dressing
75 ml/5 tbsp extra-virgin olive oil
45 ml/3 tbsp fresh lemon juice
1 garlic clove, finely chopped
salt and freshly ground black pepper

serves 6–8

1 ▲ Working near the sink, clean the squid by first peeling off the thin skin from the body section. Rinse well. Pull the head and tentacles away from the sac section. Some of the intestines will come away with the head. Remove and discard the translucent quill and any remaining insides from the sac. Sever the tentacles from the head. Discard the head and intestines. Remove the small hard beak from the base of the tentacles. Rinse the sac and tentacles well under cold running water. Drain.

2 Bring a large pan of water to the boil. Add the onion and bay leaf. Drop in the squid and cook for about 10 minutes, or until tender. Remove with a slotted spoon, and allow to cool before slicing into rings 1 cm/$^1/_2$ in wide. Cut each tentacle section into 2 pieces. Set aside.

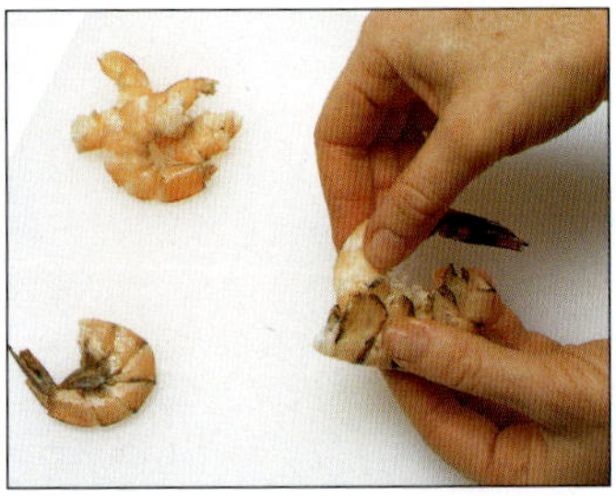

3 ▲ Drop the prawns into the same boiling water, and cook until they turn pink, about 2 minutes. Remove with a slotted spoon. Peel and devein. (The cooking liquid may be strained and kept for soup.)

4 ▲ Cut off the "beards" from the mussels. Scrub and rinse the mussels and clams well in several changes of cold water. Place in a large pan with the wine. Cover, and steam until all the shells have opened. (Discard any that do not open.) Lift the clams and mussels out.

5 ▲ Remove all the clams from their shells with a small spoon. Place in a large serving bowl. Remove all but 8 of the mussels from their shells, and add them to the clams in the bowl. Leave the remaining mussels in their half shells, and set aside. Cut the green, ferny part of the fennel away from the bulb. Chop finely and set aside. Chop the bulb into bite-size pieces, and add it to the serving bowl with the squid and prawns.

6 ▲ Make a dressing by combining the oil, lemon juice, garlic and chopped fennel green in a small bowl. Add salt and pepper to taste. Pour over the salad, and toss well. Decorate with the remaining mussels in the half shell. This salad may be served at room temperature or slightly chilled.

Prosciutto with Figs

Prosciutto crudo con fichi

The hams cured in the region of Parma are held to be the finest in Italy. Prosciutto makes an excellent appetizer sliced paper-thin and served with fresh figs or melon.

Ingredients
8 ripe green or black figs
12 paper-thin slices prosciutto crudo
crusty bread, to serve
unsalted butter, to serve
serves 4

1 ▲ Arrange the slices of prosciutto on a serving plate.

2 ▲ Wipe the figs with a damp cloth. Cut them almost into quarters but do not cut all the way through the base. If the skins are tender, they may be eaten along with the inner fruit. If you prefer, you may peel each quarter carefully by pulling the peel gently away from the pulp.

3 ▲ Arrange the figs on top of the prosciutto. Serve with bread and unsalted butter.

Cherry Tomatoes with Pesto

Pomodorini con pesto

These make a colourful and tasty appetizer to go with drinks, or as part of a buffet. Make the pesto when fresh basil is plentiful, and freeze it in batches.

Ingredients
450 g/1 lb cherry tomatoes (about 36)
For the pesto
90 g/3½ oz/1 cup fresh basil
3–4 garlic cloves
60 ml/4 tbsp pine nuts
5 ml/1 tsp salt, plus extra to taste
100 ml/4 fl oz/½ cup olive oil
50 ml/3 tbsp freshly grated parmesan cheese
90 ml/6 tbsp freshly grated pecorino cheese
freshly ground black pepper
serves 8–10 as an appetizer

1 Wash the tomatoes. Slice off the top of each tomato, and carefully scoop out the seeds with a melon baller or small spoon.

2 ▲ Place the basil, garlic, pine nuts, salt and olive oil in a blender or food processor and process until smooth. Remove the contents to a bowl with a rubber spatula. If desired, the pesto may be frozen at this point, before the cheeses are added. To use when frozen, allow to thaw, then proceed to step 3.

3 Fold in the grated cheeses (use all parmesan if pecorino is not available). Season with pepper, and more salt if necessary.

4 ▲ Use a small spoon to fill each tomato with a little pesto. This dish is at its best if chilled for about an hour before serving.

Hard-boiled Eggs with Tuna Sauce

Uova sode tonnate

The combination of eggs with a tasty tuna mayonnaise makes a nourishing first course that is quick and easy to prepare.

Ingredients
6 extra large eggs
1 x 200g/7 oz can tuna in olive oil
3 anchovy fillets
15 ml/1 tbsp capers, drained
30 ml/2 tbsp fresh lemon juice
60 ml/4 tbsp olive oil
salt and freshly ground black pepper
For the mayonnaise
1 egg yolk, at room temperature
5 ml/1 tsp Dijon mustard
5 ml/1 tsp white wine vinegar or fresh lemon juice
150 ml/$^{1}/_{4}$ pint/$^{2}/_{3}$ cup olive oil
capers and anchovy fillets, to garnish (optional)
serves 6

1 Boil the eggs for 12–14 minutes. Drain under cold water. Peel carefully and set aside.

2 ▲ Make the mayonnaise by whisking the egg yolk, mustard and vinegar or lemon juice together in a small bowl. Whisk in the oil a few drops at a time until 3 or 4 tablespoons of oil have been incorporated. Pour in the remaining oil in a slow stream, whisking constantly.

3 Place the tuna with its oil, the anchovies, capers, lemon juice and olive oil in the bowl of a blender or food processor. Process until smooth.

4 ▲ Fold the tuna sauce into the mayonnaise. Season with black pepper, and extra salt if necessary. Refrigerate for at least 1 hour.

5 ▲ To serve, cut the eggs in half lengthwise. Arrange on a serving platter. Spoon on the sauce, and garnish with capers and anchovy fillets, if desired. Serve chilled.

Tuna and Bean Salad

Tonno e fagioli

This substantial salad makes a good light meal, and can be very quickly assembled from canned ingredients.

Ingredients

2 × 400 g/14 oz cans cannellini or borlotti beans
2 × 200 g/7oz cans tuna fish, drained
60 ml/4 tbsp extra-virgin olive oil
30 ml/2 tbsp fresh lemon juice
salt and freshly ground black pepper
15 ml/1 tbsp chopped fresh parsley
3 spring onions, thinly sliced
serves 4–6

1 ▲ Pour the beans into a large strainer and rinse under cold water. Drain well. Place in a serving dish.

2 ▲ Break the tuna into fairly large flakes and arrange over the beans.

3 ▲ In a small bowl make the dressing by combining the oil with the lemon juice. Season with salt and pepper, and stir in the parsley. Mix well. Pour over the beans and tuna.

4 ▲ Sprinkle with the spring onions. Toss well before serving.

Carpaccio with Rocket

Carpaccio con rucola

Carpaccio is a fine dish of raw beef in lemon juice and olive oil. It is traditionally served with flakes of fresh Parmesan cheese. Use very fresh meat of the best quality.

Ingredients
1 garlic clove, peeled and cut in half
$1^1/_2$ lemons
50 ml/2 fl oz/$^1/_4$ cup extra-virgin olive oil
salt and freshly ground black pepper
2 bunches rocket
4 very thin slices of beef top round
115g/4 oz/1 cup Parmesan cheese, thinly shaved
serves 4

1 Rub a small bowl all over with the cut side of the garlic. Squeeze the lemons into the bowl. Whisk in the olive oil. Season with salt and pepper. Allow the sauce to stand for at least 15 minutes before using.

2 ▲ Carefully wash the rocket and tear off any thick stalks. Spin or pat dry. Arrange the rocket around the edge of a serving platter, or divide on 4 individual plates.

3 ▲ Place the beef in the centre of the platter, and pour on the sauce, spreading it evenly over the meat. Arrange the shaved Parmesan on top of the meat slices. Serve at once.

Tuna in Rolled Red Peppers

Peperoni rossi ripieni di tonno

This savoury combination originated in southern Italy. Grilled peppers have a sweet, smoky taste that combines particularly well with fish.

Ingredients
3 large red peppers
1 x 200 g/7oz can tuna fish, drained
30 ml/2 tbsp fresh lemon juice
45 ml/3 tbsp olive oil
6 green or black olives, pitted and chopped
30 ml/2 tbsp chopped fresh parsley
1 garlic clove, finely chopped
1 medium stalk celery, very finely chopped
salt and freshly ground black pepper
serves 4–6

1 Place the peppers under a hot grill, and turn occasionally until they are black and blistered on all sides. Remove from the heat and place in a paper bag.

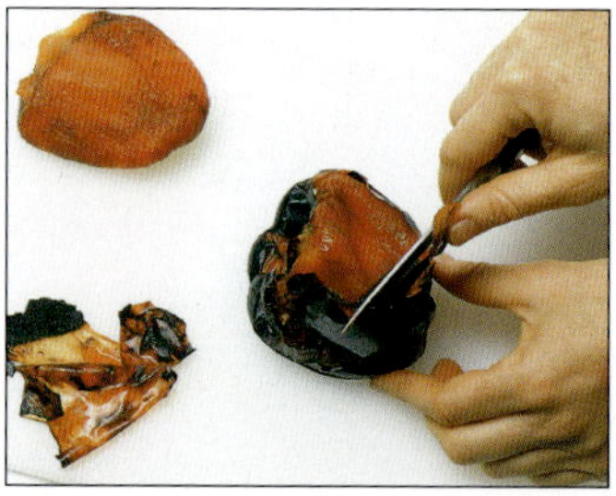

2 ▲ Leave for 5 minutes, and then peel. Cut the peppers into quarters, and remove the stems and seeds.

3 Meanwhile, flake the tuna and combine with the lemon juice and oil. Stir in the remaining ingredients. Season with salt and pepper.

4 ▲ Lay the pepper segments out flat, skin side down. Divide the tuna mixture equally between them. Spread it out, pressing it into an even layer. Roll the peppers up. Place the pepper rolls in the refrigerator for at least 1 hour. Just before serving, cut each roll in half with a sharp knife.

Stuffed Mussels

Cozze gratinate

This tasty appetizer is a speciality of southern Italy. It can be made equally well using large clams. Always use the freshest seafood available.

Ingredients
750 g/1 ½ lb large fresh mussels in their shells
75 g/3 oz/⅓ cup unsalted butter, at room temperature
25g/1 oz/¼ cup dry breadcrumbs
2 garlic cloves, finely chopped
45 ml/3 tbsp chopped fresh parsley
25 g/1 oz/¼ cup freshly grated Parmesan cheese
salt and freshly ground black pepper
serves 4

1 ▲ Scrub the mussels well under cold running water, cutting off the "beard" with a small knife. Preheat the oven to 230°C /450°F/Gas 8.

2 ▲ Place the mussels with a cupful of water in a large saucepan over a moderate heat. As soon as they open, lift them out one by one. Remove and discard the empty half shells, leaving the meat in the other half. (Discard any mussels that do not open.)

3 ▲ Combine all the remaining ingredients in a small bowl. Blend well. Place in a small pan and heat gently until the stuffing mixture begins to soften.

4 ▲ Arrange the mussel halves on a flat baking tray. Spoon a small amount of the stuffing over each mussel. Bake for about 7 minutes, or until lightly browned. Serve hot or at room temperature.

Egg and Cheese Soup

Stracciatella

In this classic Roman soup, eggs and cheese are beaten into hot broth, producing a slightly "curdled" texture characteristic of the dish.

Ingredients
3 eggs
45 ml/3 tbsp fine semolina
90 ml/6 tbsp freshly grated Parmesan cheese
pinch of nutmeg
1.5 litres/$2^1/_2$ pints/$6^1/_4$ cups meat or chicken broth
salt and freshly ground black pepper
12 rounds of French bread, to serve
serves 6

1 ▲ Beat the eggs in a bowl with the semolina and the cheese. Add the nutmeg. Beat in 1 cupful of the cool broth.

2 ▲ Meanwhile heat the remaining broth to simmering point in a large saucepan.

3 ▲ When the broth is hot, and a few minutes before you are ready to serve the soup, whisk the egg mixture into the broth. Raise the heat slightly, and bring it barely to the boil. Season with salt and pepper. Cook for 3–4 minutes. As the egg cooks, the soup will not be completely smooth.

4 ▲ To serve, toast the rounds of French bread and place 2 in the bottom of each soup plate. Ladle on the hot soup, and serve immediately.

Minestrone with Pesto

Minestrone con pesto

Minestrone is a thick mixed vegetable soup using almost any combination of seasonal vegetables. Short pasta or rice may also be added. This version includes pesto sauce.

Ingredients

1.5 litres/2$^1/_2$ pints/6$^1/_4$ cups broth or water, or a combination of both
45 ml/3 tbsp olive oil
1 large onion, finely chopped
1 leek, sliced
2 carrots, finely chopped
1 stalk celery, finely chopped
2 cloves garlic, finely chopped
2 potatoes, peeled and cut into small dice
1 bay leaf
1 sprig fresh thyme, or 1 ml/$^1/_4$ tsp dried thyme leaves
salt and freshly ground black pepper
115g/4 oz/$^3/_4$ cup peas, fresh or frozen
2–3 courgettes, finely chopped
3 medium tomatoes, peeled and finely chopped
425 g/15 oz/2 cups cooked or canned beans such as cannellini
45 ml/3 tbsp pesto sauce
freshly grated Parmesan cheese, to serve

serves 6

1 In a medium pan, heat the broth or water to simmering.

2 ▲ In a saucepan heat the olive oil in a large pan. Stir in the onion and leek, and cook for 5–6 minutes, or until the onion softens. Add the carrots, celery and garlic, and cook over moderate heat, stirring often, for another 5 minutes. Add the potatoes and cook for 2–3 minutes more.

3 Pour in the hot broth or water, and stir well. Add the herbs and seasonwith salt and pepper. Bring to the boil, reduce the heat slightly, and cook for 10–12 minutes.

4 Stir in the peas, if fresh, and the courgettes. Simmer for 5 minutes more. Add the frozen peas, if using, and the tomatoes. Cover the pan, and boil for 5–8 minutes.

5 ▲ About 10 minutes before serving the soup, uncover, and stir in the beans. Simmer for 10 minutes. Stir in the pesto sauce. Taste for seasoning. Simmer for another 5 minutes then remove from the heat. Allow the soup to stand for a few minutes, then serve with the grated Parmesan.

Pumpkin Soup

Minestrone di zucca

This beautifully coloured soup would be perfect for an autumn dinner.

Ingredients

450 g/1lb piece of peeled pumpkin
50g/2 oz/$^1/_4$ cup butter
1 medium onion, finely chopped
750 ml/1$^1/_4$ pints/3$^1/_2$ cups chicken broth or water
475 ml/16 fl oz/2 cups milk
pinch of grated nutmeg
salt and freshly ground black pepper
40 g/1$^1/_2$oz/ 7 tbsp spaghetti, broken into small pieces
90 ml/6 tbsp freshly grated Parmesan cheese

serves 4

1 Chop the piece of pumpkin into 2.5 cm/1 in cubes.

2 ▲ Heat the butter in a saucepan. Add the onion, and cook over moderate heat until it softens, 6–8 minutes. Stir in the pumpkin, and cook for 2–3 minutes more.

3 Add the broth or water, and cook until the pumpkin is soft, about 15 minutes. Remove from the heat.

4 Purée the soup in a blender or food processor. Return it to the pan. Stir in the milk and nutmeg. Season with salt and pepper. Bring the soup back to a boil.

5 Stir the broken spaghetti into the soup. Cook until the pasta is done. Stir in the Parmesan and serve at once.

Broccoli Soup

Zuppa di broccoletti

Around Rome broccoli grows abundantly and is served in this soup with garlic toasts.

Ingredients
675 g/$1\frac{1}{2}$ lb broccoli spears
1.75 litres/3 pints/$7\frac{1}{2}$ cups chicken or vegetable broth
salt and freshly ground black pepper
30 ml/1 tbsp fresh lemon juice

To serve
6 slices white bread
1 large clove garlic, cut in half
freshly grated Parmesan cheese (optional)

serves 6

1 Using a small sharp knife, peel the broccoli stems, starting from the base of the stalks and pulling gently up towards the florets. (The peel comes off very easily.) Chop the broccoli into small chunks.

2 Bring the stock to the boil in a large pan. Add the broccoli and simmer for 30 minutes, or until soft.

3 ▲ Purée about half of the soup and mix into the rest of the soup. Season with salt, pepper and lemon juice.

4 ▲ Just before serving, reheat the soup to just below boiling point. Toast the bread, rub with garlic and cut into quarters. Place 3 or 4 pieces of toast in the bottom of each soup plate. Ladle on the soup. Serve at once, with Parmesan if desired.

Tomato and Bread Soup

Pappa al pomodoro

This colourful Florentine recipe was created to use up stale bread. It can be made with very ripe fresh or canned plum tomatoes.

Ingredients
90 ml/6 tbsp olive oil
small piece of dried chilli, crumbled (optional)
175 g/6 oz/$1\frac{1}{2}$ cups stale bread, cut into 2.5 cm/1 in cubes
1 medium onion, finely chopped
2 cloves garlic, finely chopped
675 g/$1\frac{1}{2}$ lb ripe tomatoes, peeled and chopped, or 2 × 400 g/14 oz cans peeled plum tomatoes, chopped
45 ml/3 tbsp chopped fresh basil
1.5 litres/$2\frac{1}{2}$ pints/$6\frac{1}{4}$ cups light meat broth or water, or a combination of both
salt and freshly ground black pepper
extra-virgin olive oil, to serve (optional)

serves 4

1 Heat 60 ml/4 tbsp of the oil in a large saucepan. Add the chilli, if using, and stir for 1–2 minutes. Add the bread cubes and cook until golden. Remove to a plate and drain on kitchen paper.

2 ▲ Add the remaining oil, the onion and garlic, and cook until the onion softens. Stir in the tomatoes, bread and basil. Season with salt. Cook over moderate heat, stirring occasionally, for about 15 minutes.

3 Meanwhile, heat the broth or water to simmering. Add it to the pan with the tomato mixture, and mix well. Bring to the boil. Lower the heat slightly and simmer for 20 minutes.

4 ▲ Remove the soup from the heat. Use a fork to mash the tomatoes and the bread together. Season with pepper, and more salt if necessary. Allow to stand for 10 minutes. Just before serving swirl in a little extra-virgin olive oil, if desired.

White Bean Soup

Minestrone di fagioli

A thick purée of cooked dried beans is at the heart of this substantial country soup from Tuscany. It makes a warming winter lunch or supper dish.

Ingredients

350 g/12 oz/1 $^1/_2$ cups dried cannellini or other white beans
1 bay leaf
75 ml/5 tbsp olive oil
1 medium onion, finely chopped
1 carrot, finely chopped
1 stalk celery, finely chopped
3 medium tomatoes, peeled and finely chopped
2 cloves garlic, finely chopped
1 tsp fresh thyme leaves, or $^1/_2$ tsp dried thyme
750 ml/1 $^1/_4$ pints/3 $^1/_2$ cups boiling water
salt and freshly ground black pepper
extra-virgin olive oil, to serve

serves 6

1 ▲ Pick over the beans carefully, discarding any stones or other particles. Soak the beans in a large bowl of cold water overnight. Drain. Place the beans in a large saucepan of water, bring to a boil, and cook for 20 minutes. Drain. Return the beans to the pan, cover with cold water, and bring to a boil again. Add the bay leaf, and cook until the beans are tender, 1–2 hours. Drain again. Remove the bay leaf.

2 Purée about three-quarters of the beans in a food processor, or pass through a food mill, adding a little water if necessary.

3 Heat the oil in a large saucepan. Stir in the onion, and cook until it softens. Add the carrot and celery, and cook for 5 minutes more.

4 ▲ Stir in the tomatoes, garlic and thyme. Cook for 6–8 minutes more, stirring often.

5 ▲ Pour in the boiling water. Stir in the beans and the bean purée. Season with salt and pepper. Simmer for 10–15 minutes. Serve in individual soup bowls, sprinkled with a little extra-virgin olive oil.

Fish Soup

Ciuppin

Liguria is famous for its fish soups. In this one the fish are cooked in a broth with vegetables and then puréed. This soup can also be used to dress pasta.

Ingredients

1 kg/2 lb mixed fish or fish pieces (such as pollock, whiting, red mullet, red or white snapper, cod etc)
90 ml/6 tbsp olive oil, plus extra to serve
1 medium onion, finely chopped
1 stick celery, chopped
1 carrot, chopped
60 ml/4 tbsp chopped fresh parsley
175 ml/6 fl oz/$^{3}/_{4}$ cup dry white wine
3 medium tomatoes, peeled and chopped
2 cloves garlic, finely chopped
1.5 litres/2$^{1}/_{2}$ pints/6$^{1}/_{4}$ cups boiling water
salt and freshly ground black pepper
rounds of French bread, to serve

serves 6

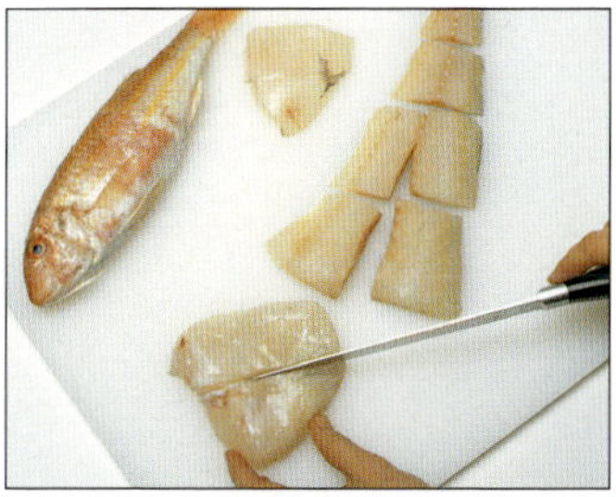

1 ▲ Scale and clean the fish, discarding all innards, but leaving the heads on. Cut into large pieces. Rinse well in cool water.

2 Heat the oil in a large saucepan and add the onion. Cook over low to moderate heat until it begins to soften. Stir in the celery and carrot, and cook for 5 minutes more. Add the parsley.

3 ▲ Pour in the wine, raise the heat, and cook until it reduces by about half. Stir in the tomatoes and garlic. Cook for 3–4 minutes, stirring occasionally. Pour in the boiling water, and bring back to a boil. Cook over moderate heat for 15 minutes.

4 Stir in the fish, and simmer for 10–15 minutes, or until the fish are tender. Season with salt and pepper.

5 ▲ Remove the fish from the soup with a slotted spoon. Discard any bones. Purée in a food processor. Taste for seasoning. If the soup is too thick, add a little more water.

6 To serve, heat the soup to simmering. Toast the rounds of bread, and sprinkle with olive oil. Place 2 or 3 in each soup plate before pouring over the soup.

~ VARIATION ~

To use the soup as a pasta dressing, cook until it reduces to the consistency of a sauce.

Barley and Vegetable Soup

Minestrone d'orzo

This soup comes from the Alto Adige region, in Italy's mountainous north. It is a thick, nourishing and warming winter soup. Serve with crusty bread.

Ingredients

225 g/8 oz/1 cup pearl barley, preferably organic
2 litres/3$^1/_2$ pints/9 cups mat broth or water, or a combination of both
45 ml/3 tbsp olive oil
2 carrots, finely chopped
1 large onion, finely chopped
2 sticks celery, finely chopped
1 leek, thinly sliced
1 large potato, finely chopped
115 g/4 oz/$^1/_2$ cup diced ham
1 bay leaf
45 ml/3 tbsp chopped fresh parsley
1 small sprig fresh rosemary
salt and freshly ground black pepper
freshly grated Parmesan cheese, to serve (optional)

serves 6–8

1 Pick over the barley, and discard any stones or other particles. Wash it in cold water. Put the barley to soak in cold water for at least 3 hours.

2 Drain the barley and place in a large saucepan with the stock or water. Bring to a boil, lower the heat and simmer for 1 hour. Skim off any scum.

3 ▲ Stir in the oil, all the vegetables and the ham. Add the herbs. If necessary add more water. The ingredients should be covered by at least 2.5 cm/1 in. Simmer for 1-1$^1/_2$ hours, or until the vegetables and barley are very tender.

4 ▲ Taste for seasoning, adding salt and pepper as necessary. Serve hot with grated Parmesan, if desired.

~ VARIATION ~

An excellent vegetarian version of this soup can be made by using vegetable broth instead of beef broth, and omitting the ham.

Rice and Broad Bean Soup

Minestra di riso e fave

This thick soup makes the most of fresh broad beans while they are in season. It works well with frozen beans for the rest of the year.

Ingredients

1 kg/2 lb broad beans in their pods, or 400g/14oz shelled frozen fava beans, thawed
90 ml/6 tbsp olive oil
1 medium onion, finely chopped
salt and freshly ground black pepper
2 medium tomatoes, peeled and finely chopped
225 g/8 oz/1 cup risotto or other non-parboiled rice
25 g/1 oz/2 tbsp butter
1 litre/1$^3/_4$ pints/4 cups boiling water
freshly grated Parmesan cheese, to serve (optional)

serves 4

1 ▲ Shell the beans if they are fresh. Bring a large pan of water to a boil, and blanch the beans, fresh or frozen, for 3-4 minutes. Rinse under cold water, and peel off the skins.

2 Heat the oil in a large saucepan. Add the chopped onion, and cook over low to moderate heat until it softens. Stir in the broad beans, and cook for about 5 minutes, stirring often to coat them with the oil. Season with salt and pepper. Add the tomatoes, and cook for 5 minutes more, stirring often.

3 Stir in the rice. After 1-2 minutes add the butter, and stir until it melts. Pour in the water, a little at a time, until the whole amount has been added. Taste for seasoning. Continue cooking the soup until the rice is tender. Serve hot, with grated Parmesan if desired.

Pasta and Dried Bean Soup

Pasta e fagioli

This peasant soup is very thick. In Italy it is made with dried or fresh beans, never canned, and served hot or at room temperature.

Ingredients

300 g/11 oz/$1^1/_2$ cups dried borlotti or cannellini beans
1 x 400g/14 oz can plum tomatoes, chopped, with their juice
3 cloves garlic, crushed
2 bay leaves
pinch coarsely ground black pepper
90 ml/6 tbsp olive oil, plus extra to serve (optional)
750 ml/ $1^1/_4$ pint/$3^1/_2$ cups water
10 ml/2 tsp salt
200 g/7 oz/$2^1/_4$ cups ditalini or other small pasta
45 ml/3 tbsp chopped fresh parsley
freshly grated Parmesan cheese, to serve

serves 4–6

1 Soak the beans in water overnight. Rinse and drain well.

2 Place the beans in a large saucepan and cover with water. Bring to a boil and cook for 10 minutes. Rinse and drain again.

3 ▲ Return the beans to the pan. Add enough water to cover them by 2.5 cm/1 in. Stir in the coarsely chopped tomatoes with their juice, the garlic, bay leaves, black pepper and the oil. Simmer for $1^1/_2$-2 hours, or until the beans are tender. If necessary, add more water.

4 ▲ Remove the bay leaves. Pass about half of the bean mixture through a food mill, or purée in a food processor. Stir into the pan with the remaining bean mixture. Add the water, and bring the soup to the boil.

5 ▲ Add the salt and the pasta. Stir, and cook until the pasta is just done. Stir in the parsley. Allow to stand for at least 10 minutes before serving. Serve with grated Parmesan passed separately. In Italy a little olive oil is poured into each serving.

Pasta and Lentil Soup

Pasta e lenticchie

The small brown lentils which are grown in central Italy are usually used in this wholesome soup, but green lentils may be substituted if preferred.

Ingredients

225g/8 oz/1 cup dried green or brown lentils
90 ml/6 tbsp olive oil
50g/2 oz/$^1/_4$ cup ham or salt pork, cut into small dice
1 medium onion, finely chopped
1 stick celery, finely chopped
1 carrot, finely chopped
2 litres/3$^1/_2$ pints/9 cups chicken broth or water, or a combination of both
1 leaf fresh sage or $^1/_8$ tsp dried
1 sprig fresh thyme or $^1/_4$ tsp dried
salt and freshly ground black pepper
175 g/6 oz/2$^1/_2$ cups ditalini or other small soup pasta

serves 4–6

1 ▲ Carefully check the lentils for small stones. Place them in a bowl, covered with cold water, and soak for 2-3 hours. Rinse and drain well.

2 ▲ In a large saucepan, heat the oil and sauté the ham or salt pork for 2-3 minutes. Add the onion, and cook gently until it softens.

3 ▲ Stir in the celery and carrot, and cook for 5 minutes more, stirring frequently. Add the lentils, and stir to coat them in the fats.

4 ▲ Pour in the broth or water and the herbs, and bring the soup to a boil. Cook over moderate heat for about 1 hour or until the lentils are tender. Add salt and pepper to taste.

5 Stir in the pasta, and cook it until it is just done. Allow the soup to stand for a few minutes before serving.

Pasta and Chickpea Soup

Pasta e ceci

Another thick soup from central Italy. The addition of a sprig of fresh rosemary provides a typically Mediterranean flavour.

Ingredients

200 g/7 oz/1 cup dried chickpeas
3 cloves garlic, peeled
1 bay leaf
90 ml/6 tbsp olive oil
pinch of freshly ground black pepper
50 g/2 oz/$^1/_4$ cup salt pork, pancetta or bacon, diced
1 sprig fresh rosemary
600 ml/1 pint/2$^1/_2$ cups water
150 g/5 oz ditalini or other short hollow pasta
salt, to taste
freshly grated Parmesan cheese, to serve (optional)

serves 4–6

1 ▲ Soak the chickpeas in water overnight. Rinse well and drain. Place the chickpeas in a large saucepan with water to cover. Boil for 15 minutes. Rinse and drain.

2 ▲ Return the chickpeas to the pan. Add water to cover, 1 clove of garlic, the bay leaf, 45 ml/3 tbsp of the oil and the ground pepper.

3 ▲ Simmer until tender, about 2 hours, adding more water as necessary. Remove the bay leaf. Pass about half the chickpeas through a food mill or purée in a food processor with a few tablespoons of the cooking liquid. Return the purée to the pan with the rest of the peas and the remaining cooking water.

4 ▲ Sauté the diced pork gently in the remaining oil with the rosemary and 2 cloves of garlic until just golden. Discard the rosemary and garlic.

5 ▲ Stir the pork with its oils into the chickpea mixture.

6 ▲ Add 600 ml/1 pint/2$^1/_2$ cups of water to the chickpeas, and bring to a boil. Correct the seasoning if necessary. Stir in the pasta, and cook until just *al dente*. Pass the Parmesan separately, if desired.

~ COOK'S TIP ~

Allow the soup to stand for about 10 minutes before serving. This will allow the flavour and texture to develop.

VEGETABLES

The colours and flavours of the Mediterranean are at the heart of this distinctive collection of vegetable dishes. Stuffed artichokes, baked fennel and grilled radicchio are some of its hearty delights.

Stuffed Artichokes

Carciofi ripieni

Artichokes grow almost wild in southern Italy and they are cooked in many different ways. In this recipe the artichokes are stuffed and baked whole.

Ingredients
1 lemon
6 large globe artichokes

For the stuffing
2 slices white bread, crusts removed (about 50 g/2 oz)
3 anchovy fillets, finely chopped
2 cloves garlic, finely chopped
30 ml/2 tbsp capers, rinsed and finely chopped
45 ml/3 tbsp finely chopped fresh parsley
60 ml/4 tbsp plain dry breadcrumbs
60 ml/4 tbsp olive oil
salt and freshly ground black pepper

For baking
1 garlic clove, cut into 3 or 4 pieces
1 sprig fresh parsley
45 ml/3 tbsp olive oil

serves 6

1 Prepare the stuffing. Soak the white bread in a little water for 5 minutes. Squeeze dry. Place in a bowl with the other stuffing ingredients and mix.

2 ▲ Squeeze the lemon, and put the juice and the squeezed halves in a large bowl of cold water. Wash the artichokes and prepare them one at a time. Cut off only the tip from the stem. Peel the stem with a small knife, pulling upwards towards the leaves. Pull off the small leaves around the stem, and continue snapping off the upper part of the dark outer leaves until you reach the taller inner leaves. Cut off the topmost part of these leaves with a sharp knife.

3 ▲ Open the artichoke slightly by spreading the leaves apart to get at the inner bristly "choke". Cut around it with the knife, and scrape it out with a small spoon. This forms a cavity inside the artichoke leaves. As soon as each artichoke has been prepared, place it in the bowl of acidulated water. This will prevent it from darkening. Preheat the oven to 190C°/375°F/gas 5.

4 ▲ Place the garlic and the parsley leaves in a baking dish large enough to hold the artichokes upright in one layer. Pour in cold water to a depth of 1 cm/$^1/_2$ inch. Remove the artichokes from the bowl, drain quickly, and fill the cavities with the stuffing. Place the artichokes upside down in the dish. Pour a little oil over each. Cover the dish tightly with foil. Bake for about 1 hour, or until tender.

Asparagus with Eggs

Asparagi alla milanese

The addition of fried eggs and grated Parmesan turns asparagus into something special. Peeling enables the asparagus to cook evenly, and makes the whole spear edible.

Ingredients

450 g/1 lb fresh asparagus
65 g/$2^1/_2$ oz/5 tbsp butter
4 eggs
60 ml/4 tbsp freshly grated Parmesan cheese
salt and freshly ground black pepper
serves 4

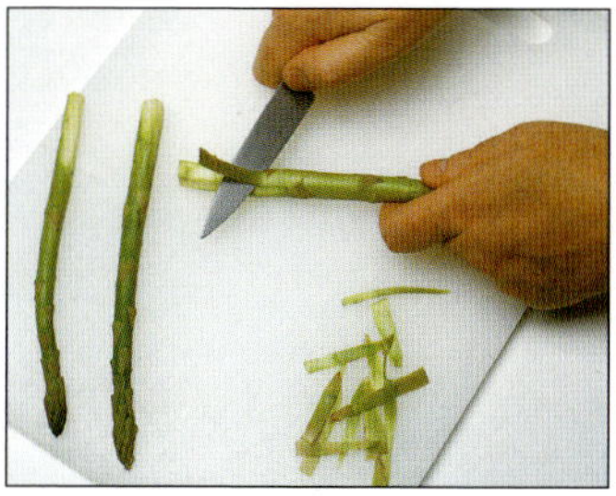

1 ▲ Cut off any woody ends from the asparagus. Peel the lower half of the asparagus spears by inserting a knife under the thick skin at the base, and pulling upwards towards the tip. Wash the asparagus in cold water.

2 Bring a large pan of water to a boil. Boil the asparagus until just tender when pierced with a knife.

3 ▲ While the asparagus is cooking, melt about a third of the butter in a frying pan. When it is bubbling, gently break in each egg, and cook until the whites have set but the yolks are still slightly soft.

4 ▲ As soon as the asparagus is cooked, remove it from the water with two slotted spoons. Place it on a cake rack covered with a clean dish towel to drain. Divide the spears between warmed individual serving plates. Place a fried egg on each, and sprinkle with the grated Parmesan.

5 ▲ Melt the remaining butter in the frying pan. As soon as it is bubbling pour it over the cheese and eggs on the asparagus. Serve at once with salt and pepper.

Stewed Artichokes

Carciofi in umido

Artichokes are eaten in many ways in Italy, sometimes sliced paper-thin and eaten raw as a salad, sometimes cut up and stewed lightly with garlic, parsley and wine, as in this recipe.

Ingredients
1 lemon
4 large or 6 small globe artichokes
25 g/1 oz/2 tbsp butter
60 ml/4 tbsp olive oil
2 cloves garlic, finely chopped
60 ml/4 tbsp chopped fresh parsley
salt and freshly ground black pepper
45 ml/3 tbsp water
90 ml/6 tbsp milk
90 ml/6 tbsp white wine
serves 6

1 Squeeze the lemon, and put the juice and the squeezed halves in a large bowl of cold water. Wash the artichokes and prepare them one at a time. Cut off only the tip from the stem. Peel the stem with a small knife, pulling upwards towards the leaves. Pull off the small leaves around the stem, and continue snapping off the upper part of the dark outer leaves until you reach the taller inner leaves.

2 ▲ Slice the topmost part of the leaves off. Cut the artichoke into 4 or 6 segments.

3 Cut out the bristly "choke" from each segment. Place in the acidulated water to prevent the artichokes from darkening while you prepare the rest.

4 Blanch the artichokes in a large pan of rapidly boiling water for 4–5 minutes. Drain.

5 ▲ Heat the butter and olive oil in a large pan. Add the garlic and parsley, and cook for 2–3 minutes. Stir in the artichokes. Season with salt and pepper. Add the water and the milk, and cook for about 10 minutes, or until the liquid has evaporated. Stir in the wine, cover and cook until the artichokes are tender. Serve hot or at room temperature.

Green Beans with Tomatoes

Fagiolini verdi con pomodori

This dish is particularly good when fresh tomatoes are used.

Ingredients
450 g/1 lb fresh green beans
45 ml/3 tbsp olive oil
1 medium onion, preferably red, very finely sliced
350 g/12oz plum tomatoes, fresh or canned, peeled and finely chopped
125 ml/4 fl oz/$^1/_2$ cup water
salt and freshly ground black pepper
5–6 leaves of fresh basil torn into pieces
serves 4–6

1 Snap or cut the stem ends off the beans, and wash well in plenty of cold water. Drain.

2 ▲ Heat the oil in a large frying pan with a cover. Add the onion slices and cook until just soft, 5–6 minutes. Add the tomatoes and cook over moderate heat until they soften, about 6–8 minutes. Stir in the water. Season with salt and pepper, and add the basil.

3 ▲ Stir in the beans, turning them in the pan to coat with the sauce. Cover the pan, and cook over moderate heat until tender, about 15–20 minutes. Stir occasionally, and add a little more water if the sauce dries out too much. Serve hot or cold.

Aubergine Baked with Cheeses

Parmigiana di melanzane

This famous dish is a speciality of Italy's southern regions.

Ingredients
1 kg/2 lb aubergines
flour, for coating
oil, for frying
35 g/1 1/2 oz/1/3 cup freshly grated Parmesan cheese
400g/14 oz/2 cups mozzarella cheese, sliced very thinly
salt and freshly ground black pepper

For the tomato sauce
60 ml/4 tbsp olive oil
1 medium onion, very finely chopped
1 clove garlic, finely chopped
450 g/1 lb tomatoes, fresh or canned, chopped, with their juice
salt and freshly ground black pepper
a few leaves fresh basil or sprigs parsley

serves 4–6

1 Wash the aubergines. Cut into rounds about 1 cm/1/2 inch wide, sprinkle with salt, and leave to drain for about 1 hour.

2 ▲ Meanwhile make the tomato sauce. Heat the olive oil in a medium saucepan. Add the chopped onion, and cook over moderate heat until it is translucent, 5–8 minutes. Stir in the chopped garlic and the tomatoes (add 45 ml/3 tbsp water if you are using fresh tomatoes). Season with salt and pepper. Add the fresh basil or parsley. Cook for 20–30 minutes. Purée in a food mill or a food processor.

3 Pat the aubergine slices dry with paper towels. Coat lightly in flour. Heat a little oil in a large frying pan (preferably non-stick). Add one layer of aubergines, and cook over low to moderate heat with the pan covered until they soften. Turn, and cook on the other side. Remove from the pan, and repeat with the remaining slices.

4 Preheat the oven to 180°C/350°F/gas 4. Grease a wide shallow baking dish or tin. Spread a little tomato sauce in the bottom. Cover with a layer of aubergine. Sprinkle with a few teaspoons of Parmesan, season with salt and pepper, and cover with a layer of mozzarella. Spoon on some tomato sauce. Repeat until all the ingredients are used up, ending with a covering of tomato sauce and a sprinkling of Parmesan. Sprinkle with a little olive oil, and bake for about 45 minutes.

Sweet and Sour Aubergines

Caponata

This delicious Sicilian dish combines aubergines and celery in a piquant sauce.

Ingredients
700 g/1 1/2 lb aubergines
30 ml/2 tbsp olive oil
1 medium onion, finely sliced
1 clove garlic, finely chopped
1 x 225g/8 oz can plum tomatoes, peeled and finely chopped
125 ml/4 fl oz/1/2 cup white wine vinegar
30 ml/2 tbsp sugar
salt and freshly ground black pepper
tender central sticks of a head of celery (about 175 g/6 oz)
30 ml/2 tbsp capers, rinsed
75 g/3 oz/1/2 cup green olives, pitted
oil, for deep-frying
30 ml/2 tbsp chopped fresh parsley

serves 4

1 Wash the aubergines and cut into small cubes. Sprinkle with salt, and leave to drain in a colander for 1 hour.

2 ▲ Heat the oil in a large pan. Stir in the onion, and cook until soft. Stir in the garlic and tomatoes, and fry over moderate heat for 10 minutes. Stir in the vinegar, sugar and pepper. Simmer until the sauce reduces, 10 minutes more. Blanch the celery sticks in boiling water until tender. Drain, and chop into 2 cm/1 in pieces. Add to the sauce with the capers and olives.

3 ▲ Pat the aubergine cubes dry with paper towels. Heat the oil to 185°C/360°F/gas 5, and deep-fry the aubergine in batches until golden. Drain on paper towels.

4 Add the aubergine to the sauce. Stir gently and season. Stir in the parsley. Allow to stand for 30 minutes. Serve at room temperature.

Carrots with Marsala

Carote al Marsala

The sweet flavour of Marsala goes surprisingly well with carrots in this Sicilian dish.

Ingredients
50 g/2 oz/4 tbsp butter
450 g/1 lb carrots, cut into sticks
5 ml/1 tsp sugar
$^{1}/_{2}$ tsp salt
50 ml/2 fl oz/$^{1}/_{4}$ cup Marsala
serves 4

1 Melt the butter in a medium saucepan, and add the carrots. Stir well to cover well with the butter. Add the sugar and salt, and mix well.

2 ▲ Stir in the Marsala, and simmer for 4–5 minutes.

3 ▲ Pour in enough water to barely cover the carrots. Cover the pan, and cook over low to moderate heat until the carrots are tender. Remove the cover, and cook until the liquids reduce almost completely. Serve hot.

Broccoli with Oil and Garlic

Broccoletti saltati con aglio

This is a very simple way of transforming steamed or blanched broccoli into a succulent Mediterranean dish. Peeling the broccoli stalks is easy, and allows for even cooking.

Ingredients
1 kg/2 lb fresh broccoli
90 ml/6 tbsp olive oil
2–3 cloves garlic, finely chopped
salt and freshly ground black pepper
serves 6

1 ▲ Wash the broccoli. Cut off any woody parts at the base of the stems. Use a small sharp knife to peel the broccoli stems. Cut any very long or wide stalks in half.

2 ▲ Boil water in the bottom of a saucepan equipped with a steamer, or bring a large pan of water to a boil. If steaming the broccoli, put it in the steamer and cover tightly. Cook for 8–12 minutes or until the stems are just tender when pierced with the point of a knife. Remove from the heat. If blanching, drop the broccoli into the pan of boiling water and blanch until just tender, 5–6 minutes. Drain.

3 ▲ In a frying pan large enough to hold all the broccoli pieces, gently heat the oil with the garlic. When the garlic is light golden (do not let it brown or it will be bitter) add the broccoli, and cook over moderate heat for 3–4 minutes, turning carefully to coat it with the hot oil. Season with salt and pepper. Serve hot or cold.

Meat-stuffed Cabbage Rolls

Involtini di verza ripieni di carne

Stuffed cabbage leaves are a good way of using up cooked meats. These rolls are quite substantial, and make a satisfying luncheon dish.

Ingredients

1 head Savoy cabbage
75 g/3 oz/$^2/_3$ cup white bread
milk, to soak bread
350 g/12 oz/1$^1/_2$ cups cooked meat, very finely chopped, or fresh minced lean beef
1 egg
30 ml/2 tbsp finely chopped fresh parsley
1 clove garlic, finely chopped
50 g/2 oz/$^1/_2$ cup freshly grated Parmesan cheese
pinch of grated nutmeg
salt and freshly ground black pepper
75 ml/5 tbsp olive oil
1 medium onion, finely chopped
250 ml/8 fl oz/1 cup dry white wine
serves 4–5

1 ▲ Cut the leaves from the cabbage. Save the innermost part for soup. Blanch the leaves a few at a time in a large pan of boiling water for 4–5 minutes. Refresh under cold water. Spread the leaves out on clean dish towels to dry.

~ VARIATION ~

Serve the rolls with a tomato sauce, spooned over just before serving.

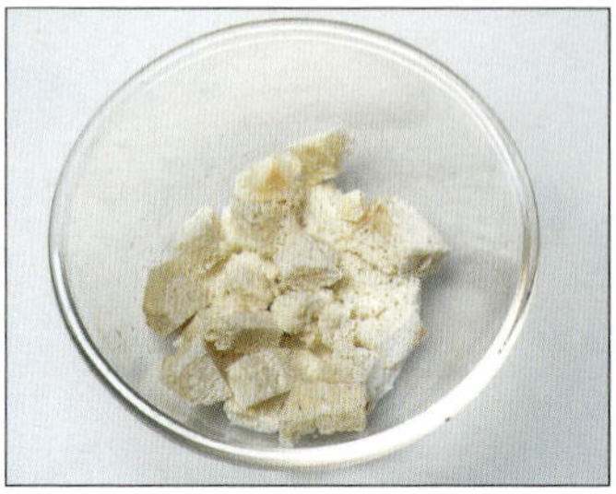

2 ▲ Cut the crusts from the bread, and discard. Soak the bread in a little milk for about 5 minutes. Squeeze out the excess moisture with your hands.

3 ▲ In a mixing bowl combine the chopped or minced meat with the egg and soaked bread. Stir in the parsley, garlic and Parmesan. Season with nutmeg, salt and pepper.

4 ▲ Divide any very large cabbage leaves in half, discarding the rib. Lay the leaves out on a flat surface. Form little sausage-shaped mounds of stuffing, and place them at the edge of each leaf. Roll up the leaves, tucking the ends in as you roll. Squeeze each roll lightly in the palm of your hand to help the leaves to stick.

5 ▲ In a large, shallow, flameproof casserole or deep frying pan large enough to hold all the cabbage rolls in one layer, heat the olive oil. Add the onion, and cook gently until it softens. Raise the heat slightly, and add the cabbage rolls, turning them over carefully with a large spoon as they begin to cook.

6 ▲ Pour in half of the wine. Cook over low to moderate heat until the wine has evaporated. Add the rest of the wine, cover the pan, and cook for 10–15 minutes more. Remove the cover, and cook until all the liquid has evaporated. Remove from the heat, and allow to rest for about 5 minutes before serving.

Broad Bean Purée with Ham

Purea di fave con prosciutto

Peeling broad beans leaves them tender and sweet. They go particularly well with the saltiness of prosciutto crudo in this Tuscan combination.

Ingredients

1 kg/2 lb fresh broad beans in their pods, or 400 g/14oz shelled broad beans, thawed if frozen
1 medium onion, finely chopped
2 small potatoes, peeled and diced
50 g/2 oz/$^1/_4$ cup prosciutto crudo
45 ml/3 tbsp extra-virgin olive oil
salt and freshly ground black pepper
serves 4

1 Place the shelled beans in a saucepan and cover with water. Bring to a boil and cook for 5 minutes. Drain. When they are cool enough to handle, peel the beans.

2 ▲ Place the peeled beans in a saucepan with the onion and potatoes. Add enough water just to cover the vegetables. Bring to the boil. Lower the heat slightly, cover, and simmer until the vegetables are very soft, 15–20 minutes. Check occasionally that all the water has not evaporated. If necessary add a few tablespoons more.

3 Chop the ham into very small dice. Heat the oil and sauté until the ham is just golden.

4 ▲ Mash or purée the bean mixture. Return it to the pan. If it is very moist, cook it over moderate heat until it reduces slightly. Stir in the oil with the ham. Season and cook for 2 minutes.

Deep-fried Cauliflower

Cavolfiore fritto

Deep-frying is very popular in Italy, and everything from cheese to fruit may be fried. The cauliflower may be eaten as a side dish or as an antipasto.

Ingredients

1 large cauliflower
1 egg
salt and freshly ground black pepper
100 g/3$^1/_2$ oz/scant 1 cup flour
175 ml/6 fl oz/$^3/_4$ cup dry white wine
oil, for deep-frying
serves 4

1 Soak the cauliflower in a bowl of salted water. In a mixing bowl, beat the egg. Season and beat in the flour. The mixture will be very thick. Add the wine. If necessary add more to make a fairly runny batter. Cover, and allow to rest for 30 minutes.

2 Steam or boil the cauliflower until just tender - do not overcook. Cut it into small florets when cool.

3 ▲ Heat the oil until a small piece of bread sizzles as soon as it is dropped in (about 185°C/360°F/ gas 5). Dip each cauliflower piece into the batter before deep-frying it until golden.

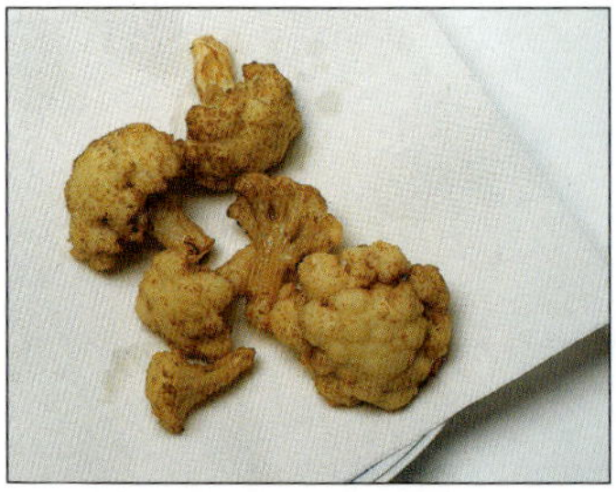

4 ▲ Remove from the oil with a slotted spoon and drain on paper towels. Sprinkle lightly with salt and serve hot.

Baked Fennel with Parmesan Cheese

Finocchio gratinato

Fennel is widely eaten in Italy, both raw and cooked. It is delicious married with the sharpness of Parmesan cheese in this quick and simple dish.

Ingredients

1 kg/2lb fennel bulbs, washed and cut in half
50 g/2 oz/4 tbsp butter
40g/$1^1/_2$ oz/$^1/_3$ cup freshly grated Parmesan cheese
serves 4–6

1 ▲ Cook the fennel in a large pan of boiling water until just soft but not mushy. Drain. Preheat the oven to 200°C/400°F/gas 6.

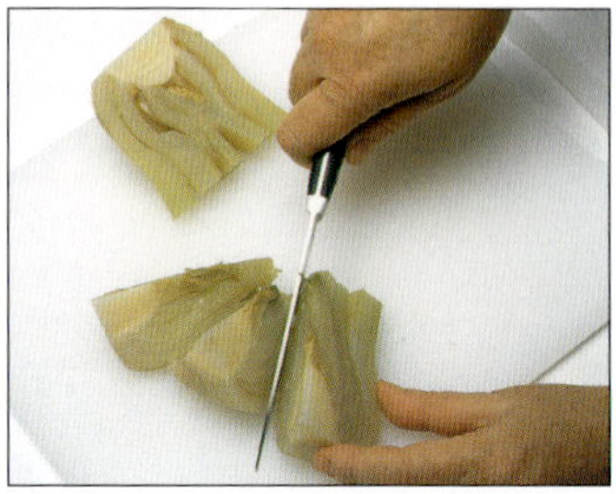

2 ▲ Cut the fennel bulbs lengthwise into 4 or 6 pieces. Place them in a buttered baking dish.

3 ▲ Dot with butter. Sprinkle with the grated Parmesan. Bake in the hot oven until the cheese is golden brown, about 20 minutes. Serve at once.

~ VARIATION ~

For a more substantial version of this dish, sprinkle 75 g/3oz chopped ham over the fennel before topping with the cheese.

Roast Mushroom Caps

Funghi arrosti

Hunting for edible wild mushrooms is one of the Italians' great passions. The most prized are porcini which grow in forests.

Ingredients

4 large mushroom caps, such as porcini or other wild types
2 cloves garlic, chopped
45 ml/3 tbsp chopped fresh parsley
salt and freshly ground black pepper
extra-virgin olive oil, for sprinkling
serves 4

1 Preheat the oven to 190°C/375°F/gas 5. Carefully wipe the mushrooms clean with a damp cloth or paper towel. Cut off the stems. (Save them for soup if they are not too woody). Oil a baking dish large enough to hold the mushrooms in one layer.

2 ▲ Place the mushroom caps in the dish, smooth side down. Mix together the chopped garlic and parsley and sprinkle on the caps.

3 ▲ Season the mushrooms with salt and pepper. Sprinkle the parsley stuffing with oil. Bake for 20–25 minutes. Serve at once.

Courgettes with Sun-dried Tomatoes

Zucchinecon pomodori

One way to preserve tomatoes for winter is to dry them in the sun, as they do all over southern Italy. These tomatoes have a concentrated, sweet flavour that goes well with courgettes.

Ingredients

10 sun-dried tomatoes, dry or preserved in oil and drained
175 ml/6 fl oz/$^3/_4$ cup warm water
75 ml/5 tbsp olive oil
1 large onion, finely sliced
2 cloves garlic, finely chopped
1 kg/2 lb courgettes, cut into thin strips
salt and freshly ground black pepper
serves 6

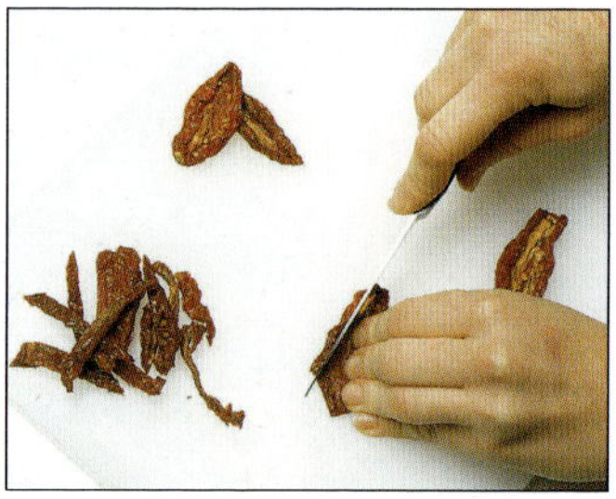

1 ▲ Slice the tomatoes into thin strips. Place in a bowl with the warm water. Allow to stand for 20 minutes.

2 ▲ In a large, deep frying pan or saucepan, heat the oil and stir in the onion. Cook over low to moderate heat until it softens but does not brown.

3 ▲ Stir in the garlic and the courgettes. Cook for about 5 minutes, continuing to stir the mixture.

4 ▲ Stir in the tomatoes and their soaking liquid. Season with salt and pepper. Raise the heat slightly and cook until the courgettes are just tender. Serve hot or cold.

Stuffed Onions

Cipolle ripiene

These savoury onions make a satisfying dish for a light lunch or supper. Small onions could be stuffed and served as an accompaniment to a meat dish.

Ingredients
6 large onions
75 g/3 oz/scant 1/2 cup ham, cut into small dice
1 egg
50 g/2 oz/1/2 cup dry breadcrumbs
45 ml/3 tbsp finely chopped fresh parsley
1 clove garic, finely chopped
pinch of grated nutmeg
75 g/3 oz/3/4 cup grated cheese, such as Parmesan or sharp Cheddar
90 ml/6 tbsp olive oil
salt and freshly ground black pepper
serves 6

1 Peel the onions without cutting through the base. Cook them in a large pan of boiling water for about 20 minutes. Drain, and refresh in plenty of cold water.

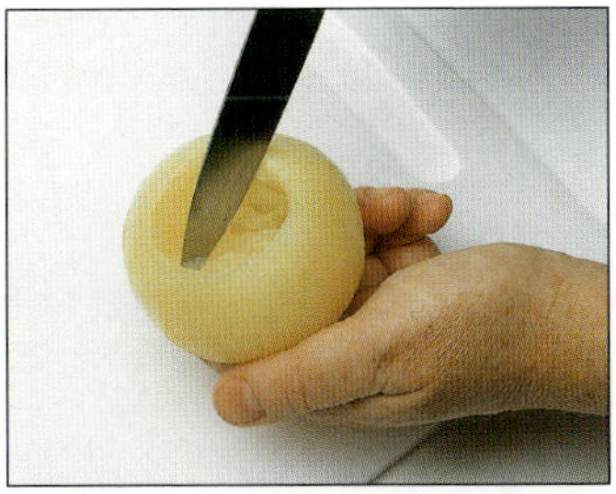

2 ▲ Using a small sharp knife, cut around and scoop out the central section. Remove about half the inside (save it for soup). Lightly salt the empty cavities, and leave the onions to drain upside down.

~ VARIATION ~

For a vegetarian version, replace the ham with chopped olives.

3 ▲ Preheat the oven to 200°C/400°F/ gas 6. In a small bowl, beat the ham into the egg. Stir in the breadcrumbs, parsley, garlic, nutmeg and all but 45 g/3 tbsp of the grated cheese. Add 45 g/3 tbsp of the oil, and season with salt and pepper.

4 Pat the insides of the onions dry with paper towels. Stuff them using a small spoon. Arrange the onions in one layer in an oiled baking dish.

5 ▲ Sprinkle the tops with the remaining cheese, and sprinkle with oil. Bake for 45 minutes, or until the onions are tender and golden on top.

Aromatic Stewed Mushrooms

Funghi trifolati

This dish from Piedmont combines both field and cultivated mushrooms, which give a balanced but not overwhelming flavour.

Ingredients
750 g/1 1/2 lb firm fresh mushrooms, field and cultivated
90 ml/6 tbsp olive oil
2 cloves garlic, finely chopped
salt and freshly ground black pepper
45 ml/3 tbsp chopped fresh parsley
serves 6

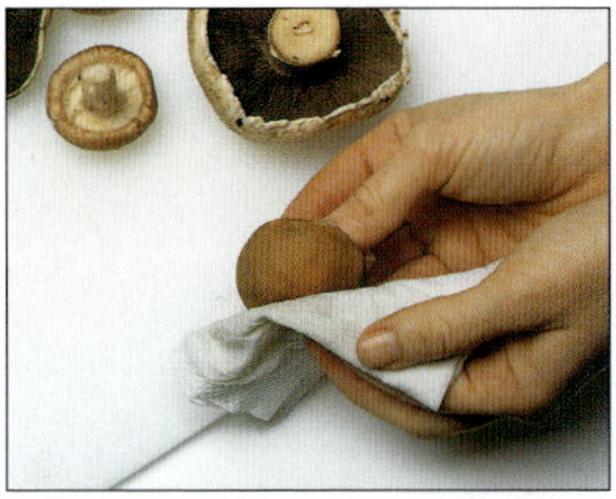

1 ▲ Clean the mushrooms carefully by wiping them with a damp cloth or paper towels.

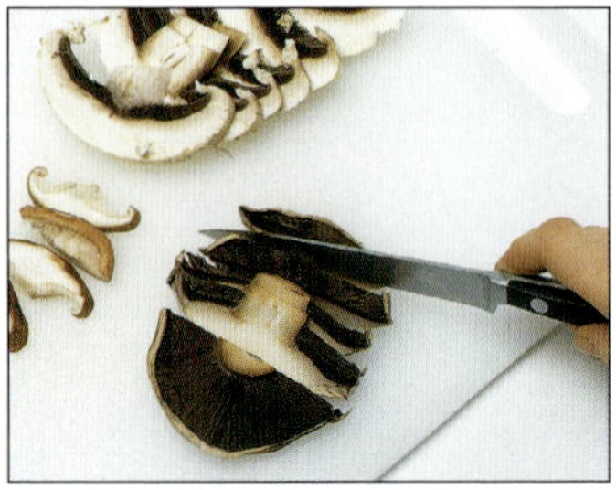

2 ▲ Cut off the woody tips of the stems and discard. Slice the stems and caps fairly thickly.

3 ▲ Heat the oil in a large frying pan. Stir in the garlic and, after about 1 minute, the mushrooms. Cook for 8–10 minutes, stirring occasionally. Season with salt and pepper, and stir in the parsley. Cook for 5 minutes more, and serve at once.

Sautéed Peas with Ham

Piselli alla fiorentina

When fresh peas are in season, they can be stewed with a little ham and onion and served as a substantial side dish.

Ingredients
45 ml/3 tbsp olive oil
115 g/4 oz/1/2 cup pancetta or ham, finely diced
45 ml/3 tbsp finely chopped onion
1 kg/2 lb whole peas (about 300 g/11oz shelled) or 275 g/10 oz frozen petits pois, thawed
30-45 ml/2–3 tbsp water
salt and freshly ground black pepper
a few leaves fresh mint or sprigs parsley
serves 4

1 Heat the oil in a medium saucepan, and sauté the pancetta or ham and onion for 2–3 minutes.

2 ▲ Stir in the shelled fresh or thawed frozen peas. Add the water. Season with salt and pepper and mix well to coat with the oil.

3 ▲ Add the fresh herbs, cover, and cook over moderate heat until tender. This may take from 5 minutes for sweet fresh peas, to 15 for tougher, older peas. Serve as a side dish to meat dishes or frittate.

Stuffed Peppers

Peperoni ripieni

Sweet peppers can be stuffed and baked with many different fillings, from leftover cooked vegetables to rice or pasta. Blanching the peppers first helps to make them tender.

Ingredients

6 medium to large peppers, any colour
200 g/7 oz/scant 1 cup rice
60 ml/4 tbsp olive oil
1 large onion, finely chopped
3 anchovy fillets, chopped
2 cloves garlic, finely chopped
3 medium tomatoes, peeled and cut into small dice
60 ml/4 tbsp white wine
45 ml/3 tbsp finely chopped fresh parsley
$^{1}/_{2}$ cup mozzarella cheese, cut into small dice
90 ml/6 tbsp freshly grated Parmesan cheese
salt and freshly ground black pepper
Basic Tomato Sauce, to serve (optional)

serves 6

1 ▲ Cut the tops off the peppers. Scoop out the seeds and fibrous insides. Blanch the peppers and their tops in a large pan of boiling water for 3–4 minutes. Remove, and stand upside down on racks to drain.

2 ▲ Boil the rice according to the instructions on the package, but drain and rinse it in cold water 3 minutes before the recommended cooking time has elapsed. Drain again.

3 ▲ In a large frying pan, heat the oil and sauté the onion until soft. Stir in the anchovy pieces and the garlic, and mash them. Add the tomatoes, and the wine, and cook for 5 minutes.

4 ▲ Preheat the oven to 190°C/375°F/gas 5. Remove the tomato mixture from the heat. Stir in the rice, parsley, mozzarella and 60 g/4 tbsp of the Parmesan cheese. Season the mixture with salt and pepper.

5 ▲ Pat the insides of the peppers dry with paper towels. Sprinkle with salt and pepper. Stuff the peppers. Sprinkle the tops with the remaining Parmesan, and sprinkle with a little oil.

6 ▲ Arrange the peppers in a shallow baking dish. Pour in enough water to come 1 cm/$^{1}/_{2}$ inch up the sides of the peppers. Bake for 25 minutes. Serve at once, with tomato sauce if desired. These peppers are also good served at room temperature.

~ COOK'S TIP ~

Choose peppers with sturdy, even bases, so they will stand on end unsupported. This will make them easier to cook and serve.

Stewed Peppers

Peperonata

This dish originated in the south of Italy, but has become a popular favourite everywhere. It can be eaten as a side dish or appetizer, and makes a delicious filling for a frittata.

Ingredients
4–5 very ripe peppers, preferably red or yellow, about 750 g/1½lb
60 ml/4 tbsp olive oil
2 medium onions, thinly sliced
3 cloves garlic, finely chopped
350 g/12oz plum tomatoes, peeled, seeded and chopped
salt and freshly ground black pepper
a few fresh basil leaves
serves 6

1 Wash the peppers. Cut them into quarters, removing the stems and seeds. Slice them into thin strips.

2 ▲ In a large, heavy pan, heat the oil and sauté the onions until soft (covering the pan will prevent the onions from browning). Add the peppers, and cook for 5–8 minutes over moderate heat, stirring frequently.

3 ▲ Stir in the garlic and tomatoes. Cover the pan, and cook for about 25 minutes, stirring occasionally. The peppers should be soft, but should still hold their shape. Season, tear the basil leaves into pieces, and stir into the peppers. Serve hot or cold.

Grilled Radicchio and Courgette

Verdure ai ferri

In Italy radicchio is often eaten grilled or barbecued. It is delicious and very easy to prepare.

Ingredients
2–3 firm heads of radicchio, round or long type
4 medium courgettes
90 ml/6 tbsp olive oil
salt and freshly ground black pepper
serves 4

1 ▲ Preheat the grill, or prepare a barbecue. Cut the radicchio in half through the root section or base. If necessary, wash in cold water. Drain.

2 ▲ Cut the courgettes into 1 cm/½in diagonal slices.

3 ▲ When the grill or barbecue is hot, brush the vegetables all over with the olive oil, and sprinkle with salt and pepper. Cook for 4–5 minutes on each side. Serve on their own or as an accompaniment to grilled fish or meat.

Potatoes Baked with Tomatoes

Patate e pomodori al forno

This simple, hearty dish from the south of Italy is best when tomatoes are in season, but can also be made with canned plum tomatoes.

Ingredients

2 large red or yellow onions, thinly sliced
1 kg/2 lb potatoes, peeled and thinly sliced
450 g/1 lb tomatoes, fresh or canned, sliced, with their juice
90 ml/6 tbsp olive oil
115 g/4 oz/1 cup freshly grated Parmesan or sharp Cheddar cheese
salt and freshly ground black pepper
a few leaves fresh basil
50 ml/2 fl oz/$^1/_4$ cup water

serves 6

1 Preheat the oven to 180°C/350°F/gas 4. Brush a large baking dish generously with oil.

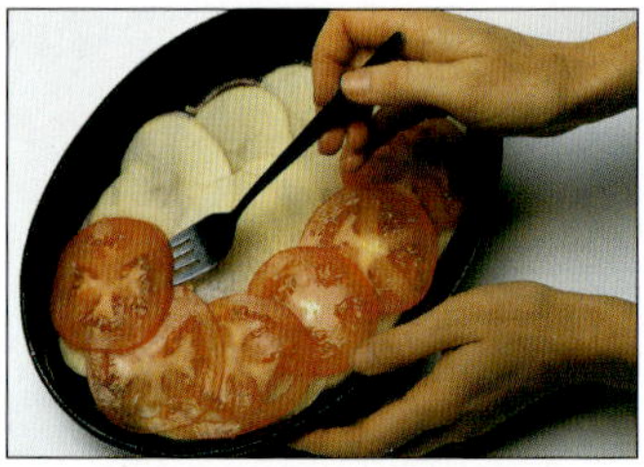

2 ▲ Arrange a layer of onions in the dish, followed by layers of potatoes and tomatoes. Pour on a little of the oil, and sprinkle with a little cheese. Season with salt and pepper.

3 ▲ Repeat until the vegetables are used up, ending with an overlapping layer of potatoes and tomatoes. Tear the basil leaves into pieces, and add them here and there among the vegetables. Sprinkle the top with cheese, and a little oil.

4 ▲ Pour on the water. Bake for 1 hour, or until tender.

5 ▲ If the top begins to brown too much, place a sheet of foil or a flat baking tray on top of the dish. Serve hot.

Tomatoes with Pasta Stuffing

Pomodori ripieni di pasta

Tomatoes are one of Italy's staple foods, appearing in more than three-quarters of all Italian savoury dishes. They can be baked with various stuffings. This one comes from the south.

Ingredients

8 large tomatoes, firm and ripe
115 g/4 oz/1$^1/_4$ cups small soup pasta
8 black olives, stoned and finely chopped
45 ml/3 tbsp finely chopped mixed fresh herbs, such as chives, parsley, basil and thyme
60 ml/4 tbsp grated Parmesan cheese
60 ml/4 tbsp olive oil
salt and freshly ground black pepper

serves 4

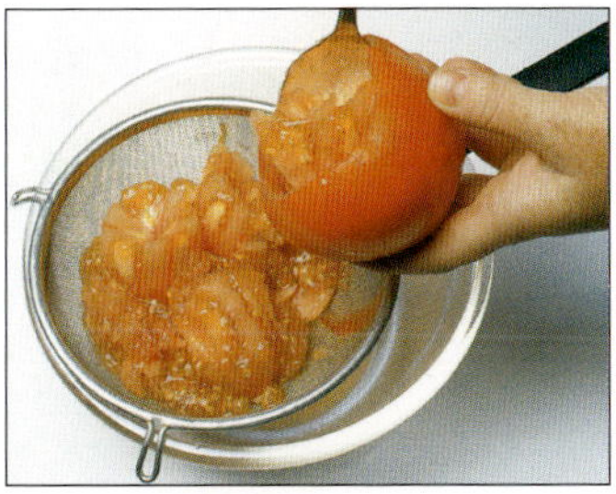

1 ▲ Wash the tomatoes. Slice off the tops, and scoop out the pulp into a strainer with a small spoon. Chop the pulp and turn the tomatoes upside down on a rack to drain.

2 ▲ Leave the pulp in a strainer, and allow the juices to drain off.. Meanwhile, boil the pasta in a pan of boiling salted water. Drain it 2 minutes before the recommended cooking time elapses.

3 ▲ Preheat the oven to 190°C/375°F/ gas 5. Combine the pasta with the remaining ingredients in a bowl. Stir in the drained tomato pulp. Season with salt and pepper.

4 ▲ Stuff the tomatoes, and replace the tops. Arrange them in one layer in a well-oiled baking dish. Bake for 15–20 minutes. Peel off the skins, if desired. Serve hot or at room temperature.

Tomato and Bread Salad

Panzanella

This salad is a traditional peasant dish from Tuscany which was created to use up bread that was several days old. It is best made with sun-ripened tomatoes.

Ingredients
400 g/14 oz/3$^1/_2$ cups stale white or brown bread or rolls
4 large tomatoes
1 large red onion, or 6 spring onions
a few leaves fresh basil, to garnish
For the dressing
60 ml/4 tbsp extra-virgin olive oil
30 ml/2 tbsp white wine vinegar
salt and freshly ground black pepper
serves 4

1 Cut the bread or rolls into thick slices. Place in a shallow bowl, and soak with cold water. Leave for at least 30 minutes.

2 ▲ Cut the tomatoes into chunks. Place in a serving bowl. Finely slice the onion or spring onions, and add them to the tomatoes. Squeeze as much water out of the bread as possible, and add it to the vegetables.

3 ▲ Make a dressing with the oil and vinegar. Season with salt and pepper. Pour it over the salad and mix well. Decorate with the basil leaves. Allow to stand in a cool place for at least 2 hours before serving.

Grilled Pepper Salad

Insalata di peperoni

This colourful salad is a southern Italian creation: all the ingredients are sun-lovers which thrive in the hot, dry Mezzogiorno.

Ingredients
4 large peppers, red or yellow or a combination of both
30 ml/2 tbsp capers in salt, vinegar, or brine, rinsed
18–20 black or green olives
For the dressing
90 ml/6 tbsp extra-virgin olive oil
2 cloves garlic, finely chopped
30 ml/2 tbsp balsamic or wine vinegar
salt and freshly ground black pepper
serves 6

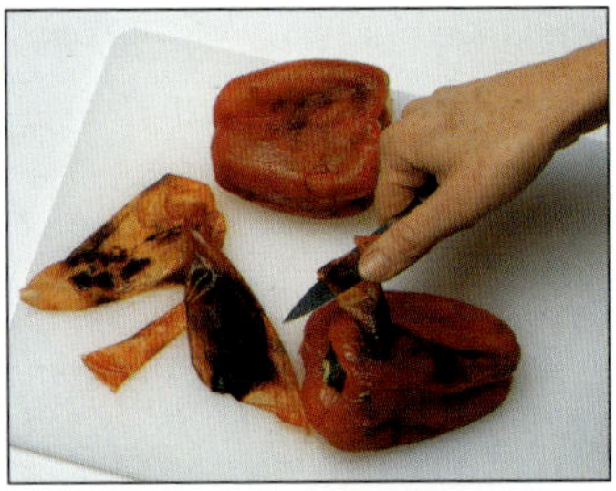

1 Place the peppers under a hot grill, and turn occasionally until they are black and blistered on all sides. Remove from the heat and place in a paper bag. Leave for 5 minutes.

2 ▲ Peel the peppers, then cut into quarters. Remove the stems and seeds.

3 Cut the peppers into strips, and arrange them in a serving dish. Distribute the capers and olives evenly over the peppers.

4 ▲ For the dressing, mix the oil and garlic together in a small bowl, crushing the garlic with a spoon to release as much flavour as possible. Mix in the vinegar, and season with salt and pepper. Pour over the dressing, mix well, and allow to stand for at least 30 minutes before serving.

Artichoke Salad with Eggs

Insalata di carciofi con uova

Artichoke bottoms are best when cut from fresh artichokes, but can also be bought frozen. This salad is easily assembled for a light lunch.

Ingredients

4 large artichokes, or 4 frozen artichoke bottoms, thawed
$^{1}/_{2}$ lemon
4 eggs, hard-boiled and shelled

For the mayonnaise

1 egg yolk
10 ml/2 tsp Dijon mustard
15 ml/1 tbsp white wine vinegar
salt and freshly ground black pepper
250 ml/ 8 fl oz/1 cup olive or vegetable oil
a few sprigs fresh parsley

serves 4

1 ▲ If using fresh artichokes, wash them. Squeeze the lemon, and put the juice and the squeezed half in a bowl of cold water. Prepare the artichokes one at a time. Cut off only the tip from the stem. Peel the stem with a small knife, pulling upwards towards the leaves. Pull off the small leaves around the stem, and continue snapping off the upper part of the dark outer leaves until you reach the taller inner leaves. Cut the tops off the leaves with a sharp knife. Place in the acidulated water. Repeat with the other artichokes.

2 Boil or steam fresh artichokes until just tender (when a leaf comes away quite easily when pulled). Cook frozen artichoke bottoms according to the package instructions. Allow to cool.

3 ▲ Make the mayonnaise. Combine the egg yolk, mustard and vinegar in a mixing bowl. Add salt and pepper to taste. Add the oil in a thin stream while beating vigorously with a wire whisk. When the mixture is thick and smooth, stir in the parsley. Blend well. Cover and refrigerate until needed.

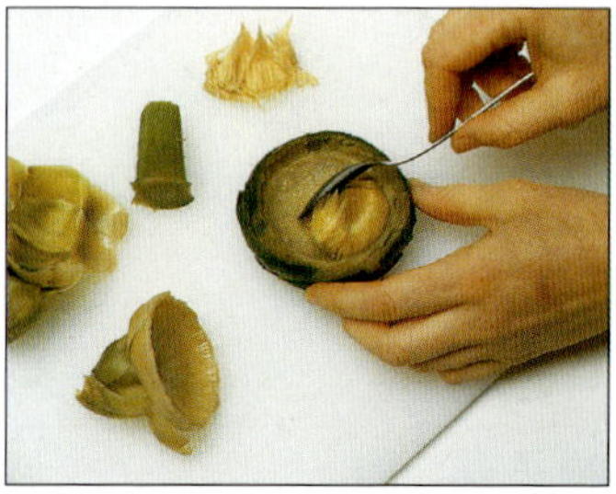

4 ▲ Pull the leaves off the fresh artichokes. Cut the stems off level with the base. Scrape the hairy "choke" off with a knife or spoon.

5 Assemble the salad by cutting the eggs and artichokes into wedges. Arrange on a serving plate, and serve garnished with the mayonnaise.

Fennel and Orange Salad

Insalata di finocchio con arancio

In seventeenth-century Italy fennel was often served at the end of the meal, sprinkled with salt. This refreshing salad originated in Sicily.

Ingredients
2 large fennel bulbs (about 700 g/1 $^{1}/_{2}$ lb)
2 sweet oranges
2 spring onions, to garnish

For the dressing
60 ml/4 tbsp extra-virgin olive oil
30 ml/2 tbsp fresh lemon juice
salt and freshly ground black pepper

serves 4

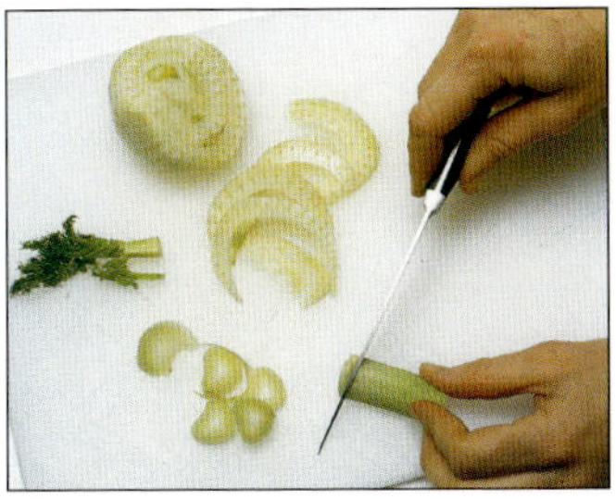

1 ▲ Wash the fennel bulbs and remove any brown or stringy outer leaves. Slice the bulbs and stems into thin pieces. Place in a shallow serving bowl.

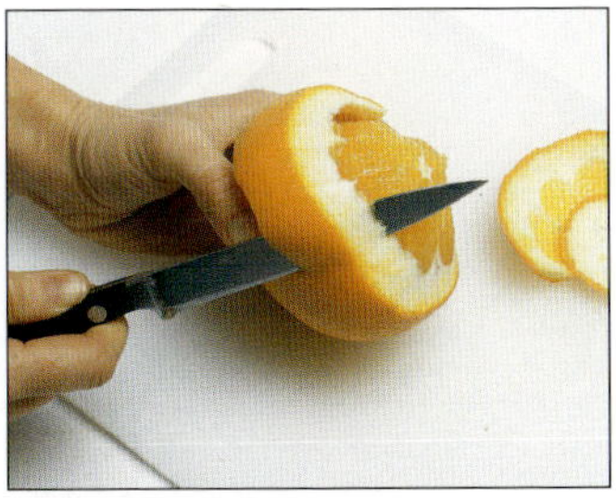

2 ▲ Peel the oranges with a sharp knife, cutting away the white pith. Slice thinly. Cut each slice into thirds. Arrange over the fennel, adding any juice from the oranges.

3 ▲ For the dressing, mix the oil and lemon juice together. Season with salt and pepper. Pour the dressing over the salad. Mix well.

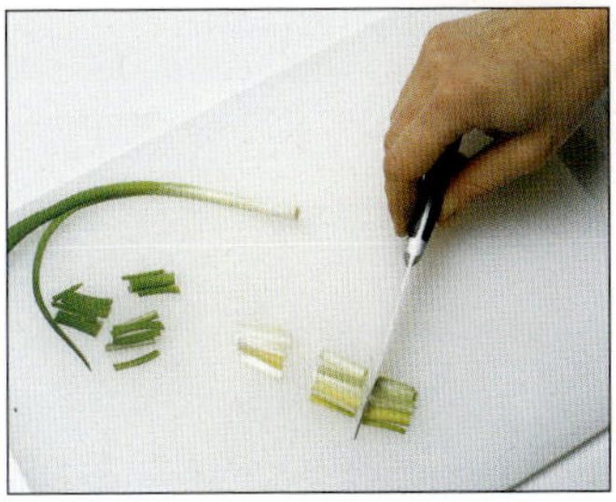

4 ▲ Slice the white and green sections of the spring onions thinly. Sprinkle over the salad.

Potato Salad

Insalata di patate

This salad is dressed while the potatoes are still warm, so the flavours are fully absorbed. Use the best olive oil available.

Ingredients
1 kg/2lb waxy potatoes
For the dressing
90 ml/6 tbsp extra-virgin olive oil
juice of 1 lemon
1 clove garlic, very finely chopped
30 ml/2 tbsp chopped fresh herbs, such as parsley, basil, thyme or oregano
salt and freshly ground black pepper
serves 6

1 Wash the potatoes, but do not peel them. Boil or steam them until tender. When they are cool enough to handle, peel them. Cut the potatoes into dice.

2 ▲ While the potatoes are cooking, mix together all the ingredients for the dressing.

3 ▲ Pour the dressing over the potatoes while they are still warm. Mix well. Serve at room temperature or cold.

Chickpea Salad

Ceci in insalata

This salad makes a good light meal, and is quickly assembled if canned chickpeas are used.

Ingredients
2 × 400 g/14 oz cans chickpeas, or 450 g/1 lb/2 cups cooked chickpeas
6 spring onions, chopped
2 medium tomatoes, cut into cubes
1 small red onion, finely chopped
12 black olives, stoned and cut in half
15 ml/1 tbsp capers, drained
30 g/2 tbsp finely chopped fresh parsley or mint
4 hard-boiled eggs, cut into quarters, to garnish
For the dressing
75 ml/5 tbsp olive oil
45 ml/3 tbsp wine vinegar
salt and freshly ground black pepper
serves 4–6

1 Rinse the chickpeas under cold water. Drain. Place in a serving bowl.

2 ▲ Mix in the other vegetables with the olives and capers.

3 ▲ Mix the dressing ingredients together in a small bowl.

4 ▲ Toss the salad. Pour the dressing over and mix well. Taste for seasoning. Allow to stand for at least 1 hour. Just before serving decorate the salad with the egg wedges.

~ VARIATION ~

Other types of canned cooked beans may be substituted in this salad, such as cannellini or borlotti.

Tuscan Baked Beans

Fagioli al forno alla toscana

Beans, both dried and fresh, are particularly popular in Tuscany, where they are cooked in many different ways. In this vegetarian dish the beans are flavoured with fresh sage leaves.

Ingredients

600 g/1lb 6oz dried beans, such as cannellini
60 ml/4 tbsp olive oil
2 cloves garlic, crushed
3 leaves fresh sage (if fresh sage is not available use 60 ml/4 tbsp chopped fresh parsley)
1 leek, finely sliced
1 x 400g/14oz can plum tomatoes, chopped, with their juice
salt and freshly ground black pepper

serves 6–8

1 ▲ Carefully pick over the beans, discarding any stones or other particles. Place the beans in a large bowl and cover with water. Soak for at least 6 hours, or overnight. Drain.

2 ▲ Preheat the oven to 180°C/350°F/ gas 4. In a small saucepan heat the oil and sauté the garlic cloves and sage leaves for 3–4 minutes. Remove from the heat.

3 ▲ In a large deep baking dish combine the beans with the leek and tomatoes. Stir in the oil with the garlic and sage. Add enough fresh water to cover the beans by 2 cm/1 inch. Mix well. Cover the dish with a lid or foil, and place in the centre of the preheated oven. Bake for $1^3/_4$ hours.

4 ▲ Remove the dish from the oven, stir the beans, and season with salt and pepper. Return the beans to the oven, uncovered, and cook for another 15 minutes, or until the beans are tender. Remove from the oven and allow to stand for 7–8 minutes before serving. Serve hot or at room temperature.

Stewed Lentils

Lenticchie in umido

In Italy lentils are very often eaten as an accompaniment to duck and to zampone or cotechino sausages, but they are also good by themselves.

Ingredients

450 g/1 lb/2 cups green or brown lentils
45 ml/3 tbsp olive oil
50 g/2 oz/$^{1}/_{4}$ cup pancetta or salt pork
1 medium onion, very finely chopped
1 stick celery, very finely sliced
1 carrot, very finely chopped
1 clove garlic
1 bay leaf
45 g/3 tbsp chopped fresh parsley
salt and freshly ground black pepper
serves 6

1 ▲ Carefully pick over the lentils, removing any stones or other particles. Place them in a large bowl and cover with water. Soak for several hours. Drain.

2 ▲ In a large heavy saucepan heat the oil. Add the pancetta or salt pork and cook for 3 or 4 minutes. Stir in the onion, and cook over low heat until it is soft.

3 ▲ Add the celery and carrot and cook for 3–4 minutes more.

4 ▲ Add the lentils to the pan, stirring to coat them with the fat. Pour in enough boiling water just to cover the lentils. Stir well, adding the whole garlic clove, the bay leaf and the parsley. Season with salt and pepper. Cook over moderate heat until the lentils are tender, about 1 hour. Discard the garlic and bay leaf. Serve hot or at room temperature.

Pasta

Dried and home-made egg pastas are easy to prepare and the varied shapes are always family favourites. Nutritious fresh sauces made from vegetables, fish, meat and cheese offer endless possibilities for first and main courses.

How to Make Egg Pasta by Hand

This classic recipe for egg noodles from Emilia-Romagna calls for just three ingredients: flour and eggs, with a little salt. In other regions of Italy water, milk or oil are sometimes added. Use plain unbleached white flour, and large eggs. As a general guide, use 70 g/$2^1/_2$ oz/$^1/_2$ cup of flour to each egg. Quantities will vary with the exact size of the eggs.

To serve 3–4
2 eggs, salt
140 g/5 oz/1 cup flour

To serve 4–6
3 eggs, salt
210 g/$7^1/_2$ oz/$1^1/_2$ cups flour

To serve 6–8
4 eggs, salt
280 g/10 oz/2 cups flour

1 Place the flour in the center of a clean smooth work surface. Make a well in the middle. Break the eggs into the well. Add a pinch of salt.

2 ▲ Start beating the eggs with a fork, gradually drawing the flour from the inside walls of the well. As the paste thickens, continue the mixing with your hands. Incorporate as much flour as possible until the mixture forms a mass. It will still be lumpy. If it still sticks to your hands, add a little more flour. Set the dough aside. Scrape off all traces of the dough from the work surface until it is perfectly smooth. Wash and dry your hands.

About Pasta

Most pasta is made from durum wheat flour and water - durum is a special kind of wheat with a very high protein content. Egg pasta, *pasta all'uova*, contains flour and eggs, and is used for flat noodles such as tagliatelle, or for lasagne. Very little whole wheat pasta is eaten in Italy, but it is quite popular in other countries.

All these types of pasta are available dried in packets, and will keep almost indefinitely. Fresh pasta is now more widely available and can be bought in most supermarkets. It can be very good, but can never compare to home-made egg pasta.

Pasta comes in countless shapes and sizes. It is very difficult to give a definite list, as the names for the shapes vary from country to country. In some cases, just within Italy, the same shape can appear with several different names, depending upon which region it is in. The pasta shapes called for in this book, as well as many others, are illustrated in the introduction. The most common names have been listed.

Most of the recipes in this book specify the pasta shape most appropriate for a particular sauce. They can, of course, be replaced with another kind. A general rule is that long pasta goes better with tomato or thinner sauces, while short pasta is best for chunkier, meatier sauces. But this rule should not be followed too rigidly. Part of the fun of cooking and eating pasta is in the endless combinations of sauce and pasta shapes.

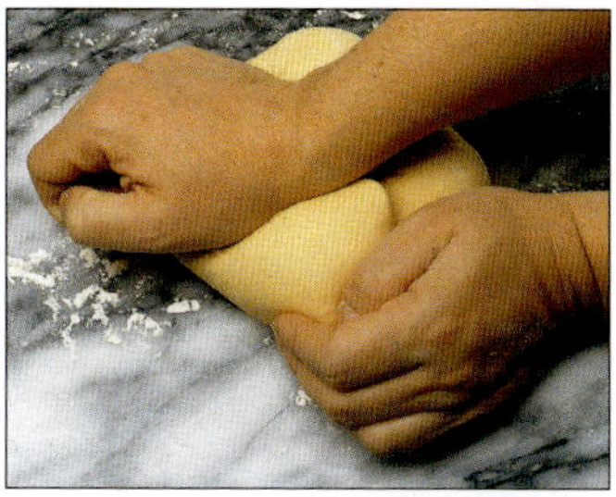

3 ▲ Lightly flour the work surface. Knead the dough by pressing it away from you with the heel of your hands, and then folding it over towards you. Repeat this action over and over, turning the dough as you knead. Work for about 10 minutes, or until the dough is smooth and elastic.

4 ▲ If you are using more than 2 eggs, divide the dough in half. Flour the rolling pin and the work surface. Pat the dough into a disc and begin rolling it out into a flat circle, rotating it one quarter turn after each roll to keep its shape round. Roll until the disc is about 3 mm/$^{1}/_{8}$ in thick.

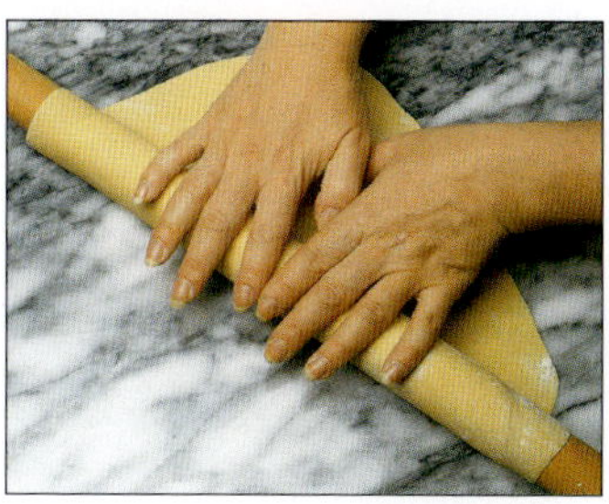

5 ▲ Roll out the dough until it is paper-thin by rolling it up on to the rolling pin and simultaneously giving a sideways stretch with the hands. Wrap the near edge of the dough around the centre of the rolling pin, and begin rolling the dough up away from you. As you roll back and forth, slide your hands from the centre towards the outer edges of the pin, stretching and thinning out the pasta.

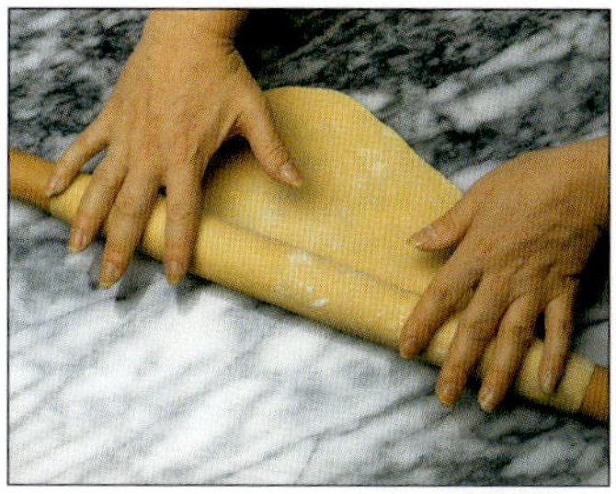

6 ▲ Quickly repeat these movements until about two-thirds of the sheet of pasta is wrapped around the pin. Lift and turn the wrapped pasta sheet about 45° before unrolling it. Repeat the rolling and stretching process, starting from a new point of the sheet each time to keep it evenly thin. By the end (this process should not last more than 8 to 10 minutes or the dough will lose its elasticity) the whole sheet should be smooth and almost transparent. If the dough is still sticky, lightly flour your hands as you continue rolling and stretching.

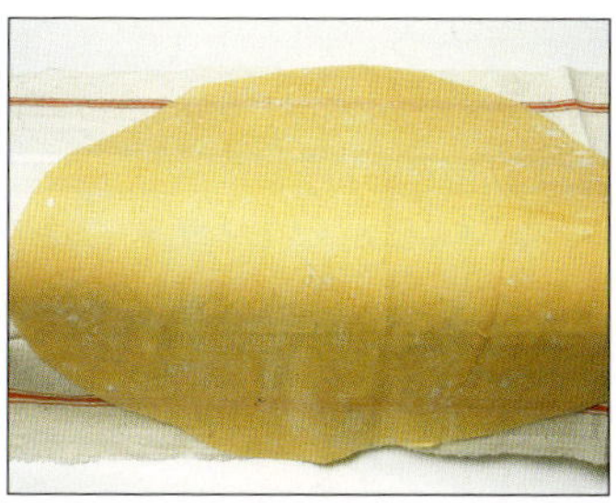

7 ▲ If you are making noodles (tagliatelle, fettuccine etc.) lay a clean dish towel on a table or other flat surface, and unroll the pasta sheet on it, letting about a third of the sheet hang over the edge of the table. Rotate the dough every 10 minutes. Roll out the second sheet of dough if you are using more than 2 eggs. After 25–30 minutes the pasta will have dried enough to cut. Do not overdry or the pasta will crack as it is cut.

8 ▲ To cut tagliatelle, fettuccine or tagliolini, fold the sheet of pasta into a flat roll about 10 cm/4 in wide. Cut across the roll to form noodles of the desired width. Tagliolini is 3 mm/$^{1}/_{8}$ in; Fettuccine is 4 mm/$^{1}/_{6}$ in; Tagliatelle is 6 mm/$^{1}/_{4}$ in. After cutting, open out the noodles, and let them dry for about 5 minutes before cooking. These noodles may be stored for some weeks without refrigeration. Allow them to dry completely before storing them, uncovered, in a dry cupboard, and use as required.

9 ▲ To cut the pasta for lasagne or pappardelle, do not fold or dry the rolled out dough. Lasagne is made by cutting rectangles approximately 13 cm/5 in by 9 cm/3$^{1}/_{2}$ in. Pappardelle are large noodles cut with a fluted pastry wheel. They are about 2 cm/$^{3}/_{4}$ in wide.

Egg Pasta Made by Machine

Making pasta with a machine is quick and easy. The results are perhaps not quite as fine as with handmade pasta, but they are certainly better than store-bought pastas.

You will need a pasta-making machine, either hand-cranked or electric. Use the same proportions of eggs, flours and salt as for Handmade Egg Pasta.

1 ▲ Place the flour in the centre of a clean smooth work surface. Make a well in the middle. Break the eggs into the well. Add a pinch of salt. Start beating the eggs with a fork, gradually drawing the flour from the inside walls of the well. As the paste thickens, continue mixing with your hands. Incorporate as much flour as possible until the mixture forms a mass. It will still be lumpy. If it sticks to your hands, add a little more flour. Set the dough aside and scrape the work surface clean.

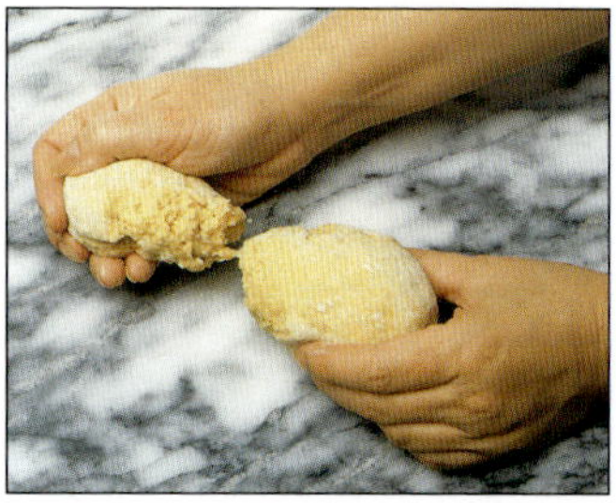

2 ▲ Set the machine rollers at their widest (kneading) setting. Pull off a piece of dough the size of a small orange. Place the remaining dough between two soup plates. Feed the dough through the rollers. Fold it in half, end to end, and feed it through again 7 or 8 times, turning it and folding it over after each kneading. The dough should be smooth and fairly evenly rectangular. If it sticks to the machine, brush with flour. Lay it out on a lightly floured work surface or on a clean dish towel, and repeat with the remaining dough, broken into pieces the same size.

3 ▲ Adjust the machine to the next line setting. Feed each strip through once only, and replace on the drying surface. Keep them in the order in which they were first kneaded.

4 ▲ Reset the machine to the next setting. Repeat, passing each strip through once. Repeat for each remaining roller setting until the pasta is the right thickness – for most purposes this is given by the next to last setting, except for very delicate strips such as tagliolini, or for ravioli. If the pasta strips get too long, cut them in half to facilitate handling.

5 ▲ When all the strips are the desired thickness they may be machine-cut into noodles, or hand-cut for lasagne or pappardelle, as described for handmade pasta earlier. When making noodles, be sure the pasta is fairly dry, but not brittle, or the noodles may stick togther when cut. Select the desired width of cutter, and feed the strips through.

6 Separate the noodles, and leave to dry for at least 15 minutes before using. They may be stored for some weeks without refrigeration. Allow them to dry completely before storing them, uncovered, in a dry cupboard. They may also be frozen, first loose on trays and then packed together.

7 If you are making stuffed pasta (ravioli, cannelloni etc.) do not let the pasta strips dry out before filling them, but proceed immediately with the individual recipes.

~ PASTA VERDE ~

Follow the same recipe, adding 50 g/2 oz/$^1/_4$ cup cooked, very finely chopped spinach (after having been squeezed very dry) to the eggs and flour. You may have to add a little more flour to absorb the moisture from the spinach. This pasta is very suitable for stuffed recipes, as it seals better than plain egg pasta.

How to Cook Dried Pasta

Store-bought and home-made pasta are cooked in the same way, though the timings vary greatly. Home-made pasta cooks virtually in the time it takes for the water to return to a boil after it is put in.

1 Always cook pasta in a large amount of rapidly boiling water. Use at least 1 litre/2 pints/5 cups of water to each 115 g/4 oz/ $^{1}/_{2}$ cup pasta.

2 ▲ The water should be salted at least 2 minutes before the pasta is added, to give the salt time to dissolve. Add about 20 g/1$^{1}/_{2}$ tbsp salt per 2 cups of pasta. You may want to vary the saltiness of the cooking water.

3 ▲ Drop the pasta into the boiling water all at once. Use a wooden spoon to help ease long pasta in as it softens, to prevent it from breaking. Stir frequently to prevent the pasta sticking to itself or to the pan. Cook the pasta at a fast boil, but be prepared to lower the heat if it boils over.

4 Timing is critical in pasta cooking. Follow package indications for store-bought pasta, but it is best in all cases to test for doneness by tasting, several times if necessary. In Italy pasta is always eaten *al dente*, which means firm to the bite. Cooked this way it is just tender, but its "soul" (the innermost part) is still firm. Overcooked pasta will be mushy.

5 ▲ Place a colander in the sink before the pasta has finished cooking. As soon as the pasta tastes done, tip it all into the colander (you may first want to reserve a cupful of the hot cooking water to add to the sauce if it needs thinning). Shake the colander lightly to remove most but not all of the cooking water. Pasta should never be over-drained.

6 ▲ Quickly turn the pasta into a warmed serving dish, and immediately toss it with a little butter or oil, or the prepared sauce. Alternatively, turn it into the cooking pan with the sauce, where it will be cooked for 1–2 minutes more as it is mixed into the sauce. Never allow pasta to sit undressed, as it will stick together and become unpalatable.

How to Cook Egg Pasta

Fresh egg pasta, especially home-made, cooks very much faster than dried pasta. Make sure everything is ready (the sauce, serving dishes etc) before you start boiling egg pasta, as there will not be time once the cooking starts, and egg pasta becomes soft and mushy very quickly.

1 Always cook pasta in a large pot with a generous amount of rapidly boiling water. Use at least 1 litre/2 pints/5 cups of water to a quantity of pasta made with 115 g/4 oz/1 cup of flour. Salt the water as for dried pasta.

2 ▲ Drop the pasta into the boiling water all at once. Stir gently to prevent the pasta sticking to itself or to the pan. Cook the pasta at a fast boil.

3 ▲ Freshly made pasta can be done as little as 15 seconds after the cooking water comes back to a boil. Stuffed pasta takes a few minutes longer. When done, turn the pasta into the colander and proceed as for dried pasta.

Basic Tomato Sauce

Sugo di pomodoro alla napoletana

Tomato sauce is without a doubt the most popular dressing for pasta in Italy. This sauce is best made with fresh tomatoes, but works well with canned plum tomatoes.

Ingredients
60 ml/4 tbsp olive oil
1 medium onion, very finely chopped
1 clove garlic, finely chopped
450 g/1lb tomatoes, fresh or canned, chopped, with their juice
salt and freshly ground black pepper
a few leaves fresh basil or sprigs parsley
for 4 servings of pasta

1 Heat the oil in a medium pan. Add the chopped onion, and cook over a moderate heat until it is translucent, 5–8 minutes.

2 ▲ Stir in the garlic and the tomatoes with their juice (add 45 ml/3 tbsp of water if you are using fresh tomatoes). Season with salt and pepper. Add the herbs. Cook for 20–30 minutes.

3 ▲ Pass the sauce through a food mill or purée in a food processor. To serve, reheat gently, correct the seasoning and pour over the drained pasta.

Special Tomato Sauce

Sugo di pomodoro

The tomatoes in this sauce are enhanced by the addition of extra vegetables. It is good served with all types of pasta or could be served as an accompaniment to stuffed vegetables.

Ingredients
700g/1 $^{2}/_{3}$lb tomatoes, fresh or canned, chopped
1 carrot, chopped
1 stick celery, chopped
1 medium onion, chopped
1 clove garlic, crushed
75 ml/5 tbsp olive oil
salt and freshly ground black pepper
a few leaves fresh basil or a small pinch dried oregano
for 6 servings of pasta

1 Place all the ingredients in a medium heavy saucepan, and simmer together for 30 minutes.

2 ▲ Purée the sauce in a food processor, or press through a sieve.

3 ▲ Return the sauce to the pan, correct the seasoning, and simmer again for about 15 minutes.

~ COOK'S TIP ~

This sauce may be spooned into freezer bags and frozen until required. Allow to thaw to room temperature before re-heating.

Linguine with Pesto Sauce

Linguine con pesto

Pesto originates in Liguria, where the sea breezes are said to give the local basil a particularly fine flavour. It is traditionally made with a mortar and pestle, but it is easier to make in a food processor or blender. Freeze any spare pesto in an ice cube tray.

Ingredients

65 g/2$^1/_2$ oz/$^3/_4$ cup fresh basil leaves
3–4 cloves garlic, peeled
45 ml/3 tbsp pine nuts
$^1/_2$ tsp salt
75 ml/5 tbsp olive oil
50 g/2 oz/$^1/_2$ cup freshly grated Parmesan cheese
60 ml/4 tbsp freshly grated pecorino cheese
freshly ground black pepper
500 g/1$^1/_4$lb linguine
serves 5–6

1 ▲ Place the basil, garlic, pine nuts, salt and olive oil in a blender or food processor and process until smooth. Remove to a bowl. (If desired, the sauce may be frozen at this point, before the cheeses are added.)

2 ▲ Stir in the cheeses (use all Parmesan if pecorino is not available). Taste for seasoning.

3 ▲ Cook the pasta in a large pan of rapidly boiling salted water until it is *al dente*. Just before draining it, take about 60 ml/4 tbsp of the cooking water and stir it into the sauce.

4 ▲ Drain the pasta and toss with the sauce. Serve immediately.

Bolognese Meat Sauce

Ragù alla bolognese

This great meat sauce is a speciality of Bologna. It is delicious with tagliatelle or short pastas such as penne or conchiglie as well as spaghetti, and is indispensable in baked lasagne. It keeps well in the refrigerator for several days and can also be frozen.

Ingredients

25 g/1 oz/2 tbsp butter
60 ml/4 tbsp olive oil
1 medium onion, finely chopped
25 g/1 oz/2 tbsp pancetta or unsmoked bacon, finely chopped
1 carrot, finely sliced
1 stick celery, finely sliced
1 garlic clove, finely chopped
350 g/12oz lean ground beef
salt and freshly ground black pepper
150 ml/$^1/_4$ pint/$^2/_3$ cup red wine
125 ml/4 fl oz/$^1/_2$ cup milk
1 x 400 g/14oz can plum tomatoes, chopped, with their juice
1 bay leaf
$^1/_4$ tsp fresh thyme leaves
for 6 servings of pasta

1 ▲ Heat the butter and oil in a heavy saucepan or earthenware pot. Add the onion, and cook over moderate heat for 3–4 minutes. Add the pancetta, and cook until the onion is translucent. Stir in the carrot, celery and garlic. Cook for 3–4 minutes more.

2 Add the beef, and crumble it into the vegetables with a fork. Stir until the meat loses its red colour. Season with salt and pepper.

3 ▲ Pour in the wine, raise the heat slightly, and cook until the liquid evaporates, 3–4 minutes. Add the milk, and cook until it evaporates.

4 ▲ Stir in the tomatoes with their juice, and the herbs. Bring the sauce to a boil. Reduce the heat to low, and simmer, uncovered for $1^1/_2$–2 hours, stirring occasionally. Correct the seasoning before serving.

Spaghetti with Garlic and Oil

Spaghetti con aglio e olio

This is one of the simplest and most satisfying pasta dishes of all. It is very popular throughout Italy. Use the best quality oil available for this dish.

Ingredients

400 g/14 oz spaghetti
60 ml/6 tbsp extra-virgin olive oil
3 cloves garlic, chopped
60 ml/4 tbsp chopped fresh parsley
salt and freshly ground black pepper
freshly grated Parmesan cheese, to serve (optional)

serves 4

1 Drop the spaghetti into a large pan of rapidly boiling salted water.

2 ▲ In a large frying pan heat the oil and gently sauté the garlic until it is barely golden. Do not let it brown or it will taste bitter. Stir in the parsley. Season with salt and pepper. Remove from the heat until the pasta is ready.

3 ▲ Drain the pasta when it is barely *al dente*. Add it to the pan with the oil and garlic, and cook together for 2–3 minutes, stirring well to coat the spaghetti with the sauce. Serve immediately in a warmed serving bowl, with Parmesan, if desired.

Spaghetti with Walnut Sauce

Spaghetti con salsa di noci

Like pesto, this sauce is traditionally ground in a mortar and pestle, but works just as well made in a food processor. It is also very good on tagliatelle and other noodles.

Ingredients

115 g/4 oz/1 cup walnut pieces or halves
45 ml/3 tbsp plain breadcrumbs
45 ml/3 tbsp olive or walnut oil
45 ml/3 tbsp chopped fresh parsley
1–2 cloves garlic (optional)
50 g/2 oz/¼ cup butter, at room temperature
30 ml/2 tbsp cream
salt and freshly ground black pepper
400 g/14oz wholewheat spaghetti
freshly grated Parmesan cheese, to serve

serves 4

1 Drop the nuts into a small pan of boiling water, and cook for 1–2 minutes. Drain. Slip off the skins. Dry on paper towels. Coarsely chop and set aside about a quarter of the nuts.

2 ▲ Place the remaining nuts, the breadcrumbs, oil, parsley and garlic, if using, in a food processor or blender. Process to a paste. Remove to a bowl, and stir in the softened butter and the cream. Season with salt and pepper.

3 ▲ Cook the pasta in a large pan of rapidly boiling salted water until *al dente*. Drain, and toss with the sauce. Sprinkle with the reserved chopped nuts, and pass the Parmesan separately.

Fusilli with Peppers and Onions

Fusilli con peperoni

Peppers are characteristic of southern Italy. When grilled and peeled they have a delicious smoky flavour, and are easily digested.

Ingredients

450 g/1 lb red and yellow peppers (about 2 large ones)
90 ml/6 tbsp olive oil
1 large red onion, thinly sliced
2 cloves garlic, minced
400 g/14 oz/4 cups fusilli or other short pasta
salt and freshly ground black pepper
45 ml/3 tbsp finely chopped fresh parsley
freshly grated Parmesan cheese, to serve

serves 4

1 ▲ Place the peppers under a hot grill and turn occasionally until they are black and blistered on all sides. Remove from the heat, place in a paper bag and leave for 5 minutes.

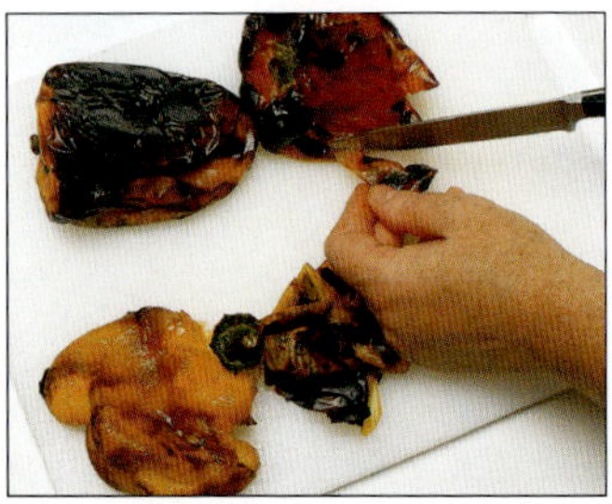

2 ▲ Peel the peppers. Cut them into quarters, remove the stems and seeds, and slice into thin strips. Bring a large pan of water to a boil.

3 ▲ Heat the oil in a large frying pan. Add the onion, and cook over moderate heat until it is translucent, 5–8 minutes. Stir in the garlic, and cook for 2 minutes more.

4 ▲ Add salt and the pasta to the boiling water, and cook until the pasta is just *al dente*.

~ COOK'S TIP ~

Peppers belong to the *Capsicum annuum* species. They were brought to Europe by Columbus who discovered them in Haiti. The large red, yellow and orange peppers are usually sweeter than the green varieties, and have a fuller flavour.

5 ▲ Meanwhile, add the peppers to the onions, and mix together gently. Stir in about 45 ml/3 tbsp of the pasta cooking water. Season with salt and pepper. Stir in the parsley.

6 ▲ Drain the pasta. Tip it into the pan with the vegetables, and cook over moderate heat for 3–4 minutes, stirring constantly to mix the pasta into the sauce. Serve with the Parmesan passed separately.

Orecchiette with Broccoli

Pasta e broccoli

Puglia, in southern Italy, specializes in imaginative pasta and vegetable combinations. Using the broccoli cooking water for boiling the pasta gives it more of the vegetable's flavour.

Ingredients

800 g/1$^3/_4$lb broccoli
450 g/1lb orecchiette or penne
90 ml/6 tbsp olive oil
3 cloves garlic, finely chopped
6 anchovy fillets in oil
salt and freshly ground black pepper
serves 6

1 Peel the stems of the broccoli, starting from the base and pulling up towards the florets with a knife. Discard the woody parts of the stem. Cut florets and stems into 5 cm/2 in pieces.

2 ▲ Bring a large pan of water to the boil. Drop in the broccoli, and boil until barely tender, about 5–8 minutes. Remove the broccoli pieces from the pan to a serving bowl. Do not discard the cooking water.

3 ▲ Add salt to the broccoli cooking water. Bring it back to a boil. Drop in the pasta, stir well, and cook until it is *al dente*.

4 ▲ While the pasta is boiling, heat the oil in a small pan. Add the garlic and, after 2–3 minutes, the anchovy fillets. Using a fork, mash the anchovies and garlic to a paste. Cook for 3–4 minutes more.

5 ▲ Before draining the pasta, ladle 1–2 cupfuls of the cooking water over the broccoli. Add the drained pasta and the hot anchovy and oil mixture. Mix well, and season with salt and pepper if necessary. Serve at once.

Spaghetti with Eggs and Bacon

Spaghetti alla carbonara

One of the classic pasta sauces, about which a debate remains: whether or not it should contain cream. Purists believe that it should not.

Ingredients
30 ml/2 tbsp olive oil
150 g/5 oz/generous $^1/_2$ cup bacon, cut into matchsticks
1 clove garlic, crushed
400 g/14 oz spaghetti
3 eggs, at room temperature
75 g/3 oz/$^3/_4$ cup freshly grated Parmesan cheese
salt and freshly ground black pepper
serves 4

1 ▲ Bring a large pan of water to the boil. In a medium frying pan, heat the oil and sauté the bacon and the garlic until the bacon renders its fat and starts to brown. Remove and discard the garlic. Keep the bacon and its fat hot until needed.

2 ▲ Add salt and the spaghetti to the boiling water, and cook until it is *al dente*.

3 ▲ While the pasta is cooking, warm a large serving bowl and break the eggs into it. Beat in the Parmesan cheese with a fork, and season with salt and pepper.

4 ▲ As soon as the pasta is done, drain it quickly, and mix it into the egg mixture. Pour on the hot bacon and its fat. Stir well. The heat from the pasta and bacon fat will cook the eggs. Serve immediately.

Short Pasta with Cauliflower

Pennoni rigati con cavolfiore

This is a pasta version of cauliflower cheese. The cauliflower water is used to boil the pasta.

Ingredients

1 medium cauliflower
500 ml/16 fl oz/2 cups milk
1 bay leaf
50 g/2 oz/$^{1}/_{4}$ cup butter
50 g/2 oz/$^{1}/_{2}$ cup flour
salt and freshly ground black pepper
75 g/3 oz/$^{3}/_{4}$ cup freshly grated Parmesan or Cheddar cheese
500 g/1$^{1}/_{4}$lb pennoni rigati, or other short pasta
serves 6

1 Bring a large pan of water to the boil. Wash the cauliflower well, and separate it into florets. Boil the florets until they are just tender, about 8–10 minutes. Remove them from the pan with a strainer or slotted spoon. Chop the cauliflower into bite-size pieces and set aside. Do not discard the cooking water.

2 ▲ Make a béchamel sauce by gently heating the milk with the bay leaf in a small saucepan. Do not let it boil. Melt the butter in a medium heavy saucepan. Add the flour, and mix it in well with a wire whisk ensuring there are no lumps. Cook for 2–3 minutes, but do not let the butter burn.

3 Strain the hot milk into the flour and butter mixture all at once, and mix smoothly with the whisk.

4 Bring the sauce to a boil, stirring constantly, and cook for 4–5 minutes more. Season with salt and pepper. Add the cheese, and stir over low heat until it melts. Stir in the cauliflower.

5 ▲ Bring the cooking water back to the boil. Add salt, and stir in the pasta. Cook until it is *al dente*. Drain, and place the pasta in a warm serving bowl. Pour over the sauce. Mix well, and serve at once.

Spaghetti with Bacon and Onion

Spaghetti all'amatriciana

This easy sauce is quickly made from ingredients that are almost always at hand.

Ingredients

30 ml/2 tbsp olive oil or lard
115 g/4 oz/$^{1}/_{2}$ cup unsmoked lean bacon, cut into matchsticks
1 small onion, finely chopped
100 ml/4 fl oz/$^{1}/_{2}$ cup dry white wine
450 g/1lb fresh or canned tomatoes, chopped
$^{1}/_{4}$ tsp thyme leaves
salt and freshly ground black pepper
600 g/1 lb 5 oz spaghetti
freshly grated Parmesan, to serve
serves 6

1 In a medium frying pan, heat the oil or lard. Add the bacon and onion, and cook over low to moderate heat until the onion is golden and the bacon has rendered its fat and is beginning to brown, about 8–10 minutes. Bring a large pan of water to the boil.

2 ▲ Add the wine to the bacon and onion, raise the heat, and cook rapidly until the liquid boils off. Add the tomatoes, thyme, salt and pepper. Cover, and cook over moderate heat for 10–15 minutes.

3 ▲ Meanwhile, add salt to the boiling water, and cook the pasta until it is *al dente*. Drain, toss with the sauce, and serve with the grated Parmesan.

Spaghetti with Olives and Capers

Spaghetti alla puttanesca

This spicy sauce originated in the Naples area, where it was named for the local women of easy virtue. It can be quickly assembled using a few kitchen cupboard staples.

Ingredients

60 ml/4 tbsp olive oil
2 cloves garlic, finely chopped
small piece of dried chilli, crumbled
50 g/2 oz can of anchovy fillets, chopped
350 g/12 oz tomatoes, fresh or canned, chopped
115 g/4 oz/$^2/_3$ cup pitted black olives
30 g/2 tbsp capers, rinsed
15 ml/1 tbsp tomato paste
400 g/14 oz spaghetti
2 tbsp chopped fresh parsley, to serve

serves 4

1 ▲ Bring a large pan of water to the boil. Heat the oil in a large frying pan. Add the garlic and the dried chilli, and cook for 2–3 minutes until the garlic is just golden.

2 ▲ Add the anchovies, and mash them into the garlic with a fork.

3 ▲ Add the tomatoes, olives, capers and tomato paste. Stir well and cook over moderate heat.

4 Add salt to the boiling water, and put in the spaghetti. Stir, and cook until the pasta is just *al dente*. Drain.

5 ▲ Turn the spaghetti into the sauce. Raise the heat, and cook for 1–2 minutes, turning the pasta constantly. Sprinkle with parsley if desired and serve. Traditionally, no cheese is served with this sauce.

Linguine with Clam and Tomato Sauce

Linguine con vongole

There are two types of traditional Italian clam sauce for pasta: one with and one without tomatoes. This tomato version can be made with bottled clams if fresh are not available.

Ingredients

1 kg/2 lb fresh clams in their shells, or 350 g/12 oz canned clams, with their liquid
90 ml/6 tbsp olive oil
1 clove garlic, crushed
400 g/14 oz tomatoes, fresh or canned, very finely chopped
350 g/12 oz linguine
60 ml/4 tbsp chopped fresh parsley
salt and freshly ground black pepper

serves 4

1 ▲ Scrub and rinse the clams well under cold running water. Place them in a large pan with a cupful of water, and heat until the clams begin to open. Lift each clam out as soon as it opens, and scoop it out of its shell using a small spoon. Place in a bowl.

2 If the clams are large, chop them into 2 or 3 pieces. Reserve any liquids from the shells in a separate bowl. When all the clams have opened (discard any that do not open) pour the cooking liquids into the juices from the clams, and strain them through a piece of paper towel to remove any sand. If using canned clams, use the liquid from the can.

3 Bring a large pan of water to a boil for the pasta. Place the olive oil in a medium saucepan with the crushed garlic. Cook over a moderate heat until the garlic is just golden.

4 ▲ Remove the garlic and discard. Add the chopped tomatoes to the oil, and pour in the clam liquid. Mix well and cook over a low to moderate heat until the sauce begins to dry out and thicken slightly. Add salt and the pasta to the boiling water.

5 ▲ A minute or two before the pasta is ready to be drained, stir the parsley and the clams into the tomato sauce, and raise the heat. Add some freshly ground black pepper, and taste for seasoning. Drain the pasta, and turn it into a serving bowl. Pour on the hot sauce, and mix well before serving.

Spaghetti with Mussels

Spaghetti con cozze

Mussels are popular in all the coastal regions of Italy, and are delicious with pasta. This simple dish is greatly improved by using the freshest mussels available.

Ingredients

1 kg/2 lb fresh mussels, in their shells
75 ml/5 tbsp olive oil
3 cloves garlic, finely chopped
60 ml/4 tbsp finely chopped fresh parsley
60 ml/4 tbsp white wine
400 g/14 oz spaghetti
salt and freshly ground black pepper
serves 4

1 ▲ Scrub the mussels well under cold running water, cutting off the "beard" with a small sharp knife.

2 ▲ Bring a large pan of water to a boil for the pasta. Place the mussels with a cupful of water in another large pan over moderate heat. As soon as they open, lift them out one by one.

3 ▲ When all the mussels have opened (discard any that do not), strain the liquid in the pan through a layer of paper towels and reserve until needed.

4 ▲ Heat the oil in a large frying pan. Add the garlic and parsley, and cook for 2–3 minutes. Add the mussels, their strained juices and the wine. Cook over moderate heat. Meanwhile add salt to the boiling water, and drop in the pasta.

5 ▲ Add a generous amount of freshly ground black pepper to the sauce. Taste for seasoning, adding salt as necessary.

6 ▲ Drain the pasta when it is *al dente*. Add it to the frying pan with the sauce, and stir well over moderate heat for 1–2 minutes more. Serve at once, without cheese.

~ COOK'S TIP ~

Mussels should be firmly closed when fresh. If a mussel is slightly open, pinch it closed. If it remains closed on its own, it is alive. If it remains open, discard it. Fresh mussels should be consumed as soon as possible after being purchased. They may be kept in a bowl of cold water in the refrigerator.

Pasta with Fresh Sardine Sauce

Pasta con sarde

In this classic Sicilian dish, fresh sardines are combined with sultanas and pine nuts.

Ingredients

30 g/1 1/4 oz/3 tbsp sultanas
450 g/1 lb fresh sardines
90 ml/6 tbsp breadcrumbs
1 small fennel bulb
90 ml/6 tbsp olive oil
1 medium onion, very thinly sliced
30 g/1 1/4 oz/3 tbsp pine nuts
1/2 tsp fennel seeds
salt and freshly ground black pepper
400 g/14 oz long hollow pasta such as percatelli, ziti, or bucatini

serves 4

1 Soak the sultanas in warm water for 15 minutes. Drain and pat dry.

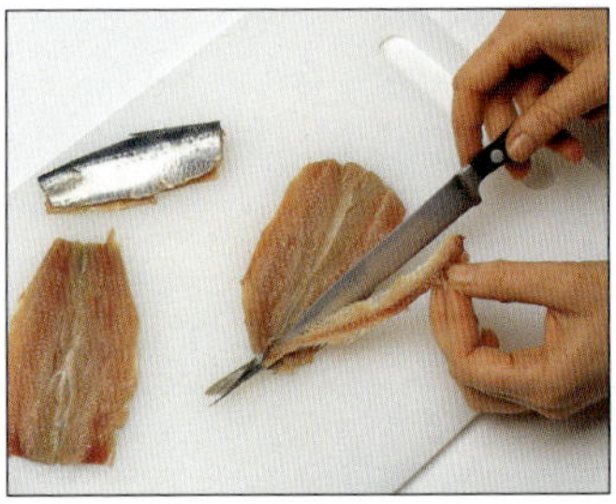

2 ▲ Clean the sardines. Open each one out flat and remove the back bone and head. Wash well and shake dry. Sprinkle with breadcrumbs.

3 ▲ Coarsely chop the top fronds of fennel and reserve. Pull off a few outer leaves and wash. Fill a large pan with enough water to cook the pasta. Add the fennel leaves and bring to a boil.

4 ▲ Heat the oil in a large frying pan and sauté the onion lightly until soft. Remove to a side dish. Add the sardines, a few at a time, and cook over moderate heat until golden on both sides, turning them once carefully. When all the sardines have been cooked, gently return them to the pan. Add the onion, and the sultanas, pine nuts and fennel seeds. Season with salt and pepper.

5 ▲ Take about 60 ml/4 tbsp of the boiling water for the pasta, and add it to the sauce. Add salt to the boiling water, and drop in the pasta. Cook until it is *al dente*. Drain, and remove the fennel leaves. Dress the pasta with the sauce. Divide between individual serving plates, arranging several sardines on each. Sprinkle with the reserved chopped fennel tops before serving.

Baked Macaroni with Cheese

Maccheroni gratinati al forno

This delicious dish is perhaps less common in Italy than other pasta dishes, but has become a family favourite around the world.

Ingredients
500 ml/16 fl oz/2 cups milk
1 bay leaf
3 blades mace, or pinch of grated nutmeg
50 g/2 oz/4 tbsp butter
35 g/$1^1/_2$ oz/$^1/_3$ cup flour
salt and freshly ground black pepper
175 g/6 oz/$1^1/_2$ cups grated Parmesan or Cheddar cheese, or a combination of both
40 g/$1^3/_4$ oz/$^1/_3$ cup breadcrumbs
450 g/1 lb macaroni or other short hollow pasta
serves 6

1 Make a béchamel sauce by gently heating the milk with the bay leaf and mace in a small saucepan. Do not let it boil. Melt the butter in a medium heavy saucepan. Add the flour, and mix it in well with a wire whisk. Cook for 2-3 minutes, but do not let the butter burn. Strain the hot milk into the flour and butter mixture all at once, and mix smoothly with the whisk. Bring the sauce to the boil, stirring constantly, and cook for another 4-5 minutes.

2 ▲ Season with salt and pepper, and the nutmeg if no mace has been used. Add all but 30 ml/2 tbsp of the cheese, and stir over low heat until it melts. Place a layer of plastic wrap right on the surface of the sauce to stop a skin from forming, and set aside.

3 ▲ Bring a large pan of water to a boil. Preheat the oven to 200°C/400°F/gas 6. Grease an ovenproof dish, and sprinkle with some breadcrumbs. Add salt and the pasta to the boiling water, and cook until it is barely *al dente*. Do not overcook, as the pasta will get a second cooking in the oven.

4 ▲ Drain the pasta, and combine it with the sauce. Pour it into the prepared ovenproof dish. Sprinkle the top with the remaining breadcrumbs and grated cheese, and place in the centre of the preheated oven. Bake for 20 minutes.

Penne with Tuna and Mozzarella

Penne con tonno e mozzarella

This tasty sauce is quickly made from store-cupboard ingredients, with the addition of fresh mozzarella. If possible, use tuna canned in olive oil.

Ingredients

400 g/14 oz penne, or other short pasta
15 ml/1 tbsp capers, in brine or salt
2 cloves garlic
45 g/3 tbsp chopped fresh parsley
1 x 200 g/7oz can of tuna, drained
75 ml/5 tbsp olive oil
salt and freshly ground black pepper
115 g/4 oz/$^{2}/_{3}$ cup mozzarella cheese, cut into small dice

serves 4

1 Bring a large pan of salted water to a boil and drop in the pasta.

2 ▲ Rinse the capers well in water. Chop them finely with the garlic. Combine with the parsley and the tuna. Stir in the oil, and season with salt and pepper, if necessary.

3 ▲ Drain the pasta when it is just *al dente*. Turn it into a large frying pan. Add the tuna sauce and the diced mozzarella, and cook over a moderate heat, stirring constantly, until the cheese just begins to melt. Serve at once.

Spaghettini with Vodka and Caviar

Spaghettini con vodka e caviale

This is an elegant yet easy way to serve spaghettini. In Rome it is an after-theatre favourite.

Ingredients

60 ml/4 tbsp olive oil
3 spring onions, thinly sliced
1 clove garlic, finely chopped
100 ml/4 fl oz/$^{1}/_{2}$ cup vodka
150 ml/$^{1}/_{4}$ pint/$^{2}/_{3}$ cup heavy cream
75 g/3 oz/$^{1}/_{2}$ cup black or red caviar
salt and freshly ground black pepper
400 g/14 oz spaghettini

serves 4

1 ▲ Heat the oil in a small frying pan. Add the spring onions and garlic, and cook gently for 4–5 minutes.

2 ▲ Add the vodka and cream, and cook over low heat for about 5–8 minutes more.

~ COOK'S TIP ~

The finest caviar is salted sturgeon roe. Red "caviar" is salmon roe, cheaper and often saltier than sturgeon roe, as is the black-dyed lump fish roe.

3 ▲ Remove from the heat and stir in half the caviar. Season with salt and pepper as necessary.

4 Meanwhile, cook the spaghettini in a large pan of rapidly boiling salted water until *al dente*. Drain the pasta, and toss with the sauce. Spoon the remaining caviar on top and serve immediately.

Pasta Bows with Prawns and Peas

Farfalle con gamberetti e piselli

A small amount of saffron in the sauce gives this dish a lovely golden colour.

Ingredients
45 ml/3 tbsp olive oil
25 g/1 oz/2 tbsp butter
2 spring onions, chopped
350 g/12oz fresh or frozen peeled prawns
225 g/8 oz/$1^1/_4$ cups frozen petits pois or peas, thawed
400 g/14 oz farfalle
250 ml/8 fl oz/1 cup dry white wine
a few whole strands saffron or $^1/_8$ tsp powdered saffron
salt and freshly ground black pepper
30 ml/2 tbsp chopped fresh fennel or dill, to serve
serves 4

1 Bring a large pan of water to a boil. Heat the oil and butter in a large frying pan and sauté the spring onions lightly. Add the peas, and cook for 2–3 minutes.

2 ▲ Add salt and the pasta to the boiling water. Add the prawns, wine and saffron to the peas. Raise the heat and cook until the wine is reduced by about half. Add salt and pepper to taste. Cover the pan and reduce the heat to low.

3 ▲ Drain the pasta when it is *al dente*. Add it to the pan with the sauce. Stir over high heat for 1–2 minutes, coating the pasta with the sauce. Sprinkle with the fresh herbs, and serve at once.

Short Pasta with Spring Vegetables

Pasta primavera

This colourful sauce makes the most of new crops of fresh tender spring vegetables.

Ingredients
1 or 2 small young carrots
2 spring onions
150 g/6 oz/1 cup courgettes
2 tomatoes
75 g/3 oz/$^1/_2$ cup shelled peas, fresh or frozen
75 g/3 oz/$^1/_2$ cup green beans
1 yellow pepper
60 ml/4 tbsp olive oil
25 g/1 oz/2 tbsp butter
1 clove garlic, finely chopped
5–6 leaves fresh basil, torn into pieces
salt and freshly ground black pepper
500 g/$1^1/_4$
lb/5 cups short coloured or plain pasta such as fusilli, penne or farfalle
freshly grated Parmesan, to serve
serves 6

1 Cut all the vegetables into small, bite-size pieces.

2 ▲ Heat the oil and butter in a large frying pan. Add the chopped vegetables, and cook over moderate heat for 5–6 minutes, stirring occasionally. Add the garlic and the basil, and season with salt and pepper. Cover the pan, and cook for 5–8 minutes more, or until the vegetables are just tender.

3 ▲ Meanwhile, cook the pasta in a large pan of rapidly boiling salted water until *al dente*. Before draining it, reserve a cupful of the pasta water.

4 Turn the pasta into the pan with the sauce, and mix well to distribute the vegetables. If the sauce seems too dry, add a few tablespoons of the reserved pasta water. Serve with the Parmesan passed separately.

Baked Seafood Spaghetti

Spaghetti cartoccio

In this dish, each portion is baked and served in an individual packet which is then opened at the table. Use parchment paper or aluminium foil to make the packets.

Ingredients

450 g/1 lb fresh mussels
100 ml/4 fl oz/$^1/_2$ cup dry white wine
60 ml/4 tbsp olive oil
2 cloves garlic, finely chopped
450 g/1 lb tomatoes, fresh or canned, peeled and finely chopped
400 g/14 oz spaghetti or other long pasta
225 g/8 oz peeled and deveined prawns, fresh or frozen
30 ml/2 tbsp chopped fresh parsley
salt and freshly ground black pepper

serves 4

1 ▲ Scrub the mussels well under cold running water, cutting off the "beard" with a small sharp knife. Place the mussels and the wine in a large saucepan and heat until they open.

2 ▲ Lift out the mussels and remove to a side dish. (Discard any that do not open.) Strain the cooking liquid through paper towels, and reserve until needed. Preheat the oven to 150°C/300°F/gas 2.

3 ▲ Bring a large pan of water to a boil. In a medium pan, heat the olive oil and garlic together for 1–2 minutes. Add the tomatoes, and cook over moderate to high heat until they soften. Stir in 150 ml/6 fl oz/ $^3/_4$ cup of the cooking liquid from the mussels. Add salt and the pasta to the boiling water, and cook until it is just *al dente*.

4 ▲ Just before draining the pasta, add the prawns and parsley to the tomato sauce. Cook for 2 minutes. Taste for seasoning, adding salt and pepper as desired. Remove from the heat.

~ VARIATION ~

Bottled mussels or clams may be substituted for fresh shellfish in this recipe. Add them to the tomato sauce with the prawns.

5 ▲ Prepare 4 pieces of parchment paper or foil approximately 30 cm × 45 cm (12 in × 18 in). Place each sheet in the center of a shallow bowl. Turn the drained pasta into a mixing bowl. Add the tomato sauce and mix well. Stir in the mussels.

6 ▲ Divide the pasta and seafood between the four pieces of paper, placing a mound in the center of each, and twisting the paper ends together to make a closed packet. (The bowl under the paper will stop the sauce from spilling while the paper parcels are being closed.) Arrange on a large baking tray, and place in the centre of the preheated oven. Bake for 10 minutes. Place one unopened packet on each individual serving plate.

Tuna Pasta Salad

Insalata di pasta con tonno

This easy pasta salad uses canned beans and tuna for a quick main dish.

Ingredients

450 g/1 lb short pasta, such as ruote, macaroni or farfalle
60 ml/4 tbsp olive oil
2 × 200 g/7 oz cans tuna, drained
2 × 400 g/14 oz cans cannellini or borlotti beans, rinsed and drained
1 small red onion
2 sticks celery
juice of 1 lemon
30 ml/2 tbsp chopped fresh parsley
salt and freshly ground black pepper
serves 6–8

1 Cook the pasta in a large pan of rapidly boiling salted water until it is *al dente*. Drain, and rinse under cold water to stop cooking. Drain well and turn into a large bowl. Toss with the olive oil, and set aside. Allow to cool completely before mixing with the other ingredients.

2 ▲ Mix the flaked tuna and the beans into the cooked pasta. Slice the onion and celery very thinly and add them to the pasta.

3 ▲ Combine the lemon juice with the parsley. Mix into the other ingredients. Season with salt and pepper. Allow the salad to stand for at least 1 hour before serving.

Chicken Pasta Salad

Insalata di pasta con pollo

This salad uses leftover chicken from a roast, or a cold poached chicken breast.

Ingredients

350 g/12 oz short pasta, such as mezze rigatoni, fusilli or penne
45 ml/3 tbsp olive oil
225 g/8 oz/$1\frac{1}{2}$ cups cold cooked chicken
2 small red and yellow peppers (about 200 g/7 oz)
50 g/2 oz/$\frac{1}{3}$ cup pitted green olives
4 spring onions, chopped
45 ml/3 tbsp mayonnaise
1 tsp Worcestershire sauce
15 ml/1 tbsp wine vinegar
salt and freshly ground black pepper
a few leaves fresh basil, to garnish
serves 4

1 Cook the pasta in a large pan of rapidly boiling salted water until it is *al dente*. Drain, and rinse under cold water to stop the cooking. Drain well and turn into a large bowl. Toss with the olive oil, and set aside. Allow to cool completely.

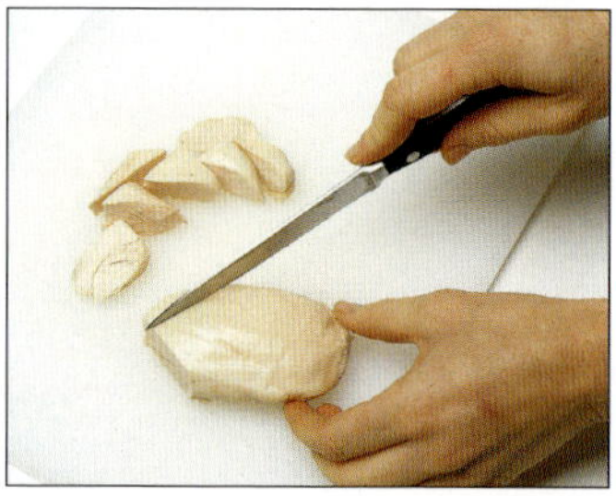

2 ▲ Cut the chicken into bite-size pieces, removing any bones. Cut the peppers into small pieces, removing the seeds and stems.

3 ▲ Combine all the ingredients except the pasta in a medium bowl. Taste for seasoning, then mix into the pasta. Garnish with the basil, and serve chilled.

Wholewheat Pasta Salad

Insalata di pasta integrale

This substantial vegetarian salad is easily assembled from any combination of seasonal vegetables. Use raw or lightly blanched vegetables, or a mixture of both.

Ingredients

450 g/1 lb short wholewheat pasta, such as fusilli or penne
45 ml/3 tbsp olive oil
2 medium carrots
1 small bunch broccoli, halved
175 g/6 oz/1 cup shelled peas, fresh or frozen
1 red or yellow pepper
2 sticks celery
4 spring onions
1 large tomato
75 g/3 oz/$^{1}/_{2}$ cup stoned olives, halved

For the dressing

45 ml/3 tbsp wine or balsamic vinegar
60 ml/4 tbsp olive oil
15 ml/1 tbsp Dijon style mustard
15 ml/1 tbsp sesame seeds
10 ml/2 tsp finely chopped mixed fresh herbs, such as parsley, thyme and basil
salt and freshly ground black pepper
115 g/4 oz/$^{2}/_{3}$ cup diced Cheddar or mozzarella, or a combination of both

serves 8

1 Cook the pasta in a large pan of rapidly boiling salted water until it is *al dente*. Drain, and rinse under cold water to stop the cooking. Drain well and turn into a large bowl. Toss with 45ml/3 tbsp of the olive oil, and set aside. Allow to cool completely before mixing with the other ingredients.

2 ▲ Lightly blanch the carrots, broccoli and peas in a large pan of boiling water. Refresh under cold water. Drain well.

3 ▲ Chop the carrots and broccoli into bite-size pieces and add to the pasta with the peas. Slice the pepper, celery, spring onions and tomato into small pieces. Add them to the salad with the olives.

4 ▲ Make the dressing in a small bowl by combining the vinegar with the oil and mustard. Stir in the sesame seeds and herbs. Mix the dressing into the salad. Taste for seasoning, adding salt, pepper or more oil and vinegar as necessary. Stir in the cheese. Allow the salad to stand for 15 minutes before serving.

Pasta Salad with Olives

Insalata di pasta con olive

This delicious salad combines all the flavours of the Mediterranean. It is an excellent way of serving pasta and is particularly nice on hot summer days.

Ingredients
450 g/1 lb short pasta, such as medium shells, farfalle or penne
60 ml/4 tbsp extra-virgin olive oil
10 sun-dried tomatoes, thinly sliced
30 ml/2 tbsp capers, in brine or salted
115 g/4 oz/$^2/_3$ cup black olives, pitted
2 cloves garlic, finely chopped
45 ml/3 tbsp balsamic vinegar
salt and freshly ground black pepper
45 ml/3 tbsp chopped fresh parsley
serves 6

1 ▲ Cook the pasta in a large pan of rapidly boiling salted water until it is *al dente*. Drain, and rinse under cold water to stop the cooking. Drain well and turn into a large bowl. Toss with the olive oil, and set aside.

2 ▲ Soak the tomatoes in a bowl of hot water for 10 minutes. Do not discard the water. Rinse the capers well. If they have been preserved in salt, soak them in a little hot water for 10 minutes. Rinse again.

3 ▲ Combine the olives, tomatoes, capers, garlic and vinegar in a small bowl. Season with salt and pepper.

4 ▲ Stir this mixture into the pasta, and toss well. Add 2 or 3 spoons of the tomato soaking water if the salad seems too dry. Toss with the parsley, and allow to stand for 15 minutes before serving.

Fettuccine with Ham and Cream

Fettuccine con prosciutto

Prosciutto is perfect for this rich and delicious dish, which makes an elegant first course.

Ingredients
115 g/4 oz/$^1/_2$ cup slice prosciutto crudo or other unsmoked ham (raw or cooked)
50 g/2 oz/$^1/_4$ cup butter
2 shallots, very finely chopped
salt and freshly ground black pepper
150 ml/$^1/_4$ pint/$^3/_4$ cup heavy cream
350 g/12 oz fettuccine (made with 3 eggs)
50 g/2 oz/$^1/_2$ cup grated Parmesan cheese
sprig fresh parsley, to garnish
serves 4

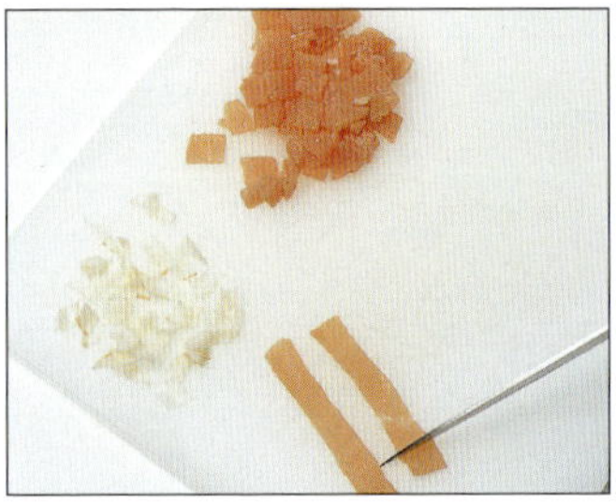

1 ▲ Cut the fat from the ham, and chop both lean and fat parts separately into small squares.

2 ▲ Melt the butter in a medium frying pan, and add the shallots and the squares of ham fat. Cook until golden. Add the lean ham, and cook for 2 minutes more. Season with black pepper. Stir in the cream, and keep warm over low heat while the pasta is cooking.

3 ▲ Boil the pasta in a large pan of rapidly boiling salted water. Drain when *al dente*. Turn into a warmed serving bowl, and toss with the sauce. Stir in the cheese and serve at once, garnished with a sprig of parsley.

~ VARIATION ~

Substitute 170 g/6 oz fresh or frozen peas for the ham. Add to the pan with the shallots.

Tagliatelle with Smoked Salmon

Tagliatelle con salmone affumicato

In Italy smoked salmon is imported, and quite expensive. This elegant creamy sauce makes a little go a long way. Use a mixture of green and white pasta if you wish.

Ingredients
115 g/4 oz/$^3/_4$ cup smoked salmon slices or ends, fresh or frozen
300 ml/$^1/_2$ pint/1$^1/_4$ cups single cream
pinch of ground mace or nutmeg
350g/12 oz green and white tagliatelle (made with 3 eggs)
salt and freshly ground black pepper
45 ml/3 tbsp chopped fresh chives, to garnish
serves 4–5

1 Cut the salmon into thin strips about 5 cm/2 in long. Place in a bowl with the cream and the mace or nutmeg. Stir, cover, and allow to stand for at least 2 hours in a cool place.

2 ▲ Bring a large pan of water to a boil for the pasta. While the water is heating, gently warm the cream and salmon mixture in a small saucepan without boiling it.

3 ▲ Add salt to the boiling water. Drop in the pasta all at once. Drain when it is just *al dente*. Pour the sauce over the pasta and mix well. Season and garnish with the chives.

Baked Lasagne with Meat Sauce

Lasagne al forno

This lasagne made from egg pasta with home-made meat and béchamel sauces is exquisite.

Ingredients

1 recipe Bolognese Meat Sauce
egg pasta sheets made with 3 eggs, or 400 g/14 oz dried lasagne
115 g/4 oz/1 cup grated Parmesan cheese
40 g/3 tbsp butter

For the béchamel sauce

700 ml/1 $^1/_4$ pints/3 cups milk
1 bay leaf
3 blades mace
115 g/4 oz/$^1/_2$ cup butter
75 g/3 oz/$^3/_4$ cup flour
salt and freshly ground black pepper

serves 8–10

1 Prepare the meat sauce and set aside. Butter a large shallow baking dish, preferably rectangular or square.

2 Make the béchamel sauce by gently heating the milk with the bay leaf and mace in a small saucepan. Melt the butter in a medium heavy pan. Add the flour, and mix it in well with a wire whisk. Cook for 2–3 minutes. Strain the hot milk into the flour and butter mixture, and combine smoothly with the whisk. Bring the sauce to a boil, stirring constantly, and cook for 4–5 minutes more. Season with salt and pepper, and set aside.

3 ▲ Make the pasta. Do not let it dry out before cutting it into rectangles approximately 11 cm/4$^1/_2$ in wide and the same length as the baking dish (this will make it easier to assemble). Preheat the oven to 200°C/400°F/gas 6.

4 ▲ Bring a very large pan of water to a boil. Place a large bowl of cold water near the stove. Cover a large work surface with a tablecloth. Add salt to the rapidly boiling water. Drop in 3 or 4 of the egg pasta rectangles. Cook very briefly, about 30 seconds. Remove them from the pan using a slotted spoon, and drop them into the bowl of cold water for about 30 seconds. Pull them out of the water, shaking off the excess water. Lay them out flat without overlapping on the tablecloth. Continue with all the remaining pasta and trimmings.

5 ▲ To assemble the lasagne, have all the elements at hand: the baking dish, béchamel and meat sauces, pasta strips, grated Parmesan and butter. Spread one large spoonful of the meat sauce over the bottom of the dish. Arrange a layer of pasta in the dish, cutting it with a sharp knife so that it fits well inside the dish.

6 ▲ Cover with a thin layer of meat sauce, then one of béchamel. Sprinkle with a little cheese. Repeat the layers in the same order, ending with a layer of pasta coated with béchamel. Do not make more than about 6 layers of pasta. (If you have a lot left over, make another small lasagne in a little ovenproof dish.) Use the pasta trimmings to patch any gaps in the pasta. Sprinkle the top with Parmesan, and dot with butter.

7 Bake in the preheated oven for 20 minutes or until brown on top. Remove from the oven and allow to stand for 5 minutes before serving. Serve directly from the baking dish, cutting out rectangular or square sections for each helping.

~ VARIATION ~

If you are using dried or bought pasta, follow step 4, but boil the lasagne in just two batches, and stop the cooking about 4 minutes before the recommended cooking time on the package has elapsed. Rinse in cold water and lay the pasta out the same way as for the egg pasta.

Tagliolini with Asparagus

Tagliolini con asparagi

Tagliolini are very thin home-made egg noodles, more delicate in texture than spaghetti. They go well with this subtle cream sauce flavoured with asparagus.

Ingredients

450 g/1 lb fresh asparagus
egg pasta sheets made with 2 eggs, or 350 g/12 oz fresh tagliolini or other egg noodles
50 g/2 oz/$^1/_4$ cup butter
3 spring onions, finely chopped
3–4 leaves fresh mint or basil, finely chopped
150 ml/$^1/_4$ pint/$^2/_3$ cup double cream
salt and freshly ground black pepper
50 g/2 oz/$^1/_2$ cup freshly grated Parmesan cheese

serves 4

1 ▲ Peel the asparagus by inserting a small sharp knife at the base of the stalks and pulling upwards towards the tips. Drop them into a large pan of rapidly boiling water, and boil until just tender, 4–6 minutes.

2 ▲ Remove from the water, reserving the cooking water. Cut the tips off, and then cut the stalks into 4 cm/1$^1/_2$ in pieces. Set aside.

3 Make the egg pasta sheets, and fold and cut into thin noodles, or feed them through the narrowest cutters of a machine. Open the noodles out, and let them dry for at least 5–10 minutes.

4 ▲ Melt the butter in a large frying pan. Add the spring onions and herbs, and cook for 3–4 minutes. Stir in the cream and asparagus, and heat gently, but do not boil. Season to taste.

5 Bring the asparagus cooking water back to the boil. Add salt. Drop the noodles in all at once. Cook until just tender (freshly made noodles will cook in a few seconds). Drain.

6 ▲ Turn the pasta into the pan with the sauce, raise the heat slightly, and mix well. Stir in the Parmesan. Mix well and serve at once.

Ravioli with Ricotta and Spinach

Ravioli ripieni di magro

Home-made ravioli are fun to make, and can be stuffed with different meat, cheese or vegetable fillings. This filling is easy to make, and lighter than the normal meat variety.

Ingredients
400 g/14 oz fresh spinach or 175 g/6oz frozen spinach
175 g/6 oz/¾ cup ricotta cheese
1 egg
50 g/2 oz/½ cup grated Parmesan cheese
pinch of grated nutmeg
salt and freshly ground black pepper
egg pasta sheets made with 3 eggs
For the sauce
75 g/3 oz/⅓ cup butter
5–6 sprigs fresh sage
serves 4

1 Wash fresh spinach well in several changes of water. Place in a saucepan with only the water that is clinging to the leaves. Cover, and cook until tender, about 5 minutes. Drain. Cook frozen spinach according to the instructions on the package. When the spinach is cool, squeeze out as much moisture as possible. Chop finely.

2 Combine the chopped spinach with the ricotta, egg, Parmesan and nutmeg. Mix well. Season with salt and pepper. Cover the bowl and set aside.

3 Prepare the sheets of egg pasta. Roll out very thinly by hand or machine. Do not let the pasta dry out.

4 ▲ Place small teaspoons of filling along the pasta in rows 5 cm/2 in apart. Cover with another sheet of pasta, pressing down gently to avoid forming air pockets.

5 ▲ Use a fluted pastry wheel to cut between the rows to form small squares with filling in the centre of each. If the edges do not stick well, moisten with milk or water, and press together with a fork. Place the ravioli on a lightly floured surface, and allow to dry for at least 30 minutes. Turn occasionally so they dry on both sides. Bring a large pan of salted water to the boil.

6 Heat the butter and sage together over very low heat, taking care that the butter melts but does not darken.

7 ▲ Drop the ravioli into the boiling water. Stir gently to prevent them from sticking. They will be cooked in very little time, about 4–5 minutes. Drain carefully and arrange in individual serving dishes. Spoon on the sauce, and serve at once.

Baked Vegetable Lasagne

Lasagne al forno con funghi e pomodori

Following the principles of the classic meat sauce lasagne, other combinations of ingredients can be used most effectively. This vegetarian lasagne uses fresh vegetables and herbs.

Ingredients

egg pasta sheets made with 3 eggs
30 ml/2 tbsp olive oil
1 medium onion, very finely chopped
500 g/1 $^{1}/_{4}$lb tomatoes, fresh or canned, chopped
salt and freshly ground black pepper
675 g/1 $^{1}/_{2}$ lb cultivated or wild mushrooms, or a combination of both
75 g/3 oz/$^{1}/_{3}$ cup butter
2 cloves garlic, finely chopped
juice of $^{1}/_{2}$ lemon
1 litre/1 $^{3}/_{4}$ pints/4 $^{1}/_{2}$ cups béchamel sauce
1 $^{1}/_{2}$ cups freshly grated Parmesan or Romano cheese, or a combination

serves 8

1 Butter a large shallow baking dish, preferably rectangular or square.

2 ▲ Make the egg pasta. Do not let it dry out before cutting it into rectangles approximately 11 cm/4 $^{1}/_{2}$in wide and the same length as the baking dish (this will make it easier to assemble).

3 In a small frying pan heat the oil and sauté the onion until translucent. Add the chopped tomatoes, and cook for 6–8 minutes, stirring often. Season with salt and pepper, and set aside.

4 ▲ Wipe the mushrooms carefully with a damp cloth. Slice finely. Heat 35 g/1 $^{1}/_{2}$ oz/2 tbsp of the butter in a frying pan, and when it is bubbling, add the mushrooms. Cook until the mushrooms start to exude their juices. Add the garlic and lemon juice, and season with salt and pepper. Cook until the liquids have almost all evaporated and the mushrooms are starting to brown. Set aside.

5 ▲ Preheat the oven to 200°C/400°F/gas 6. Bring a very large pan of water to the boil. Place a large bowl of cold water near the stove. Cover a large work surface with a tablecloth. Add salt to the rapidly boiling water. Drop in 3 or 4 of the egg pasta rectangles. Cook very briefly, about 30 seconds. Remove them from the pan using a slotted spoon, and drop them into the bowl of cold water for about 30 seconds. Remove and lay out to dry. Continue with the remaining pasta.

6 ▲ To assemble the lasagne have all the elements at hand: the baking dish, fillings, pasta, cheeses and butter. Spread one large spoonful of the béchamel sauce over the bottom of the dish. Arrange a layer of pasta in the dish, cutting it with a sharp knife so that it fits well. Cover the pasta with a thin layer of mushrooms, then one of béchamel sauce. Sprinkle with a little cheese.

7 ▲ Make another layer of pasta, spread with a thin layer of tomatoes, and then one of béchamel. Sprinkle with cheese. Repeat the layers in the same order, ending with a layer of pasta coated with béchamel. Do not make more than about 6 layers of pasta. Use the pasta trimmings to patch any gaps in the pasta. Sprinkle with cheese, and dot with butter.

8 Bake for 20 minutes. Remove from the oven and allow to stand for 5 minutes before serving.

Tortelli with Pumpkin Stuffing

Tortelli di zucca

During autumn and winter the northern Italian markets are full of bright orange pumpkins, which are used to make soups and pasta dishes. This dish is a speciality of Mantua.

Ingredients
1 kg/2 lb pumpkin (weight with shell)
75 g/3 oz/1 $^{1}/_{2}$ cups amaretti, finely crushed
2 eggs
75 g/3 oz/$^{3}/_{4}$ cup freshly grated Parmesan cheese
pinch of grated nutmeg
salt and freshly ground black pepper
plain breadcrumbs, as required
egg pasta sheets made with 3 eggs
To serve
115 g/4 oz/$^{1}/_{2}$ cup butter
75 g/3 oz/$^{3}/_{4}$ cup freshly grated Parmesan cheese
serves 6–8

1 Preheat the oven to 190°C/375°F/gas 5. Cut the pumpkin into 10 cm/4 in pieces. Leave the skin on. Place the pumpkin pieces in a covered casserole, and bake for 45-50 minutes. When cool, cut off the skins. Purée the flesh in a food mill or food processor or press through a sieve.

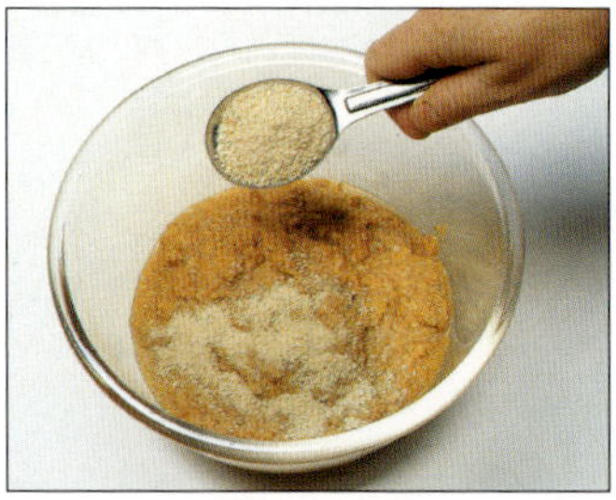

2 ▲ Combine the pumpkin purée with the biscuit crumbs, eggs, Parmesan and nutmeg. Season with salt and pepper. If the mixture is too wet, add 15-30 g/1-2 tbsp of breadcrumbs. Set aside.

3 Prepare the sheets of egg pasta. Roll out very thinly by hand or machine. Do not let the pasta dry out before filling it.

4 ▲ Place tablespoons of filling every 6-7 cm/2$^{1}/_{2}$ in along the pasta in rows 5 cm/2 in apart. Cover with another sheet of pasta, and press down gently. Use a fluted pastry wheel to cut between the rows to form rectangles with filling in the centre of each. Place the tortelli on a lightly floured surface, and allow to dry for at least 30 minutes. Turn them occasionally so they dry on both sides.

5 Bring a large pan of salted water to a boil. Gently heat the butter over very low heat, taking care that it does not darken.

6 ▲ Drop the tortelli into the boiling water. Stir to prevent from sticking. They will be cooked in 4-5 minutes. Drain and arrange in individual dishes. Spoon on the melted butter, sprinkle with Parmesan or Romano, and serve.

Stuffed Pasta Half-moons

Mezzelune ripiene di formaggi

These stuffed egg pasta half-moons are filled with a delicate mixture of cheeses. They make an elegant first course.

Ingredients
225 g/8 oz/$1\frac{1}{4}$ cups fresh ricotta or curd cheese
225 g/8 oz/$1\frac{1}{4}$ cups mozzarella cheese
115 g/4 oz/1 cup freshly grated Parmesan cheese
2 eggs
45 ml/3 tbsp finely chopped fresh basil
salt and freshly ground black pepper
egg pasta sheets made with 3 eggs
milk

For the sauce
450 g/1 lb fresh tomatoes
30 ml/2 tbsp olive oil
1 small onion, very finely chopped
90 ml/6 tbsp cream

serves 6–8

1 ▲ Press the ricotta or curd cheese through a sieve or strainer. Chop the mozzarella into very small cubes. Combine all three cheeses in a bowl. Beat in the eggs and basil, season and set aside.

2 Make the sauce by dropping the tomatoes into a small pan of boiling water for 1 minute. Remove, and peel using a small sharp knife to pull the skins off. Chop the tomatoes finely. Heat the oil in a medium pan. Add the onion and cook over moderate heat until soft and translucent. Add the tomatoes and cook until soft, about 15 minutes. Season with salt and pepper. (The sauce may be pressed through a sieve to make it smooth.) Set aside.

3 Prepare the sheets of egg pasta. Roll out very thinly by hand or machine. Do not let the pasta dry out.

4 ▲ Using a water glass or pastry cutter, cut out rounds approximately 10 cm/4in in diameter. Spoon one large tablespoon of the filling onto one half of each pasta round and fold over.

5 Press the edges closed with a fork. Re-roll any trimmings and use to make more rounds. Allow the half-moons to dry for at least 10–15 minutes. Turn them over so they dry evenly.

6 Bring a large pan of salted water to a boil. Place the tomato sauce in a small saucepan and heat gently while the pasta is cooking. Stir in the cream. Do not boil.

7 Gently drop the stuffed pasta into the boiling water, and stir carefully to prevent them from sticking. Cook for 5-7 minutes. Scoop them out of the water, drain carefully, and arrange in individual dishes. Spoon on some of the sauce, and serve at once.

Cannelloni Stuffed with Meat

Cannelloni ripieni di carne

Cannelloni are rectangles of egg pasta which are spread with a filling, rolled up and baked in a sauce. In this recipe, they are baked in a béchamel sauce.

Ingredients

30 ml/2 tbsp olive oil
1 medium onion, very finely chopped
225 g/8 oz/1 1/2 cups very lean minced beef
75 g/3 oz/1/2 cup cooked ham (either boiled or baked), finely chopped
15 ml/1 tbsp chopped fresh parsley
30 ml/2 tbsp tomato paste, softened in 15 ml/1 tbsp warm water
1 egg
salt and freshly ground black pepper
egg pasta sheets made with 2 eggs
750 ml/1 1/4 pints/3 1/4 cups béchamel sauce
50 g/2 oz/1/2 cup freshly grated Parmesan cheese
40 g/1 1/2 oz/3 tbsp butter

serves 6–8

1 ▲ Prepare the meat filling by heating the oil in a medium saucepan. Add the onion, and sauté gently until translucent. Stir in the beef, crumbling it with a fork, and stirring constantly until it has lost its raw red colour. Cook for 3–4 minutes.

2 ▲ Remove from the heat, and turn the beef mixture into a bowl with the ham and parsley. Add the tomato paste and the egg, and mix well. Season with salt and pepper. Set aside.

3 ▲ Make the egg pasta sheets with a machine or by hand. Do not let the pasta dry before cutting it into rectangles 12–13 cm/5–6 in long and as wide as they come from the machine (8–9 cm/3 in if you are not using a machine).

4 Bring a very large pan of water to a boil. Place a large bowl of cold water near the stove. Cover a large work surface with a tablecloth. Add salt to the rapidly boiling water. Drop in 3 or 4 of the egg pasta rectangles. Cook very briefly, about 30 seconds. Remove and drop them into the bowl of cold water for about 30 seconds more. Pull them out of the water, shaking off the excess water. Lay them out flat on the tablecloth. Continue with the remaining pasta.

5 Preheat the oven to 220°C/425°F/gas 7. Select a shallow baking dish large enough to accommodate all the cannelloni in one layer. Butter the dish, and smear 2–3 tbsp of béchamel sauce over the bottom.

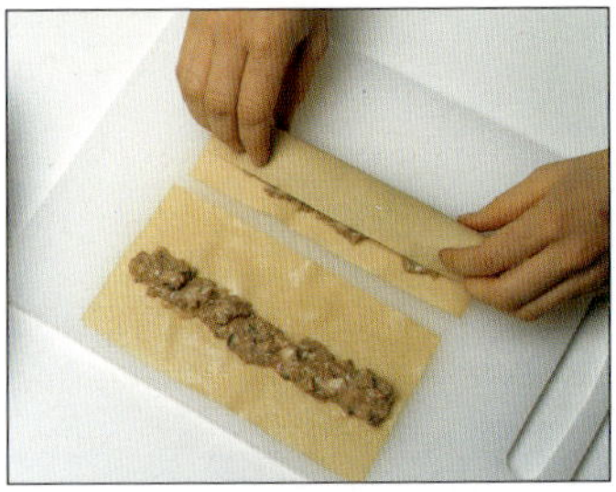

6 ▲ Stir about one-third of the béchamel into the meat filling. Spread a thin layer of filling on each pasta rectangle. Roll the rectangles up loosely starting from the long side, Swiss-roll style. Place the cannelloni into the baking dish with their open edges down.

7 ▲ Spoon the rest of the sauce over the cannelloni, pushing a little down between each pasta roll. Sprinkle the top with the grated Parmesan, and dot with butter. Bake for about 20 minutes. Allow to rest for 5–8 minutes before serving.

Rice, Polenta, Eggs and Cheese

Classic risottos are wonderfully creamy, flavoured subtly with mushrooms, asparagus or prawns. Thick yellow polenta goes well with meat or vegetable stews or cheeses and can be easily mastered by following the steps.

Risotto with Parmesan Cheese

Risotto alla parmigiana

Risotto is distinguished from other rice dishes by its unique cooking method.

Ingredients

1.1 litres/2 pints/$5^1/_2$ cups meat, chicken or vegetable broth, preferably home-made
65 g/5 tbsp butter
1 small onion, finely chopped
275 g/10 oz/$1^1/_2$ cups medium-grain risotto rice, such as arborio
100 ml/4 fl oz/$^1/_2$ cup dry white wine
salt and freshly ground black pepper
$^3/_4$ cup freshly grated Parmesan cheese
serves 3–4

1 Heat the stock in a medium saucepan, and keep it simmering until it is needed.

2 In a large heavy frying pan, melt two-thirds of the butter. Stir in the onion, and cook gently until it is soft and golden. Add the rice, mixing it well to coat it with butter. After 1-2 minutes pour in the wine.

3 ▲ Raise the heat slightly, and cook until the wine evaporates. Add one small ladleful of the hot stock. Over moderate heat cook until the stock is absorbed or evaporates, stirring the rice with a wooden spoon to prevent it from sticking to the pan. Add a little more stock, and stir until the rice dries out again. Continue stirring and adding the liquid a little at a time. After about 20 minutes of cooking time, taste the rice. Add salt and pepper.

4 Continue cooking, stirring and adding the liquid until the rice is *al dente*, or tender but still firm to the bite. The total cooking time of the risotto may be from 20-35 minutes. If you run out of stock, use hot water, but do not worry if the rice is done before you have used up all the stock.

5 ▲ Remove the risotto pan from the heat. Stir in the remaining butter and the cheese. Taste again for seasoning. Allow the risotto to rest for 3-4 minutes before serving.

Risotto with Prawns

Risotto con gamberi

This prawn risotto is given a soft pink colour by the addition of a little tomato purée.

Ingredients

325 g/12oz fresh prawns in their shells
1.1 litres/2 pints/5 cups water
1 bay leaf
1–2 sprigs of parsley
5 ml/1 tsp whole peppercorns
2 cloves garlic, peeled
65 g/$2^1/_2$ oz/5 tbsp butter
2 shallots, finely chopped
275 g/10 oz/$1^1/_2$ cups medium-grain risotto rice, such as arborio
15 ml/1 tbsp tomato purée softened in 100 ml/4 fl oz/$^1/_2$ cup dry white wine
salt and freshly ground black pepper
serves 4

1 Place the prawns in a large saucepan with the water, herbs, peppercorns and garlic. Bring to a boil and cook for about 1 minute. Remove the prawns, peel, and return the shells to the saucepan. Boil the shells for another 10 minutes. Strain. Return the broth to a pan, and simmer until needed.

2 Slice the prawns in half lengthwise, removing the dark vein along the back. Set 4 halves aside for garnish and roughly chop the rest.

3 Heat two-thirds of the butter in a casserole. Add the shallots and cook until golden. Stir in the prawns. Cook for 1-2 minutes.

4 ▲ Add the rice, mixing well to coat it with butter. After 1-2 minutes pour in the tomato paste and wine. Follow steps 3-5 for Risotto with Parmesan, omitting the cheese and garnishing with the reserved prawn halves.

Risotto with Mushrooms

Risotto con funghi

The addition of wild mushrooms gives this risotto a wonderful woodsy flavour.

Ingredients

25 g/1 oz/$^1/_3$ cup dried wild mushrooms, preferably porcini
175 g/6 oz/1$^1/_2$ cups fresh cultivated mushrooms
juice of $^1/_2$ lemon
75 g/3 oz/$^1/_3$ cup butter
30 ml/2 tbsp finely chopped parsley
900 ml/1$^2/_3$ pints/4 cups meat or chicken broth, preferably home-made
30 ml/2 tbsp olive oil
1 small onion, finely chopped
275 g/10 oz/1$^1/_2$ cups medium-grain risotto rice, such as arborio
100 ml/4 fl oz/$^1/_2$ cup dry white wine
salt and freshly ground black pepper
45 ml/3 tbsp freshly grated Parmesan cheese

serves 3–4

1 Place the dried mushrooms in a small bowl with about 350 ml/12 fl oz/1$^1/_2$ cups warm water. Soak for at least 40 minutes. Rinse the mushrooms thoroughly. Filter the soaking water through a strainer lined with paper towels, and reserve.

2 ▲ Wipe the fresh mushrooms with a damp cloth, and slice finely. Place in a bowl and toss with the lemon juice. In a large heavy frying pan or casserole melt one-third of the butter. Stir in the fresh sliced mushrooms and cook over moderate heat until they give up their juices, and begin to brown. Stir in the parsley, cook for 30 seconds more, and remove to a side dish.

3 Place the broth in a saucepan. Add the soaking water from the mushrooms, and simmer until needed.

4 ▲ Heat another third of the butter with the olive oil in the same pan the mushrooms were cooked in. Stir in the onion, and cook until it is soft and golden. Add the rice, stirring for 1–2 minutes to coat it with the oils. Add the soaked and sautéed mushrooms, and mix well.

5 ▲ Pour in the wine, and cook over moderate heat until it evaporates. Follow steps 3–4 for Risotto with Parmesan Cheese.

6 Remove the risotto pan from the heat. Stir in the remaining butter and the Parmesan or Romano. Grind in a little black pepper, and taste again for salt. Allow the risotto to rest for 3–4 minutes before serving.

Risotto with Asparagus

Risotto con asparagi

This is an elegant risotto to make when asparagus is in season.

Ingredients

225 g/8 oz asparagus, lower stalks peeled
700 ml/$1^1/_4$ pints/3 cups vegetable or meat broth, preferably home-made
65 g/$2^1/_2$ oz/5 tbsp butter
1 small onion, finely chopped
400 g/14 oz/2 cups medium-grain risotto rice, such as arborio
salt and freshly ground black pepper
75 g/3 oz/$^3/_4$ cup freshly grated Parmesan cheese

serves 4–5

1 Bring a large pan of water to the boil. Add the asparagus. Bring the water back to the boil, and blanch for 5 minutes. Lift the asparagus out, reserving the cooking water. Rinse the asparagus under cold water. Drain. Cut the asparagus diagonally into 4 cm/$1^1/_2$ in pieces. Keep the tip and next-highest sections separate from the stalk sections.

2 Place the broth in a saucepan. Measure out 850 ml/$1^1/_2$ pints/$3^3/_4$ cups of the asparagus cooking water, and add it to the broth. Heat the liquid to simmering, and keep it hot until it is needed.

3 ▲ Heat two-thirds of the butter in a large heavy frying pan or casserole. Add the chopped onion and cook until it is soft and golden. Stir in all the asparagus except the top two sections. Cook for 2–3 minutes. Add the rice, mixing well to coat it with butter for 1–2 minutes.

4 ▲ Stir in half a ladleful of the hot liquid. Using a wooden spoon, stir constantly until the liquid has been absorbed or evaporated. Add another half ladleful of the liquid, and stir until it has been absorbed. Continue stirring and adding the liquid, a little at a time, for about 10 minutes.

5 ▲ Add the remaining asparagus sections, and proceed as for step 4 of Risotto with Parmesan Cheese.

6 Remove the risotto pan from the heat. Stir in the remaining butter and the Parmesan. Grind in a little black pepper, and taste again for salt. Serve at once.

Polenta

Polenta

Polenta is a form of cornmeal. It is eaten in northern Italy in place of rice or pasta.

Ingredients
1.5 litres/2$^1/_2$ pints/6$^1/_4$ cups water
15 ml/1 tbsp salt
350 g/12 oz/2$^1/_2$ cups polenta flour
serves 4–6

1 ▲ Bring the water to a boil in a large heavy saucepan. Add the salt. Reduce the heat to a simmer, and begin to add the polenta flour in a fine rain. Stir constantly with a whisk until the polenta has all been incorporated.

2 ▲ Switch to a long-handled wooden spoon, and continue to stir the polenta over low to moderate heat until it is a thick mass, and pulls away from the sides of the pan. This may take from 25–50 minutes, depending on the type of polenta used. For best results, never stop stirring the polenta until you remove it from the heat.

3 ▲ When the polenta is cooked, spoon it into a large slightly wet bowl, wait 5 minutes, and turn it out onto a serving platter. Serve it with a meat or tomato sauce, or follow the instructions given in the recipes on the following pages.

Fried Polenta

Polenta fritta

Leftover polenta can be fried, making a crispy appetizer to serve with drinks or antipasti.

Ingredients
cold leftover polenta
oil, for deep-frying
flour, for dredging
salt and freshly ground black pepper
serves 6–8 as an appetizer

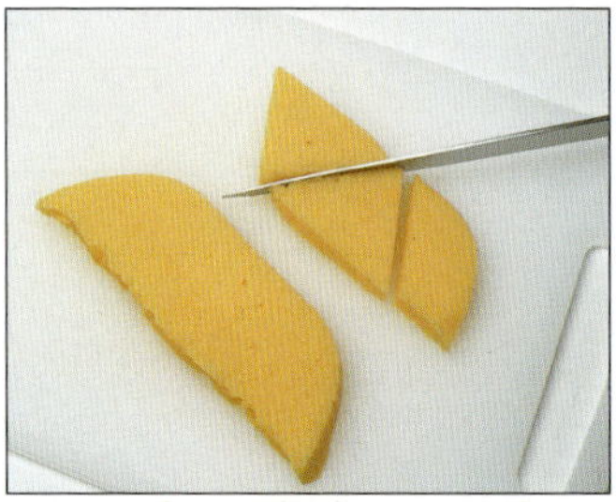

1 ▲ Cut the polenta into slices about 1 cm/$^1/_2$ inch thick. Cut the slices into triangles or rounds.

2 Heat the oil until a small piece of bread sizzles as soon as it is dropped in (about 185°C/360°F).

3 ▲ Season the flour with salt and pepper. Dredge the pieces lightly in the flour, shaking off any excess.

4 ▲ Fry the polenta, a few pieces at a time, until golden and crisp. Drain on paper towels while the remaining pieces are frying. Serve at once.

Polenta with Mushrooms

Polenta con funghi

This dish is delicious made with a mixture of wild and cultivated mushrooms. Just a few dried porcini mushrooms will help to give cultivated mushrooms a more interesting flavour.

Ingredients

10 g/$^1/_4$ oz/2 tbsp dried porcini mushrooms (omit if using wild mushrooms)
60 ml/4 tbsp olive oil
1 small onion, finely chopped
700 g/1$^1/_2$lb mushrooms, wild or cultivated, or a combination of both
2 cloves garlic, finely chopped
45 ml/3 tbsp chopped fresh parsley
3 medium tomatoes, peeled and diced
15 ml/1 tbsp tomato paste
175 ml/6 fl oz/$^3/_4$ cup warm water
$^1/_4$ tsp fresh thyme leaves, or $^1/_8$ tsp dried thyme
1 bay leaf
salt and freshly ground black pepper
a few sprigs fresh parsley, to garnish

For the polenta

1.5 litres/2$^1/_2$ pints/6$^1/_4$ cups water
15 ml/1 tbsp salt
350 g/12 oz/2$^1/_2$ cups polenta flour

serves 6

1 ▲ Soak the dried mushrooms, if using, in a small cup of warm water for 20 minutes. Remove the mushrooms with a slotted spoon, and rinse them well in several changes of cool water. Filter the soaking water through a layer of paper towels placed in a sieve, and reserve.

2 In a large frying pan heat the oil, and sauté the onion over low heat until soft and golden.

3 ▲ Clean the fresh mushrooms by wiping them with a damp cloth. Cut into slices. When the onion is soft add the mushrooms to the pan. Stir over moderate to high heat until they give up their liquid. Add the garlic, parsley and diced tomatoes. Cook for 4–5 minutes more.

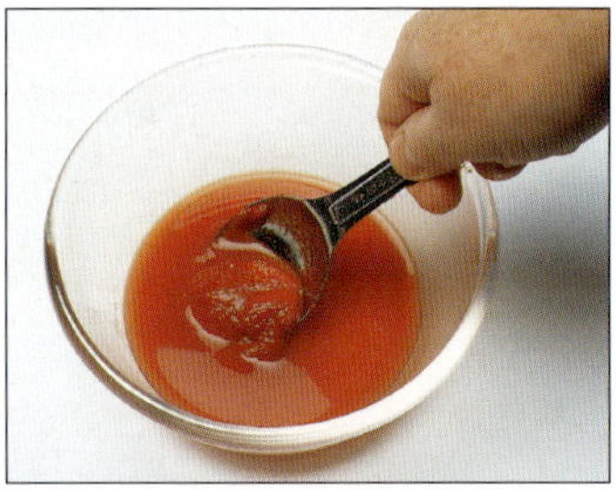

4 ▲ Soften the tomato paste in the warm water (use only 100 ml/4 fl oz/$^1/_2$ cup water if you are using dried mushrooms). Add it to the pan with the herbs. Add the dried mushrooms and soaking liquid, if using them. Mix well and season with salt and pepper. Lower the heat to low to moderate and cook for 15–20 minutes. Set aside while you make the polenta.

5 ▲ Bring the water to a boil in a large heavy saucepan. Add the salt. Reduce the heat to a simmer, and begin to add the polenta in a fine rain. Stir constantly with a whisk until the polenta has all been incorporated.

6 Switch to a long-handled wooden spoon, and continue to stir the polenta over low to moderate heat until it is a thick mass, and pulls away from the sides of the pan. This may take from 25–50 minutes, depending on the type of polenta used. For best results, never stop stirring the polenta until you remove it from the heat.

7 ▲ When the polenta has almost finished cooking, gently reheat the mushroom sauce. To serve, spoon the polenta onto a warmed serving platter. Make a well in the centre. Spoon some of the mushroom sauce into the well, and garnish with parsley. Serve at once, passing the remaining sauce in a separate bowl.

Grilled Polenta with Gorgonzola

Polenta alla griglia

Grilled polenta is delicious, and is a good way of using up cold polenta. Try it with any soft flavourful cheese. Plain broiled polenta is a good accompaniment to stews and soups.

Ingredients

1.5 litres/$2^1/_2$ pints/$6^1/_4$ cups water
15 ml/1 tbsp salt
350 g/12 oz/$2^1/_2$ cups polenta flour
225 g/8 oz/$1^1/_4$ cups Gorgonzola or other cheese, at room temperature
serves 6–8 as a snack or appetizer

1 ▲ Bring the water to a boil in a large heavy-bottomed saucepan. Add the salt. Reduce the heat to a simmer, and begin to add the polenta in a fine rain. Stir constantly with a whisk until the polenta has all been incorporated.

2 ▲ Switch to a long-handled wooden spoon, and continue to stir the polenta over low to moderate heat until it is a thick mass, and pulls away from the sides of the pan. This may take from 25–50 minutes, depending on the type of polenta used. For best results, never stop stirring the polenta until you remove it from the heat.

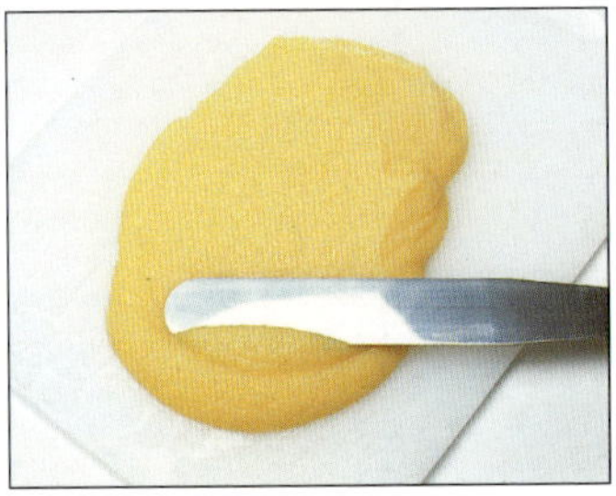

3 ▲ When the polenta is cooked, sprinkle a work surface or large board with a little water. Spread the polenta out onto the surface in a layer 1.5 cm/$^3/_4$in thick. Allow to cool completely. Preheat the grill.

4 ▲ Cut the polenta into triangles. Grill until hot and speckled with brown on both sides. Spread with the Gorgonzola or other cheese. Serve immediately.

Polenta Baked with Cheese

Polenta pasticciata

Cold polenta can be cut into slices and baked in layers with cheese and other ingredients. The traditional way of cutting it is with a wooden knife or a piece of thick thread.

Ingredients
75 g/3 oz/generous $^1/_3$ cup butter
warm cooked polenta, made with 250 g/ 9 oz/2 cups polenta flour
45 ml/3 tbsp olive oil
2 medium onions, thinly sliced
pinch of grated nutmeg
salt and freshly ground black pepper
150 g/5 oz/$^3/_4$ cup mozzarella or sharp Cheddar cheese, cut into thin slices
45 ml/3 tbsp finely chopped fresh parsley
$^1/_3$ cup freshly grated Parmesan cheese
serves 4–6

1 ▲ Stir a third of the butter into the cooked polenta. Sprinkle a work surface with a little water. Spread the polenta out in a layer 1 cm/$^1/_2$in thick. Allow to cool. Cut into 6 cm/2$^1/_2$in rounds.

2 ▲ Heat the oil in a medium pan with 15 g/$^1/_2$ oz/1 tbsp of the remaining butter. Add the onions, and stir over low heat until soft.

3 ▲ Season the onions with nutmeg, salt and pepper. Preheat the oven to 190°C/375°F/Gas 5. Butter an ovenproof dish. Spread a few of the onion slices in the bottom of the dish. Cover with a layer of polenta rounds. Dot with butter.

4 ▲ Add a layer of the sliced mozzarella or Cheddar, and a sprinkling of parsley and Parmesan. Season with salt and pepper. Make another layer of the onions, and continue the layers in order, ending with the Parmesan. Dot the top with butter and bake for 20–25 minutes, or until the cheese has melted. Serve from the baking dish.

Timballo of Rice with Peas

Timballo di riso con piselli

The timballo is named because it looks like an inverted kettledrum (*timballo *or* timpano*). It is made like a risotto, but is given a final baking in the oven, and then unmoulded.

Ingredients

75 g/3 oz/$^1/_3$ cup butter
30 ml/2 tbsp olive oil
1 small onion, finely chopped
50 g/2 oz/$^1/_3$ cup ham, cut into small dice
45 ml/3 tbsp finely chopped fresh parsley, plus a few sprigs to garnish
2 cloves garlic, very finely chopped
225 g/8 oz/1 cup shelled peas, fresh or frozen and thawed
salt and freshly ground black pepper
60 ml/4 tbsp water
1.25 litres/2$^1/_4$ pints/5$^1/_2$ cups meat or vegetable broth, preferably home-made
275 g/10 oz/1$^1/_2$ cups medium-grain risotto rice, such as arborio
75 g/3 oz/$^3/_4$ cup freshly grated Parmesan cheese
175 g/6 oz/$^3/_4$ cup fontina cheese, very thinly sliced
a few sprigs parsley, to garnish

serves 4

1 ▲ Heat half the butter and all the oil in a large heavy frying pan or casserole. Add the chopped onion, and cook for a few minutes until it softens. Add the diced ham, and stir over moderate heat for 3–4 minutes. Stir in the parsley and garlic. Cook for 1 or 2 minutes. Add the peas, mix well, season with salt and pepper and add the water. Cover the pan, and cook for about 8 minutes for fresh peas, 4 minutes for frozen peas. Remove the cover, and cook until all the liquid has evaporated. Remove half the pea mixture to a dish.

2 Heat the broth, and keep it simmering until needed. Butter a round, flat-bottomed ovenproof dish and line the bottom with a round of buttered greaseproof paper.

3 ▲ Stir the rice into the pea mixture remaining in the pan. After 1–2 minutes, add a small ladleful of the hot broth. Cook over moderate heat until the broth is absorbed, stirring the rice with a wooden spoon to prevent it from sticking. Add a little more stock, and stir until the rice dries out again. Continue stirring and adding the liquid.

4 ▲ Preheat the oven to 180°C/350°F. After about 20 minutes of cooking time, taste the rice. As soon as the rice is just *al dente*, or tender but still firm to the bite, remove the pan from the heat. Correct the seasoning. Mix most of the remaining butter and half the grated Parmesan into the rice.

5 Assemble by sprinkling a little Parmesan into the bottom of the dish. Spoon about half the rice into the dish. Follow with a thin layer of the fontina and a layer of reserved cooked peas and ham. Sprinkle with grated Parmesan.

6 ▲ Cover with the remaining fontina slices and end with the rice. Sprinkle with Parmesan, and dot with butter. Bake in the preheated oven for 10–15 minutes. Remove from the oven, and allow to stand for 10 minutes.

7 ▲ To unmould, slip a knife around between the rice and the dish. Place a serving plate upside down on top of the dish. Wearing oven mitts, pick up the dish and turn it over while still holding the plate. If the rice does not drop down, give it a sharp knock with your gloved hand. Peel off the greaseproof paper. Garnish with parsley. Serve by cutting the timballo into wedges.

Fried Rice Balls Stuffed with Cheese

Supplì

These deep-fried balls of risotto are stuffed with an inner filling of mozzarella cheese. They are very popular snacks in Rome and central Italy.

Ingredients

1 recipe Risotto with Parmesan Cheese or Risotto with Mushrooms
3 eggs
115 g/4 oz/$^2/_3$ cup mozzarella cheese, cut into small dice
plain breadcrumbs, as required
oil, for deep-frying
flour, to coat

serves 4

1 ▲ Allow the risotto to cool completely. (These are even better when formed from risotto made the day before.) Beat 2 of the eggs, and mix them well into the cold risotto.

2 ▲ Use your hands to form the rice mixture into balls the size of a large egg. If the mixture is too moist to hold its shape well, stir in a few tablespoons of breadcrumbs as necessary. Poke a hole into the centre of each ball, fill it with a few small cubes of mozzarella, and close the hole over again with the rice mixture.

3 Heat the oil until a small piece of bread sizzles as soon as it is dropped in (about 185°C/360°F).

4 ▲ Spread some flour on a plate. Beat the remaining egg in a shallow bowl. Sprinkle another plate with breadcrumbs. Roll the balls in the flour, then in the egg, and finally in the breadcrumbs.

5 ▲ Fry them a few at a time in the hot oil until golden and crisp. Drain on paper towels while the remaining balls are frying. Serve hot.

Potato Gnocchi

Gnocchi di patate

Gnocchi are little dumplings made either with mashed potato and flour, as here, or with semolina. They should be light in texture, and must not be overworked while being made.

Ingredients
1 kg/2 lb waxy potatoes, scrubbed
15 ml/1 tbsp salt
250–300 g/9–11 oz/2–2$^1/_2$ cups flour
1 egg
pinch of grated nutmeg
25 g/1 oz/2 tbsp butter
freshly grated Parmesan, to serve
serves 4–6

1 Place the unpeeled potatoes in a large pan of salted water. Bring to a boil, and cook until the potatoes are tender but not falling apart. Drain. Peel as soon as possible, while the potatoes are still hot.

2 On a work surface spread out a layer of flour. Mash the hot potatoes with a food mill, dropping them directly onto the flour, dropping them directly onto the flour. Sprinkle with about half of the remaining flour and mix very lightly into the potatoes. Break the egg into the mixture, add the nutmeg, and knead lightly, drawing in more flour as necessary. When the dough is light to the touch and no longer moist or sticky it is ready to be rolled. Do not overwork or the gnocchi will be heavy.

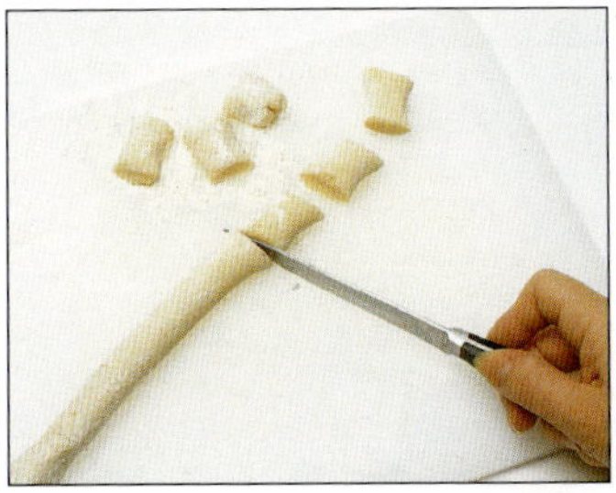

3 ▲ Divide the dough into 4 parts. On a lightly floured board form each into a roll about 2 cm/$^3/_4$ inch in diameter. Cut the rolls crosswise into pieces about 2 cm/$^3/_4$ inch long.

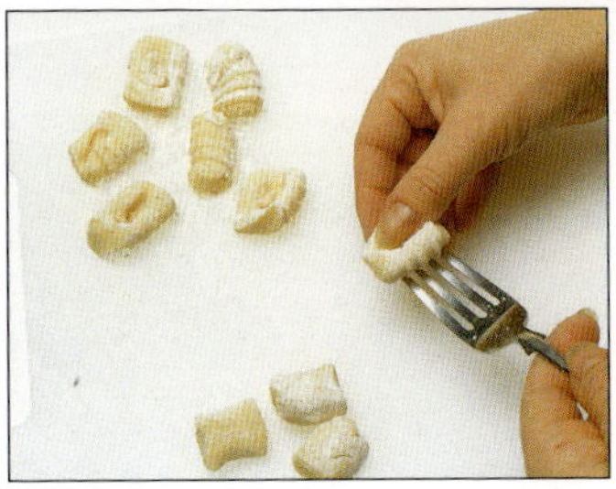

4 ▲ Hold an ordinary table fork with long tines sideways, leaning on the board. One by one press and roll the gnocchi lightly along the tines of the fork towards the points, making ridges on one side, and a depression from your thumb on the other.

5 Bring a large pan of water to a fast boil. Add salt, and drop in about half the gnocchi.

6 ▲ When the gnocchi rise to the surface, after 3–4 minutes, they are cooked. Scoop them out of the water, allow to drain, and place in a warmed serving bowl. Dot with butter. Keep warm while the remaining gnocchi are boiling. As soon as they are cooked, toss the gnocchi with the butter or a heated sauce, sprinkle with grated Parmesan, and serve.

Potato and Spinach Gnocchi

Gnocchi di patate e spinaci

These green gnocchi are made in the same way as potato gnocchi, with the addition of fresh or frozen spinach. Serve tossed with butter or with a tomato sauce.

Ingredients

750 g/1 $^{1}/_{2}$lb fresh spinach, or 400 g/ 14oz frozen leaf spinach
1 kg/2lb waxy potatoes, scrubbed
salt, to taste
250 g-300g/9–11 oz/2–2$^{1}/_{2}$ cups flour
1 egg
pinch of grated nutmeg
50 g/2 oz/$^{1}/_{4}$ cup butter
freshly grated Parmesan cheese, to serve

serves 6

1 Wash fresh spinach in several changes of cold water. Pull off any tough stalks. Place in a large saucepan with only the water that is clinging to the leaves. Cover the pan, and cook over moderate heat, stirring occasionally, until the spinach is tender, about 5-8 minutes. Cook uncovered for the last 2-3 minutes to boil off some of the water. Remove from the heat. Drain.

2 ▲ Cook frozen spinach according to the instructions on the packet. Spread the spinach over a clean dish towel, roll it up and wring out all excess moisture. Chop the spinach finely with a sharp knife.

3 Place the unpeeled potatoes in a large pan of salted water. Bring to a boil, and cook until the potatoes are tender but not falling apart. Drain. Peel as soon as possible, while the potatoes are still hot.

4 ▲ On a work surface spread out a layer of flour. Mash the hot potatoes with a food mill, dropping them directly onto the flour. Add the spinach, and mix lightly into the potatoes. Sprinkle with about half of the remianing flour and mix in lightly.

5 Break the egg into the mixture, add the nutmeg, and knead lightly, drawing in more flour as necessary. When the dough is light to the touch and no longer moist or sticky it is ready to be rolled. Do not overwork or the gnocchi will be heavy.

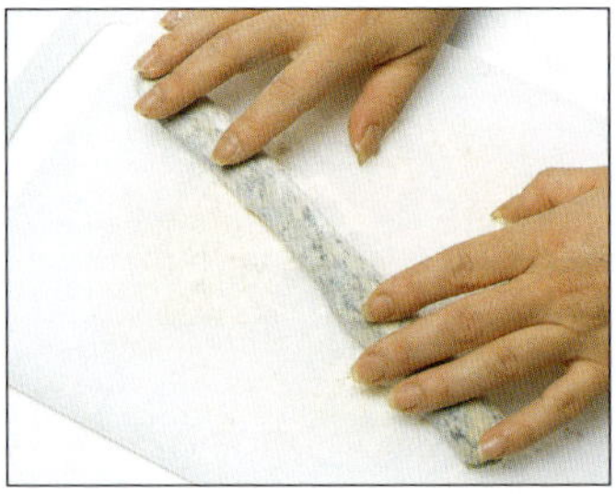

6 ▲ Divide the dough into 4 parts. On a lightly floured board form each into a roll about 2 cm/$^{3}/_{4}$ inch in diameter. Cut the rolls crosswise into pieces about 2 cm/$^{3}/_{4}$ inch long.

7 ▲ Hold an ordinary table fork with long tines sideways, leaning on the board. One by one press and roll the gnocchi lightly along the tines of the fork towards the points, making ridges on one side, and a depression from your thumb on the other.

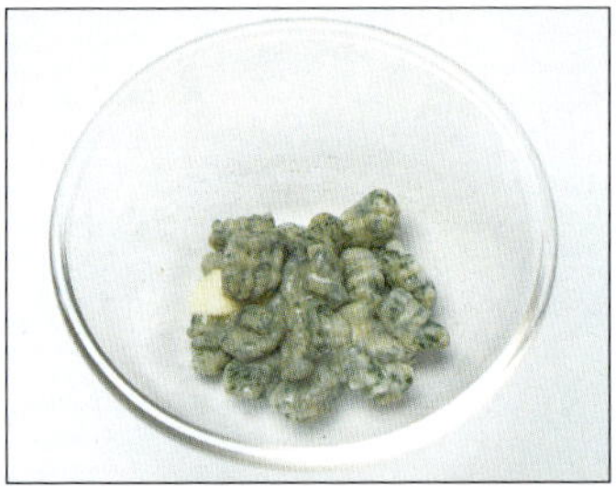

8 ▲ Bring a large pan of water to a fast boil. Add salt and drop about half the gnocchi in. They will sink to the bottom of the pan. When they rise to the surface, after 3-4 minutes, the gnocchi are done. Scoop them out with a large slotted spoon, and place in a warmed serving bowl. Keep warm while the remaining gnocchi are boiling. As soon as they are cooked, toss the gnocchi with the butter or a heated sauce, sprinkle with grated Parmesan, and serve.

Semolina Gnocchi

Gnocchi di semola

This famous Roman dish is made with coarsely ground semolina, which is cooked in a similar way to polenta. The rich paste is cut into flat discs, and baked with butter and cheese.

Ingredients

1 litre/1¾ pints/4½ cups milk
pinch of salt
35 g/1½ oz/3 tbsp butter
250 g/9 oz/generous 2 cups coarsely ground semolina
3 egg yolks
3 tbsp freshly grated Parmesan cheese

For baking

60 g/2¼ oz/5 tbsp butter, melted
60 g/2¼ oz/½ cup freshly grated Parmesan cheese
pinch of grated nutmeg

serves 4

1 ▲ Heat the milk with the salt and a third of the butter in a heavy or non-stick saucepan. When it boils sprinkle in the semolina, stirring with a wire whisk to prevent lumps from forming. Bring the mixture to the boil. Lower the heat and simmer for 15–20 minutes, stirring occasionally. The mixture will be very thick.

~ COOK'S TIP ~

Semolina is ground durum wheat, which is the kind used to make dried pasta. Buy semolina in small batches and store in an air-tight container as it goes stale when kept for too long.

2 ▲ Remove from the heat and beat in the remaining butter, and then the egg yolks one at a time. Stir in the grated Parmesan. Season with salt. Sprinkle a little cold water onto a work surface. Spread the hot semolina mixture out onto it in an even layer about 1 cm/½ inch thick. Allow to cool for at least 2 hours.

3 ▲ Preheat the oven to 220°C/425°F/gas 7. Butter a shallow baking dish. Use a biscuit cutter to cut the semolina into 6 cm/2½in rounds.

4 ▲ Place the trimmings in an even layer in the bottom of the dish. Pour over a little melted butter, and sprinkle with cheese. Cover with a layer of the cut-out circles, overlapping them slightly. Sprinkle with nutmeg, cheese and butter. Continue the layering until all the ingredients have been used up.

5 Bake for about 20 minutes, or until the top is browned. Remove from the oven and allow to stand for 5 minutes before serving.

Frittata with Sun-dried Tomatoes

Frittata con pomodori secchi

Adding just a few sun-dried tomatoes gives this frittata a distinctly Mediterranean flavour.

Ingredients

6 sun-dried tomatoes, dry or in oil and drained
60 ml/4 tbsp olive oil
1 small onion, finely chopped
pinch of fresh thyme leaves
salt and freshly ground black pepper
6 eggs
50 g/2 oz/$^{1}/_{2}$ cup freshly grated Parmesan cheese

serves 3–4

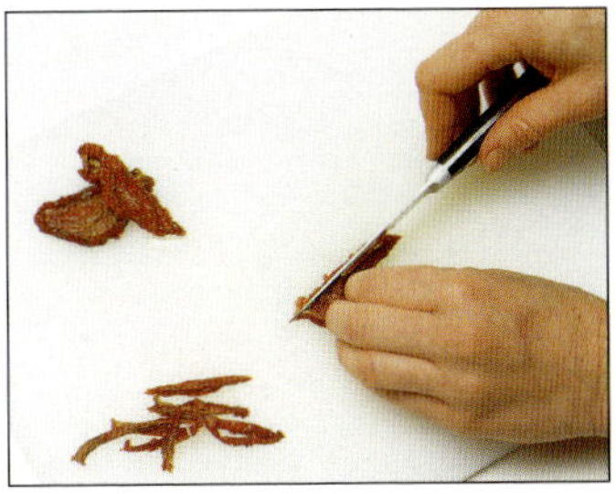

1 ▲ Place the tomatoes in a small bowl, and pour on enough hot water to just cover them. Soak for about 15 minutes. Lift the tomatoes out of the water, and slice them into thin strips. Reserve the soaking water.

2 ▲ Heat the oil in a large non-stick or heavy frying pan. Stir in the onion, and cook for 5-6 minutes or until soft and golden. Add the tomatoes and thyme, and stir over moderate heat for 2-3 minutes. Season with salt and pepper.

3 ▲ Break the eggs into a bowl and beat lightly with a fork. Stir in 45-60 ml/3-4 tbsp of the tomato soaking water and the grated Parmesan. Raise the heat under the pan. When the oil is sizzling pour in the eggs. Mix them quickly into the other ingredients, and stop stirring. Lower the heat to moderate, and cook for about 4-5 minutes, or until the frittata is puffed and golden brown.

4 ▲ Take a large plate, place it upside down over the pan, and holding it firmly with oven gloves, turn the pan and the frittata over onto it. Slide the frittata back into the pan, and continue cooking until golden brown on the second side, 3-4 minutes more. Remove from the heat. The frittata can be served hot, at room temperature, or cold. Cut it into wedges to serve.

Frittata of Leftover Pasta

Frittata di pasta avanzata

This is a great way to use up cold leftover pasta, whatever the sauce.

Ingredients
5–6 eggs
225–275 g/8–10 oz/1 $^{1}/_{2}$–2 cups cold cooked pasta, with any sauce
50 g/2 oz/$^{1}/_{2}$ cup freshly grated Parmesan cheese
salt and freshly ground black pepper
65 g/2 $^{1}/_{2}$ oz/5 tbsp butter
serves 4

1 ▲ In a medium bowl beat the eggs lightly with a fork. Stir in the pasta and the Parmesan. Season to taste.

2 ▲ Heat half the butter in a large non-stick or heavy frying pan. As soon as the foam subsides pour in the pasta mixture. Cook over moderate heat, without stirring, for 4–5 minutes, or until the bottom is golden brown. Loosen the frittata by shaking the pan backwards and forwards.

3 ▲ Take a large plate, place it upside down over the pan and, holding it firmly with oven gloves, turn the pan and the frittata over onto it. Add the remaining butter to the pan. As soon as it stops foaming slide the frittata back into the pan, and continue cooking until golden brown on the second side, 3–4 minutes more. Remove from the heat. The frittata can be served hot, at room temperature, or cold. Cut it into wedges to serve.

Frittata with Onions

Frittata con cipolle

Gently cooked onions add a sweet flavour to the basic frittata mixture.

Ingredients
60 ml/4 tbsp olive oil
2 medium onions, thinly sliced
salt and freshly ground black pepper
30 ml/2 tbsp chopped fresh parsley
6 eggs
serves 3–4

1 Heat the oil in a large non-stick or heavy frying pan. Stir in the onions, and cook over low heat until they are soft and golden. This may take 10–15 minutes. Season with salt and pepper. Stir in the herbs.

2 Break the eggs into a bowl, and beat them lightly with a fork. Raise the heat under the onions to moderate, and when they are sizzling pour in the eggs. Quickly stir them into the onions to distribute them. Stop stirring.

3 ▲ Cook for about 5 minutes, or until the frittata is puffed and golden brown underneath. If the frittata seems to be sticking to the pan, shake the pan back and forth to release it.

4 ▲ Take a large plate, place it upside down over the pan and, holding it firmly with oven mitts, turn the pan and the frittata over onto it. Slide the frittata back into the pan, and continue cooking until golden brown on the second side, 3–4 minutes more. Remove from the heat. Cut it into wedges to serve.

Frittata with Spinach and Ham

Frittata con spinaci e prosciutto

In Italy, frittate are often used as fillings for sandwiches.

Ingredients

200 g/7 oz/1 cup cooked leaf spinach, fresh or frozen
45 ml/3 tbsp olive oil
4 spring onions, finely sliced
1 clove garlic, finely chopped
50 g/2 oz/$^1/_3$ cup ham or prosciutto, cut into small dice
salt and freshly ground black pepper
8 eggs

serves 6

1 ▲ Squeeze any excess moisture out of the spinach with your hands. Chop it roughly and set aside.

2 ▲ Heat the oil in a large non-stick or heavy frying pan. Stir in the spring onions, and cook for 3–4 minutes. Add the garlic and ham, and stir over moderate heat until just golden. Stir in the spinach, and cook for 3–4 minutes, or until just heated through. Season with salt and pepper.

3 ▲ Break the eggs into a bowl and beat lightly with a fork. Raise the heat under the vegetables. After about 1 minute pour in the eggs. Mix them quickly into the other ingredients, and stop stirring. Cook over moderate heat for about 5–6 minutes, or until the frittata is puffed and golden brown underneath. If the frittata seems to be sticking to the pan, shake the pan backwards and forwards to release it.

4 ▲ Take a large plate, place it upside down over the pan and, holding it firmly with oven gloves, turn the pan and the frittata over onto it. Slide the frittata back into the pan, and continue cooking until golden brown on the second side, 3–4 minutes more. Remove from the heat. The frittata can be served hot, at room temperature, or cold. Cut it into wedges to serve.

Sliced Frittata Salad

Frittata fredda in insalata

This dish - cold frittata with a tomato sauce - is ideal for a light summer lunch.

Ingredients
6 eggs
30 ml/2 tbsp mixed fresh herbs,finely chopped,such as basil, parsley, thyme or tarragon
35 g/1$^1/_2$ oz/$^1/_4$ cup freshly grated Parmesan cheese
salt and freshly ground black pepper
45 ml/3 tbsp olive oil

For the tomato sauce
30 ml/2 tbsp olive oil
1 small onion, finely chopped
350 g/12oz fresh tomatoes, or 1x 400 g/14oz can tomatoes, chopped
1 clove garlic, chopped
60 ml/4 tbsp water
salt and freshly ground black pepper

serves 3–4

1 To make the frittata, break the eggs into a bowl, and beat them lightly with a fork. Beat in the herbs and cheese. Season with salt and pepper. Heat the oil in a large non-stick or heavy frying pan until hot but not smoking.

2 ▲ Pour in the egg mixture. Cook, without stirring, until the frittata is puffed and golden brown underneath.

3 Take a large plate, place it upside down over the pan, and holding it firmly with oven gloves, turn the pan and the frittata over onto it. Slide the frittata back into the pan, and continue cooking until golden brown on the second side, 3–4 minutes more. Remove from the heat and allow to cool completely.

4 ▲ To make the tomato sauce, heat the oil in a medium heavy pan. Add the onion, and cook slowly until it is soft. Add the tomatoes, garlic and water, and season with salt and pepper. Cover the pan and cook over moderate heat until the tomatoes are soft, about 15 minutes.

5 Remove from the heat, and cool slightly before passing the sauce through a food mill or strainer. Leave to cool completely.

6 ▲ To assemble the salad, cut the frittata into thin slices. Place them in a serving bowl and toss lightly with the sauce. Serve the salad at room temperature or chilled.

Baked Eggs with Tomatoes

Uova al piatto con pomodori

These eggs simply baked over a fresh tomato sauce make an easy dish for a light supper. Allow 1 or 2 eggs per person.

Ingredients
60 ml/4 tbsp olive oil
1 small onion, finely chopped
450 g/1lb tomatoes, peeled, seeded and chopped
30 ml/2 tbsp chopped fresh basil
6 eggs
salt and freshly ground black pepper
15 g/1 tbsp butter
chopped fresh parsley, to garnish
3 large or 6 small servings

1 ▲ Heat the oil in a shallow flameproof dish. Add the onion, and cook until soft and golden.

2 ▲ Preheat the oven to 190°C/375°F/ gas 5. When the onion is soft and golden, add the tomatoes and cook for 5–10 minutes, or until the tomatoes are very soft. Stir in the chopped basil.

~ VARIATION ~

Sprinkle 30–45 ml/2–3 tbsp of freshly grated Parmesan cheese over the eggs before baking for a richer, tastier dish.

3 ▲ Break the eggs one at a time and slip them into the dish in one layer on top of the tomatoes. Season with salt and pepper. Dot with butter. Cover the dish, and bake in the oven for 7–10 minutes, or until the egg whites have just set, but the yolks are still soft. Serve at once.

Baked Eggs with Cheese

Uova al piatto alla parmigiana

Grated Parmesan makes a tasty addition to this simple dish.

Ingredients
6 eggs
salt and freshly ground black pepper
35 g/1$^{1}/_{2}$ oz/3 tbsp ham, cut into thin matchsticks
90 ml/6 tbsp freshly grated Parmesan cheese
25 g/1 oz/2 tbsp butter
3–4 leaves fresh parsley, to garnish
rounds of crusty bread, warmed, to serve
3 large or 6 small servings

1 Preheat the oven to 200°C/400°F/ gas 6. Butter a shallow ovenproof dish (or dishes, if you prefer to bake the eggs individually).

2 ▲ Break the eggs into the dish. Season with salt and pepper. Sprinkle the ham over the whites. Sprinkle the top with the Parmesan.

3 ▲ Dot with butter. Cover the dish, and bake for 7–10 minutes, or until the whites have set and the cheese has melted. Garnish with the parsley. Serve hot with warmed bread.

Fonduta with Steamed Vegetables

Fonduta con verdure

Fonduta is a creamy cheese sauce from the mountainous Val d'Aosta region. Traditionally it is garnished with slices of white truffles and eaten with toasted bread rounds.

Ingredients
assorted vegetables, such as fennel, broccoli, carrots, cauliflower and courgettes
115 g/4 oz/$^1/_2$ cup butter
12–16 rounds of Italian or French baguette

For the fonduta
300 g/11 oz/1$^2/_3$ cups fontina cheese
15 ml/ 1 tbsp flour
milk, as required
50 g/2 oz/$^1/_4$ cup butter
50 g/2 oz/$^1/_2$ cup freshly grated Parmesan cheese
pinch of grated nutmeg
salt and freshly ground black pepper
2 egg yolks, at room temperature
a few slivers of white truffle (optional)
serves 4

1 ▲ About 6 hours before you want to serve the fonduta, cut the fontina into chunks and place in a bowl. Sprinkle with the flour. Pour in enough milk to barely cover the cheese, and set aside in a cool place. If you put the bowl in the refrigerator, take it out at least 1 hour before cooking the fonduta. It should be at room temperature before being cooked.

2 Just before preparing the fonduta, steam the vegetables until tender. Cut into pieces. Place on a serving platter, dot with butter, and keep warm.

3 Butter the bread rounds and toast lightly in the oven or under the grill.

4 ▲ For the fonduta, melt the butter in a mixing bowl set over a pan of simmering water, or in the top of a double boiler. Strain the fontina and add it, with 45–60 ml/3–4 tbsp of its soaking milk. Cook, stirring, until the cheese melts. When it is hot, and has formed a homogeneous mass, add the Parmesan and stir until melted. Season with nutmeg, salt and pepper.

5 ▲ Remove from the heat and immediately beat in the egg yolks which have been passed through the strainer. Spoon into warmed individual serving bowls, garnish with the white truffle if using, and serve with the vegetables and toasted bread.

Fried Mozzarella

Mozzarella fritta

These cheese slices make a good informal lunch. They originate from the Neapolitan area, where much mozzarella is produced. They must be made just before serving.

Ingredients

300 g/11 oz/1$^3/_4$ cups mozzarella cheese
oil, for deep-frying
2 eggs
flour seasoned with salt and freshly ground black pepper, for coating
plain dry breadcrumbs, for coating
serves 2–3

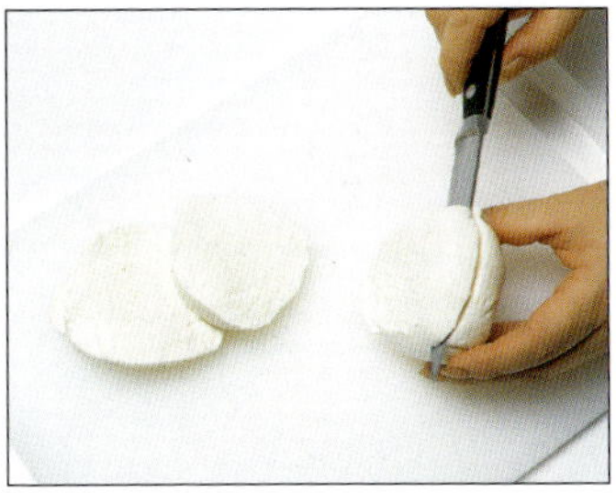

1 ▲ Cut the mozzarella into slices about 1 cm/$^1/_2$ inch thick. Gently pat off any excess moisture with a paper towel.

2 ▲ Heat the oil until a small piece of bread sizzles as soon as it is dropped in (about 185°C/360°F). While the oil is heating beat the eggs in a shallow bowl. Spread some flour on one plate, and some breadcrumbs on another.

3 ▲ Press the cheese slices into the flour, coating them evenly with a thin layer of flour. Shake off any excess. Dip them into the egg, then into the breadcrumbs. Dip them once more into the egg, and then again into the breadcrumbs.

4 ▲ Fry immediately in the hot oil until golden brown. (You may have to do this in two batches but do not let the breaded cheese wait for too long or the breadcrumb coating will separate from the cheese while it is being fried.) Drain quickly on paper towels, and serve hot.

Grilled Cheese Sandwiches

Panini alla griglia

Garlic, herbs and tomatoes make these open sandwiches very Mediterranean.

Ingredients
45 ml/3 tbsp olive oil
4 or 5 canned plum tomatoes, finely chopped
a few leaves fresh basil, torn into pieces
salt and freshly ground black pepper
4–6 medium slices of Italian or crusty bread
1 clove garlic, peeled and cut in half
75 g/3 oz/$^1/_2$ cup scamorza, mozzarella or Cheddar cheese, sliced
serves 4

1 Heat the oil in a small frying pan. Add the tomatoes and basil, and season with salt and pepper. Cook over low to moderate heat for about 8–10 minutes, or until the tomatoes start to dry out. Preheat the grill.

2 ▲ Lightly toast the bread. When it has cooled slightly rub it on one side with the garlic.

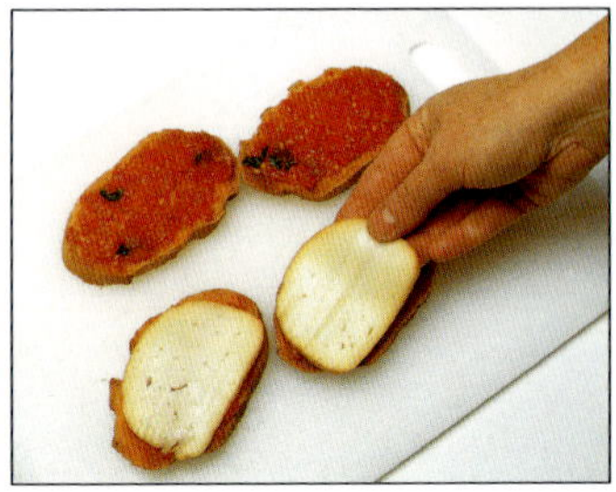

3 ▲ Spread some of the tomatoes on each piece of bread, and top with the sliced cheese. Place under the hot grill until the cheese melts and begins to bubble, 5–8 minutes. Serve hot.

Mozzarella, Tomato and Basil Salad

Insalata caprese

This very popular and easy salad is considered rather patriotic in Italy, as its three ingredients are the colours of the national flag.

Ingredients
4 large tomatoes
400 g/14 oz/2 cups mozzarella cheese, from cow or buffalo milk
8–10 leaves fresh basil
60 ml/4 tbsp extra-virgin olive oil
salt and freshly ground black pepper
serves 4

1 ▲ Slice the tomatoes and mozzarella into thick rounds.

2 ▲ Arrange the tomatoes and cheese in overlapping slices on a serving dish. Decorate with basil.

3 ▲ Sprinkle with olive oil and a little salt. Serve with the black pepper passed separately.

~ COOK'S TIP ~

In Italy the most sought-after mozzarella is made from the milk of water buffalo. It is found mainly in the south and in Campania.

Pizzas, Pastries and Bread

Pizzas are fun to make at home. Personalize them with combinations of your favourite ingredients. Italian flatbreads and breadsticks can be topped with herbs and seeds for tasty accompaniments, appetizers or unusual snacks.

Basic Pizza Dough

Pizza dough is leavened with yeast. It usually rises once before being rolled out and filled. The dough can be baked in pizza pans or baked directly on a flat baking sheet.

Ingredients

25 g/1 oz/$2^{1}/_{2}$ tbsp fresh bread yeast or 15 g/$^{1}/_{2}$ oz/$1^{1}/_{2}$ tbsp active dried yeast
250 ml/ 8 fl oz/1 cup lukewarm water
pinch of sugar
5 ml/1 tsp salt
350–400 g/12–14 oz/3–$3^{1}/_{2}$ cups plain flour, preferably strong

serves 4 as a main course or 8 as an appetizer

1 ▲ Warm a medium mixing bowl by swirling some hot water in it. Drain. Place the yeast in the bowl, and pour on the warm water. Stir in the sugar, mix with a fork, and allow to stand until the yeast has dispersed and starts to foam, 5-10 minutes.

2 ▲ Use a wooden spoon to mix in the salt and about one-third of the flour. Mix in another third of the flour, stirring with the spoon until the dough forms a mass and begins to pull away from the sides of the bowl.

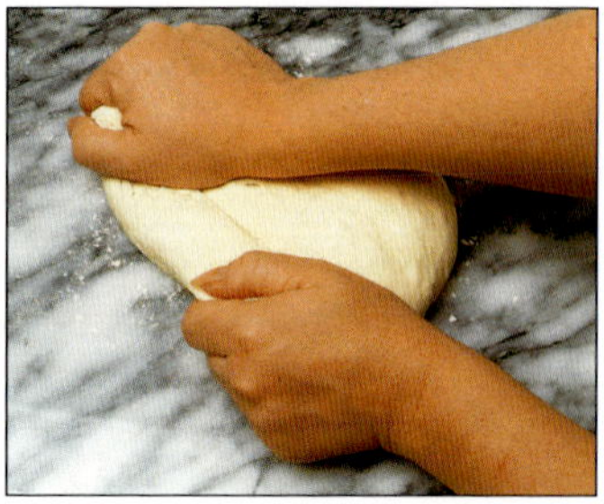

3 ▲ Sprinkle some of the remaining flour onto a smooth work surface. Remove the dough from the bowl and begin to knead it, working in the remaining flour a little at a time. Knead for 8-10 minutes. By the end the dough should be elastic and smooth. Form it into a ball.

4 Lightly oil a mixing bowl. Place the dough in the bowl. Stretch a moistened and wrung-out dish towel across the top of the bowl, and leave it to stand in a warm place until the dough has doubled in volume, about 40-50 minutes or more, depending on the type of yeast used. (If you do not have a warm enough place, turn the oven on to medium heat for 10 minutes before you knead the dough. Turn it off. Place the bowl with the dough in it in the turned-off oven with the door closed and let it rise there.) To test whether the dough has risen enough, poke two fingers into the dough. If the indentations remain, the dough is ready.

5 ▲ Punch the dough down with your fist to release the air. Knead for 1-2 minutes.

6 If you want to make 2 medium pizzas, divide the dough into 2 balls. If you want to make 4 individual pizzas (in pans 26 cm/$10^{1}/_{2}$ in in diameter), divide the dough into 4 balls. Pat the ball of dough out into a flat circle on a lightly floured surface. With a rolling pin, roll it out to a thickness of about 5-7 mm/$^{3}/_{8}$-$^{1}/_{4}$in. If you are using a pizza pan, roll the dough out about 7 mm/$^{1}/_{4}$ in larger than the size of the pan to allow for the rim of the crust.

7 ▲ Place in the lightly oiled pan, folding the extra dough under to make a thicker rim around the edge. If you are baking the pizza without a round pan, press some of the dough from the center of the circle towards the edge, to make a thicker rim. Place it on a lightly oiled flat baking sheet. The dough is now ready for filling.

~ COOK'S TIP ~

This basic dough can be used for other recipes in this book, such as Focaccia, Breadsticks, Calzone and Sicilian Closed Pizza. The dough may be frozen at the end of step 7, and thawed before filling.

Wholewheat Pizza Dough

Pizza dough can also be made with wholewheat flour, although it is easier to handle and more elastic if a proportion of white flour is used. This dough can be used in any recipe calling for Basic Pizza Dough.

Ingredients

25 g/1 oz/2 1/2 tbsp fresh bread yeast or 15 g/1/2 oz/1 1/2 tbsp active dried yeast
250 ml/8 fl oz/1 cup lukewarm water
pinch of sugar
30 ml/2 tbsp olive oil
5 ml/1 tsp salt
150 g/5 oz/1 1/4 cups plain white flour
250 g/ 9 oz/2 cups stoneground wholewheat flour

serves 4 as a main course or 8 as an appetizer

1 Warm a medium mixing bowl by swirling some hot water in it. Drain. Place the yeast in the bowl, and pour on the warm water. Stir in the sugar, mix with a fork, and allow to stand until the yeast has dispersed and starts to foam, 5–10 minutes.

2 ▲ Use a wooden spoon to mix in the olive oil and the salt, and the white flour. Mix in about half of the wholewheat flour, stirring with the spoon until the dough forms a mass and begins to pull away from the sides of the bowl.

3 ▲ Proceed with steps 3–7 as for Basic Pizza Dough, punching down the risen dough, and kneading until ready to roll out and place in a pan.

To Make the Dough in a Food Processor

1 ▲ Have all the ingredients ready and measured out. In a small pitcher or bowl add the yeast to the warm water. Stir in the sugar, and allow to stand until the yeast has dissolved, 5–10 minutes.

2 ▲ Fit the food processor with the metal blades. Place the salt and three-quarters of the flour in the bowl of the food processor. Turn it on, and pour in the yeast mixture and olive oil through the opening at the top. Continue processing until the dough forms one or two balls. Turn the machine off, open it, and touch the dough. If it still feels sticky, add a little more flour, and process again until it is incorporated.

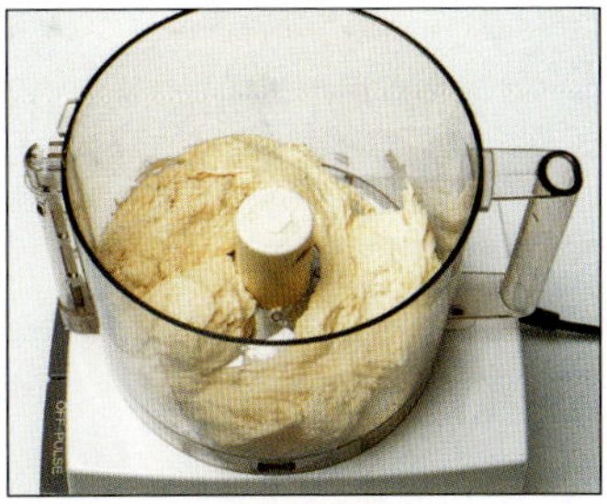

3 ▲ Remove the dough from the processor. Knead it for about 2–3 minutes on a surface dusted with the remaining flour. Form the dough into a ball, and proceed with Step 4 of Basic Pizza Dough.

Cheese and Tomato Pizza

Pizza alla Margherita

The Margherita is named after the nineteenth-century Queen of Italy, and is one of the most popular of all pizzas.

Ingredients
450 g/1 lb peeled plum tomatoes, fresh or canned, weighed whole, without extra juice
1 recipe Basic Pizza Dough, rolled out
350 g/12 oz/1$^{3}/_{4}$ cups mozzarella cheese, cut into small dice
10–12 leaves fresh basil, torn
60 ml/4 tbsp freshly grated Parmesan cheese (optional)
salt and freshly ground black pepper
45 ml/3 tbsp olive oil
serves 4

1 Preheat the oven to 250°C/475°F/ gas 9 for at least 20 minutes before baking. Strain the tomatoes through the medium holes of a food mill placed over a bowl, scraping in all the pulp.

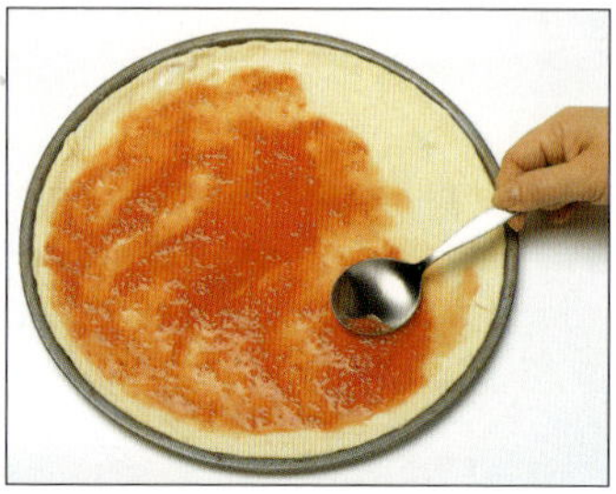

2 ▲ Spread the puréed tomatoes onto the prepared pizza dough, leaving the rim uncovered.

3 ▲ Sprinkle evenly with the mozzarella. Dot with basil. Sprinkle with Parmesan if using, salt and pepper and olive oil. Immediately place the pizzas in the oven. Bake for about 15–20 minutes, or until the crust is golden brown and the cheeses are melted and bubbling.

Pizza with Mozzarella and Anchovies

Pizza alla napoletana

If you ask for a pizza in the Neapolitan manner anywhere in Italy other than in Naples, you will be given this pizza with anchovies.

Ingredients
450 g/1 lb peeled plum tomatoes, fresh or canned, weighed whole, without extra juice
1 recipe Basic Pizza Dough, rolled out
40 g/1$^{1}/_{2}$ oz/3 tbsp anchovy fillets in oil, drained and cut into pieces
350 g/12 oz/1$^{3}/_{4}$ cups mozzarella cheese, cut into small dice
5 ml/1 tsp oregano leaves, fresh or dried
salt and freshly ground black pepper
45 ml/3 tbsp olive oil
serves 4

1 Preheat the oven to 250°C/475°F/ gas 9 for at least 20 minutes before baking. Strain the tomatoes through the medium holes of a food mill placed over a bowl, scraping in all the pulp.

2 ▲ Spread the puréed tomatoes on the pizza dough, leaving the rim uncovered. Dot with the anchovy pieces and the mozzarella.

3 ▲ Sprinkle with oregano, salt and pepper, and olive oil. Immediately place the pizza in the oven. Bake for about 15–20 minutes, or until the crust is golden brown and the cheese is bubbling.

Four Seasons Pizza

Pizza quattro stagioni

The topping on this pizza is divided into four quarters, one for each "season". You may replace the suggested ingredients with any other seasonal flavours.

Ingredients

450 g/1lb peeled plum tomatoes, fresh or canned, weighed whole, without extra juice
75 ml/5 tbsp olive oil
115 g/4 oz/1 cup mushrooms, thinly sliced
1 clove garlic, finely chopped
1 recipe Basic Pizza Dough, rolled out
350 g/12 oz/1$^{3}/_{4}$ cups mozzarella cheese, cut into small dice
4 thin slices of ham, cut into 5 cm/2in squares
32 black olives, stoned and halved
8 artichoke hearts marinated in oil, drained and cut in half
5 ml/1 tsp oregano leaves, fresh or dried
salt and freshly ground black pepper
serves 4

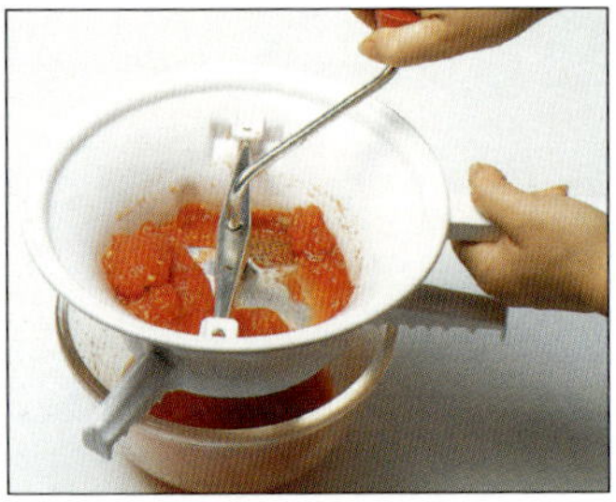

1 ▲ Preheat the oven to 250°C/475°F/ Gas 9 for at least 20 minute before baking the pizza. Strain the tomatoes through the medium holes of a food mill placed over a bowl, scraping in all the pulp.

2 Heat 30 ml/2 tbsp of the oil in a frying pan and lightly sauté the mushrooms. Stir in the garlic and set aside.

3 ▲ Spread the puréed tomato on the prepared pizza dough, leaving the rim uncovered. Sprinkle evenly with the mozzarella. Spread mushrooms over one-quarter of each pizza.

4 ▲ Arrange the ham on another quarter, and the olives and artichoke hearts on the two remaining quarters. Sprinkle with oregano, salt and pepper, and the remaining olive oil. Immediately place the pizza in the oven. Bake for about 15–20 minutes, or until the crust is golden brown and the topping is bubbling.

Pizza with Fresh Vegetables

Pizza all'ortolana

This pizza can be made with any combination of fresh vegetables. Most will benefit from being blanched or sautéed before being baked on the pizza.

Ingredients

400 g/14 oz peeled plum tomatoes, fresh or canned, weighed whole, without extra juice
2 medium broccoli spears
225 g/8oz fresh asparagus
2 small courgettes
75 ml/5 tbsp olive oil
50 g/2 oz/$^{1}/_{3}$ cup shelled peas, fresh or frozen
4 spring onions, sliced
1 recipe Basic Pizza Dough, rolled out
75 g/3 oz/$^{1}/_{2}$ cup mozzarella cheese, cut into small dice
10 leaves fresh basil, torn
2 cloves garlic, finely chopped
salt and freshly ground black pepper
serves 4

1 Preheat the oven to 250°C/475°F/ gas 9 for at least 20 minutes before baking the pizza. Strain the tomatoes through the medium holes of a food mill placed over a bowl, scraping in all the pulp.

2 ▲ Peel the broccoli stems and the lower parts of the asparagus, and blanch with the courgette in a large pan of boiling water for 4–5 minutes. Drain. Cut into bite-size pieces.

3 Heat 30 ml/2 tbsp of the olive oil in a small pan. Stir in the peas and spring onions, and cook for 5–6 minutes, stirring often. Remove from the heat.

4 ▲ Spread the puréed tomatoes onto the pizza dough, leaving the rim uncovered. Add the other vegetables, spreading them evenly over the tomatoes.

5 ▲ Sprinkle with the mozzarella, basil, garlic, salt and pepper, and remaining olive oil. Immediately place the pizza in the oven. Bake for about 20 minutes, or until the crust is golden brown and the cheese has melted.

Pizza with Sausage

Pizza con salsicce

Use sausages with a high meat content for this topping.

Ingredients

450 g/1 lb peeled plum tomatoes, fresh or canned, weighed whole, without extra juice
1 recipe Basic Pizza Dough, rolled out
350 g/12 oz/1 $^3/_4$ cups mozzarella cheese, cut into small dice
225 g/8 oz/1 $^1/_2$ cups sausage meat, removed from the casings and crumbled
5 ml/1 tsp oregano leaves, fresh or dried
salt and freshly ground black pepper
45 ml/3 tbsp olive oil
serves 4

1 Preheat the oven to 250°C/475°F/ gas 9 for at least 20 minutes before baking the pizza. Strain the tomatoes through the medium holes of a food mill placed over a bowl, scraping in all the pulp.

2 ▲ Spread some of the puréed tomatoes on the prepared pizza dough, leaving the rim uncovered. Sprinkle evenly with the mozzarella. Add the sausage meat in a layer.

3 ▲ Sprinkle with oregano, salt and pepper, and olive oil. Immediately place the pizza in the preheated oven. Bake for about 15–20 minutes, or until the crust is golden brown and the cheese is bubbling.

Pizza with Four Cheeses

Pizza con quattro formaggi

Any combination of cheeses can be used, but choose cheeses which are different in character.

Ingredients

1 recipe Basic Pizza Dough, rolled out
75 g/3 oz/ $^1/_2$ cup Gorgonzola or other blue cheese, thinly sliced
75 g/3 oz/ $^1/_2$ cup mozzarella cheese, finely diced
75 g/3 oz/ $^1/_2$ cup goat's cheese, thinly sliced
75 g/3 oz/ $^1/_2$ cup sharp Cheddar cheese, coarsely grated
4 leaves fresh sage,torn into pieces, or 45 ml/3 tbsp chopped fresh parsley
salt and freshly ground black pepper
45 ml/3 tbsp olive oil
serves 4

1 Preheat the oven to 250°C/475°F/ gas 9 for at least 20 minutes before baking the pizza. Arrange the Gorgonzola on one quarter of the pizza and the mozzarella on another, leaving the edge free.

2 ▲ Arrange the goat's and Cheddar cheeses on the remaining two quarters.

~ VARIATION ~

For an unusual taste, substitute 75 g/3oz sliced smoked cheese for one of the cheeses.

3 ▲ Sprinkle with the herbs, salt and pepper, and olive oil. Immediately place the pizza in the oven. Bake for about 15–20 minutes, or until the crust is golden brown and the cheeses are bubbling.

Mediterranean Pizza

Pizza mediterranea

The combination of favourite Mediterranean ingredients makes a delicious modern pizza topping.

Ingredients

12 sun-dried tomatoes, dry or in oil, drained
350 g/12 oz/1 $^{3}/_{4}$ cups goat's cheese, sliced as thinly as possible
1 recipe Basic Pizza Dough, rolled out
30 g/2 tbsp capers in brine or salt, rinsed
10 leaves fresh basil
salt and freshly ground black pepper
60 ml/3 tbsp olive oil
serves 4

1 Preheat the oven to 250°C/475°F/gas 9 for at least 20 minutes before baking the pizza. Place the tomatoes in a small bowl, cover with hot water, and leave to soak for 15 minutes. Drain and cut into thin slices. (The soaking water may be saved to add to a pasta sauce or soup.)

2 ▲ Arrange the cheese on the prepared pizza dough, leaving the rim uncovered. Dot the pizza with the tomato slices.

3 ▲ Sprinkle with the capers and basil leaves. Allow to rise for 10 minutes before baking.

4 Sprinkle with salt, pepper and olive oil. Place the pizza in the oven. Bake for about 15–20 minutes, or until the crust is golden brown.

Pizza with Onions and Olives

Pizza con cipolle e olive

Onions cooked slowly to release their sweetness contrast with the salty bitterness of the olives.

Ingredients

90 ml/6 tbsp olive oil
4 medium onions, finely sliced
salt and freshly ground black pepper
1 recipe Basic Pizza Dough, rolled out
350 g/12 oz/1 $^{3}/_{4}$ cups mozzarella cheese, cut into small dice
32 black olives, pitted and halved
60 ml/3 tbsp chopped fresh parsley
serves 4

1 Preheat the oven to 250°C/475°F/gas 9 for at least 20 minutes before baking the pizza. Heat half the olive oil in a large frying pan. Add the sliced onions, and cook over low heat until soft, translucent, and just beginning to turn brown, 12–15 minutes. Season with salt and pepper, and remove from the heat.

2 ▲ Spread the onions over the prepared pizza dough in an even layer, leaving the rim uncovered. Sprinkle with the mozzarella.

3 ▲ Dot with the olives. Sprinkle with parsley and the remaining olive oil. Immediately place the pizza in the oven. Bake for about 15–20 minutes, or until the crust is golden brown and the cheese is bubbling.

Pizza with Seafood

Pizza con frutti di mare

Any combination of shellfish or other seafood can be used as a pizza topping.

Ingredients

450 g/1 lb peeled plum tomatoes, fresh or canned, weighed whole, without extra juice
175 g/6 oz small squid
225 g/8 oz fresh mussels
1 recipe Basic Pizza Dough, rolled out
175 g/6 oz prawns, raw or cooked, peeled and deveined
2 cloves garlic, finely chopped
45 ml/3 tbsp chopped fresh parsley
salt and freshly ground black pepper
45 ml/3 tbsp olive oil

serves 4

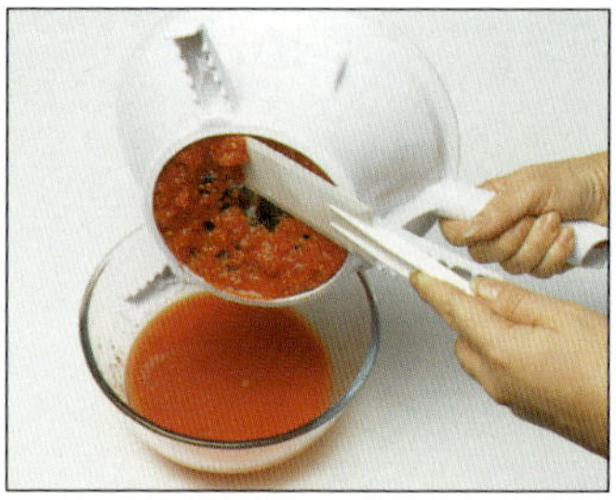

1 ▲ Preheat the oven to 250°C/475°F/ gas 6 for at least 20 minutes before baking the pizza. Strain the tomatoes through the medium holes of a food mill placed over a bowl, scraping in all the pulp.

2 ▲ Working near the sink, clean the squid by first peeling off the thin skin from the body section. Rinse well. Pull the head and tentacles away from the sac section. Some of the intestines will come away with the head.

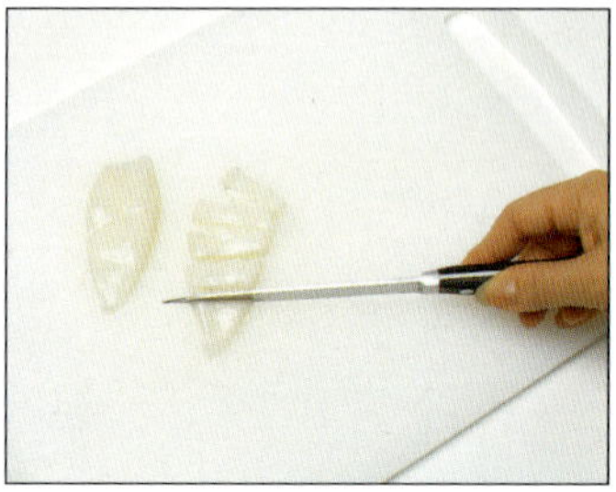

3 ▲ Remove and discard the translucent quill and any remaining insides from the sac. Sever the tentacles from the head, and discard the head and intestines. Remove the small hard beak from the base of the tentacles. Rinse the sac and tentacles under running water. Drain. Slice the sacs into rings 5mm/$^1/_4$ in thick.

4 ▲ Scrape any barnacles off the mussels, and scrub well with a stiff brush. Rinse in several changes of cold water. Place the mussels in a saucepan and heat until they open. Lift them out with a slotted spoon, and remove to a side dish. (Discard any that do not open.) Break off the empty half shells, and discard.

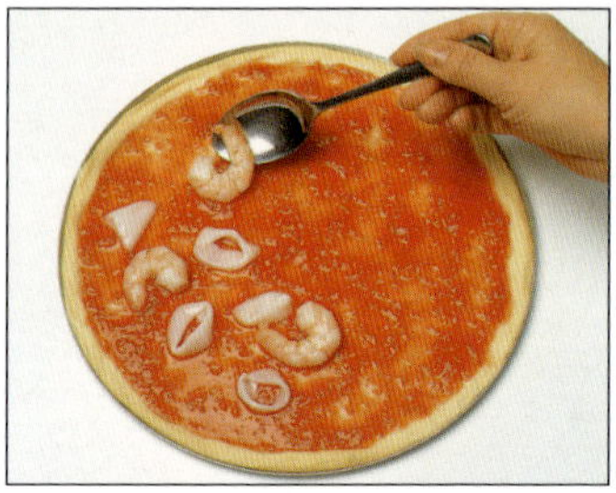

5 ▲ Spread the puréed tomatoes on the prepared pizza dough, leaving the rim uncovered. Dot evenly with the prawns and squid rings and tentacles. Sprinkle with the garlic, parsley, salt and pepper, and olive oil. Immediately place the pizza in the oven. Bake for about 8 minutes.

6 ▲ Remove from the oven, and add the mussels in the half shells. Return to the oven and bake for 7–10 minutes more, or until the crust is golden.

~ VARIATION ~

Fresh clams may be added: scrub them well under cold running water. Cook them in the same way as the mussels. Discard any that do not open. Break off the empty half shells, and discard. Add to the pizza after 8 minutes of baking.

Pizza with Herbs

Pizza in bianco con erbe aromatiche

This simple topping of mixed fresh herbs, olive oil and salt makes a delicious hot pizza which can also be eaten as a bread. In Italy it is often served in pizzerias as an appetizer.

Ingredients

1 recipe Basic Pizza Dough, rolled out
60 ml/4 tbsp chopped mixed fresh herbs, such as thyme, rosemary, basil, parsley or sage
salt, to taste
90 ml/6 tbsp extra-virgin olive oil
serves 4

1 ▲ Preheat the oven to 250°C/475°F/ gas 9 for at least 20 minutes before baking the pizza. Sprinkle the prepared dough with the herbs, and salt.

2 ▲ Sprinkle with olive oil. Immediately place the pizza in the oven. Bake for about 20 minutes, or until the crust is golden brown.

Sicilian Closed Pizza

Sfinciuni

These can be stuffed with any pizza topping.

Ingredients

1 recipe Basic Pizza Dough, risen once
30 ml/2 tbsp coarse cornmeal
3 hard-boiled eggs, peeled and sliced
50 g/2 oz/$^1/_4$ cup anchovy fillets, drained and chopped
12 olives, stoned and halved
8 leaves fresh basil, torn into pieces
6 medium tomatoes, peeled, seeded and diced
2 cloves garlic, finely chopped
freshly ground black pepper
175 g/6 oz/1$^1/_2$ cups grated caciocavallo or Pecorino cheese
olive oil, for brushing
serves 4–6

1 Preheat the oven to 230°C/450°F/ gas 8. Punch the dough and knead lightly for 3–4 minutes. Divide the dough into two pieces, one slightly larger than the other. Lightly oil a round pizza pan 38 cm/15 inches in diameter. Sprinkle with the cornmeal. Roll or press the larger piece of dough into a round slightly bigger than the pan.

2 ▲ Transfer to the pan, bringing the dough up the sides of the pan to the rim. Fill the pie by placing the sliced eggs in the bottom in a layer, leaving the edges of the dough uncovered. Dot with the anchovies, olives and basil.

3 Spread the diced tomatoes over the other ingredients. Sprinkle with garlic and pepper. Top with the grated cheese.

4 ▲ Roll or press the other piece of dough into a circle the same size as the pan. Place it over the filling. Roll the edge of the bottom dough over it, and crimp together to make a border.

5 Brush the top and edges of the pie with olive oil. Bake for 30–40 minutes, or until the top is golden brown. Allow to stand for 5–8 minutes before slicing into wedges.

Calzones

Calzone

A calzone is a pizza folded over to enclose its filling. It can be made large or small, and stuffed with any of the flat pizza fillings. Calzones can be eaten hot or cold.

Ingredients

1 recipe Basic Pizza Dough, risen once
350 g/12 oz/1 1/2 cups ricotta cheese
175 g/6 oz/3/4 cup ham, cut into small dice
6 medium tomatoes, peeled, seeded and diced
8 leaves fresh basil, torn into pieces
175 g/6 oz/1 cup mozzarella cheese, cut into small dice
60 ml/4 tbsp freshly grated Parmesan cheese
salt and freshly ground black pepper
olive oil, for brushing

serves 4

1 ▲ Preheat the oven to 250°C/475°F/gas 9 for at least 20 minutes before baking the calzoni. Punch the dough down and knead it lightly. Divide the dough into 4 balls.

2 ▲ Roll each ball out into a flat circle about 5mm/1/4 inch thick.

3 ▲ Combine all the filling ingredients in a bowl, and mix well. Season with salt and pepper.

4 ▲ Divide the filling between the 4 circles of dough, placing it on half of each circle and allowing a border of 1 in all around.

5 ▲ Fold the other half of the circle over. Crimp the edges of the dough together with your fingers to seal.

6 ▲ Place the calzones on lightly oiled baking sheets. Brush the tops lightly with olive oil. Bake in the preheated oven for about 15–20 minutes, or until the tops are golden brown and the dough is puffed.

~ COOK'S TIP ~

The calzone is a speciality of Naples. Calzone means "trouser leg" in Italian. This pizza was so named because it resembled a leg of the baggy trousers worn by Neapolitan men in the 18th and 19th centuries. Calzones are now usually round but were traditionally made from rectangular pieces of dough folded over a long central filling.

Focaccia

Focaccia

Focaccia is an antique form of flat bread which is oiled before baking. It is traditionally made on a large baking tray, and sold in bakeries cut into squares.

Ingredients
1 recipe Basic Pizza Dough, risen once
45 ml/3 tbsp olive oil
coarse sea salt
serves 6–8 as a side dish

1 ▲ After punching the dough down, knead it for 3–4 minutes. Brush a large shallow baking pan with 15 ml/1 tbsp of oil.

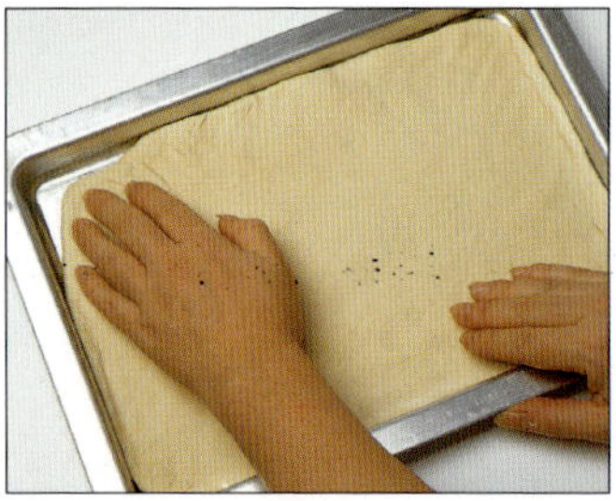

2 ▲ Place the dough in the pan, and use your fingers to press it into an even layer 2 cm/1 in thick. Cover the dough with a cloth, and leave to rise in a warm place for 30 minutes. Preheat the oven to 200°C/400°F/gas 6.

~ COOK'S TIP ~

To freeze, allow to cool to room temperature after baking. Wrap in foil and freeze. Thaw and place in a warm oven before serving.

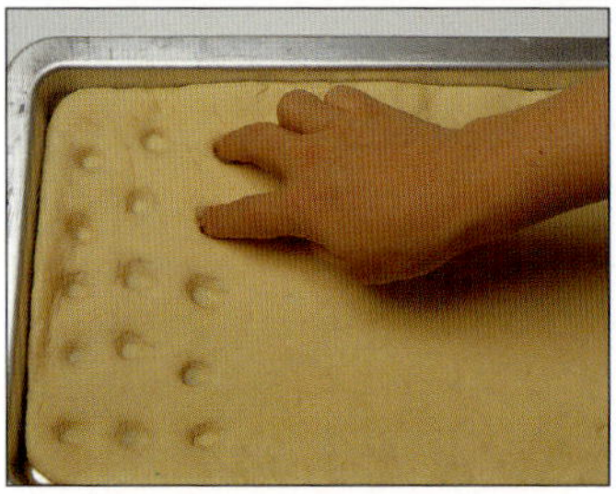

3 ▲ Just before baking, use your fingers to press rows of light indentations into the surface of the focaccia dough.

4 ▲ Brush with the remaining oil, and sprinkle lightly with coarse salt. Bake for about 25 minutes, or until just golden. Cut into squares or wedges and serve as an accompaniment to a meal, or alone, warm or at room temperature.

Focaccia with Onions

Focaccia con cipolle

This appetizing flat bread has a topping of sautéed onions. It can be split and filled with prosciutto or cheese for an unusual sandwich.

Ingredients

1 recipe Basic Pizza Dough, risen once
75 ml/5 tbsp olive oil
1 medium onion, sliced very thinly and cut into short lengths
1/2 tsp fresh thyme leaves
coarse sea salt
serves 6–8 as a side dish

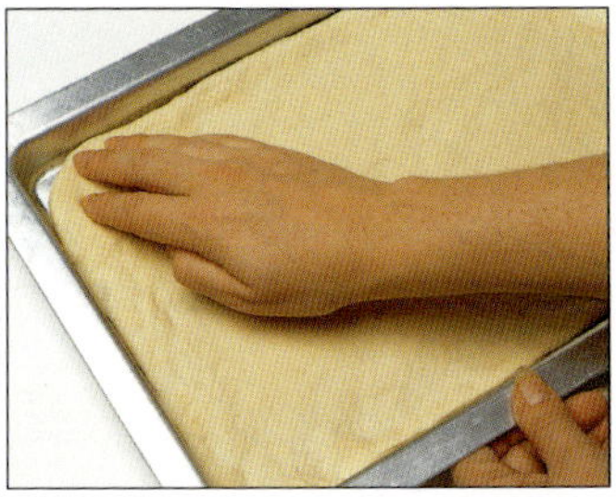

1 ▲ After punching the dough down, knead it for 3–4 minutes. Brush a large shallow baking pan with 15 ml/1 tbsp of the oil. Place the dough in the pan, and use your fingers to press it into an even layer 2 cm/1 inch thick. Cover the dough with a cloth, and leave to rise in a warm place for 30 minutes. Preheat the oven to 200°C/400°F/gas 6 for 30 minutes during this time.

2 ▲ While the focaccia is rising, heat 45 ml/3 tbsp of the oil in a medium frying pan. Add the onion, and cook over low heat until soft. Stir in the thyme.

3 ▲ Just before baking, use your fingers to press rows of light indentations into the surface of the focaccia. Brush with the remaining oil.

4 ▲ Spread the onions evenly over the top, and sprinkle lightly with coarse salt. Bake for about 25 minutes, or until just golden. Cut into squares or wedges and serve as an accompaniment to a meal, or alone, either warm or at room temperature.

Focaccia with Olives

Focaccia con olive

For this topping, pieces of pitted green olives are pressed onto the dough before baking.

Ingredients

1 recipe Basic Pizza Dough, risen once
45 ml/3 tbsp olive oil
10–12 large green olives, stoned and cut in half lengthwise
coarse sea salt

serves 6–8 as a side dish

1 After punching the dough down, knead it for 3–4 minutes. Brush a large shallow baking pan with 15 ml/1 tbsp of the oil. Place the dough in the pan, and use your fingers to press it into an even layer 2 cm/1in thick. Cover the dough with a cloth, and leave to rise in a warm place for 30 minutes. Preheat the oven to 200°C/400°F/gas 6 for 30 minutes during this time.

2 ▲ Just before baking, use your fingers to press rows of light indentations into the surface of the focaccia. Brush with the remaining oil.

3 ▲ Dot the bread evenly with the olive pieces, and sprinkle with a little coarse salt. Bake for about 25 minutes, or until just golden. Cut into squares or wedges and serve alone or as an accompaniment to a meal, warm or at room temperature.

Focaccia with Rosemary

Focaccia con rosmarino

One of the most popular breads. If possible, use fresh rosemary for this recipe.

Ingredients

1 recipe Basic Pizza Dough, risen once
45 ml/3 tbsp olive oil
2 medium sprigs fresh rosemary, coarse stalks removed
coarse sea salt

serves 6–8 as a side dish

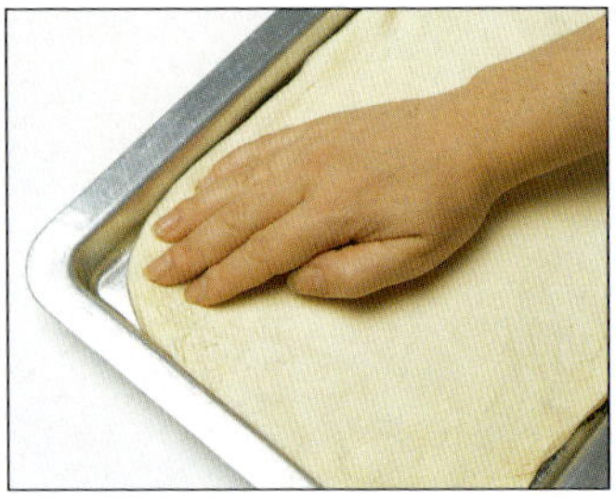

1 ▲ After punching the dough down, knead it for 3–4 minutes. Brush a large shallow baking pan with 15 ml/1 tbsp of the oil. Place the dough in the pan, and use your fingers to press it into an even layer 2 cm/1 inch thick.

2 ▲ Sprinkle with the rosemary leaves. Cover the dough with a cloth, and leave to rise in a warm place for 30 minutes. Preheat the oven to 200°C/400°F/gas 6 for 30 minutes during this time.

3 ▲ Just before baking, use your fingers to press rows of light indentations into the surface of the focaccia. Brush with the remaining oil, and sprinkle lightly with coarse salt. Bake for about 25 minutes, or until just golden. Cut into squares or wedges and serve as an accompaniment to a meal, or alone, warm or at room temperature.

Italian Bread Sticks

Grissini

These typically Italian bread sticks are especially delicious when hand-made. They are still sold loose in many bakeries in Turin and the north of Italy.

Ingredients

15 g/$^1/_2$ oz/1 tbsp fresh bread yeast or
7 g/$^1/_4$ oz/$^1/_2$ tbsp active dried yeast
100 ml/4 fl oz/$^1/_2$ cup lukewarm water
pinch of sugar
10 ml/2 tsp malt extract (optional)
1 tsp salt
200–225/7–8 oz/1$^3/_4$–2 cups plain flour
makes about 30

1 ▲ Warm a medium mixing bowl by swirling some hot water in it. Drain. Place the yeast in the bowl, and pour on the warm water. Stir in the sugar, mix with a fork, and allow to stand until the yeast has dispersed and starts to foam, 5–10 minutes.

2 ▲ Use a wooden spoon to mix in the malt extract, if using, the salt and about one-third of the flour. Mix in another third of the flour, stirring with the spoon until the dough forms a mass and begins to pull away from the sides of the bowl.

3 ▲ Sprinkle some of the remaining flour onto a smooth work surface. Remove all of the dough from the bowl, and begin to knead it, working in the remaining flour a little at a time. Knead for 8–10 minutes. By the end the dough should be elastic and smooth. Form it into a ball.

4 ▲ Tear a lump the size of a small walnut from the ball of dough. Roll it lightly between your hands into a small sausage shape. Set it aside on a lightly floured surface. Repeat until all the dough is used up. There should be about 30 pieces.

~ VARIATION ~

Grissini are also good when rolled lightly in poppy or sesame seeds before being baked.

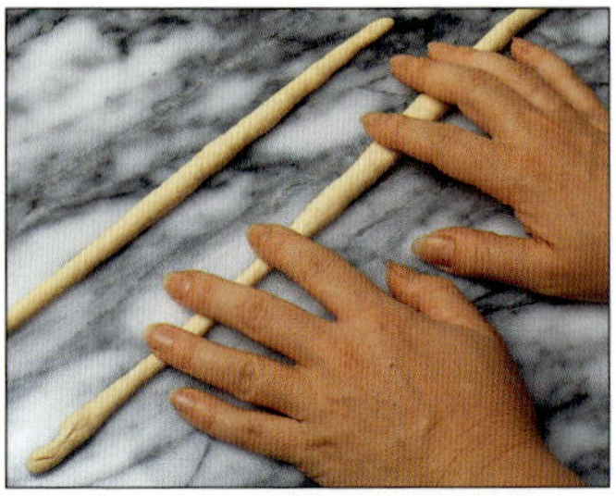

5 ▲ Place one piece of dough on a clean smooth work surface without any flour on it. Roll the dough under the spread-out fingers of both hands, moving your hands backwards and forwards to lengthen and thin the dough into a long strand about 1 cm/$^3/_8$ inch thick. Transfer to a very lightly greased baking tray. Repeat with the remaining dough pieces, taking care to roll all the grissini to about the same thickness.

6 ▲ Preheat the oven to 200°C/400°F/gas 6. Cover the tray with a cloth, and place the grissini in a warm place to rise for 10–15 minutes while the oven is heating. Bake for about 8–10 minutes. Remove from the oven. Turn the grissini over, and return them to the oven for 6–7 minutes more. Do not let them brown. Allow to cool. Grissini should be crisp when served. If they lose their crispness on a damp day, warm them in a moderate oven for a few minutes before serving.

Bread with Grapes

Schiacciata con uva

This bread is made to celebrate the grape harvest in central Italy. Use small black grapes with or without seeds; in Italy wine grapes are used.

Ingredients

750 g/1 $^{1}/_{2}$ lb small black grapes
115 g/4 oz/$^{1}/_{2}$ cup sugar
1 recipe Basic Pizza Dough, risen once
30 ml/2 tbsp olive oil
serves 6–8

1 ▲ Remove the grapes from their stems. Wash them well, and pat dry with paper towels. Place in a bowl and sprinkle with the sugar. Set aside until they are needed.

2 ▲ Knead the dough lightly. Divide it into two halves. Roll out or press one half into a circle about 1cm/$^{1}/_{2}$ inch thick. Place on a lightly oiled flat baking sheet. Sprinkle with half of the sugared grapes.

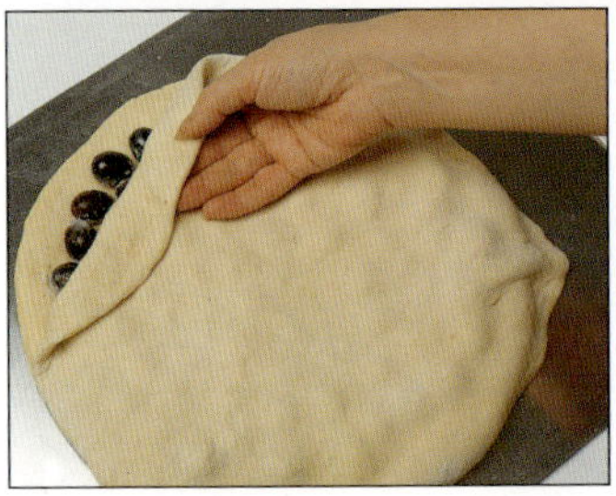

3 ▲ Roll out or press the second half of the dough into a circle the same size as the first. Place it on top of the first.

4 ▲ Crimp the edges together. Sprinkle the top with the remaining grapes. Cover with a dish towel and leave in a warm place to rise for 30 minutes. Preheat the oven to 190°C/375°F/gas 5. Sprinkle the bread with the oil, and bake for 50–60 minutes, until risen and golden. Allow to cool before cutting into wedges.

Tomato and Basil Tart

Torta di pomodoro e basilico

This tart is similar to a pizza, but uses shortcrust pastry instead of yeast dough for the base.

Ingredients
175 g/6 oz/1 1/2 cups flour
1/2 tsp salt, plus more to sprinkle
115 g/4 oz/1/2 cup butter or margarine, chilled
45-75 ml/3–5 tbsp cold water
30 ml/2 tbsp extra-virgin olive oil

For the filling
175 g/6 oz/1 cup mozzarella cheese, sliced as thinly as possible
12 leaves fresh basil
4–5 medium tomatoes, cut into 5 mm/1/4in slices
salt and freshly ground black pepper
60 ml/4 tbsp freshly grated Parmesan cheese

serves 6–8

1 ▲ Make the pastry by placing the flour and salt in a mixing bowl. Using a pastry blender, cut the butter or margarine into the dry ingredients until the mixture resembles coarse meal. Add 45 ml/3 tbsp of water, and combine with a fork until the dough holds together. If it is too crumbly, mix in a little more water.

2 Gather the dough into a ball and flatten it into a disc. Wrap in greaseproof paper and refrigerate for at least 40 minutes. Preheat the oven to 190°C/375°F/gas 5.

3 Roll the pastry out between two sheets of greaseproof paper to a thickness of 5 mm/1/4 inch. Line a 28 cm/11 in a tart or pie pan, trimming the edges evenly. Refrigerate for 20 minutes. Prick the bottom all over with a fork.

4 ▲ Line the pastry with a sheet of baking parchment. Fill with dried beans. Place the pie pan on a baking tray and bake about 15 minutes. Remove from the oven.

5 Remove the beans and paper. Brush the pastry with oil. Line with the mozzarella. Tear half of the basil into pieces, and sprinkle on top.

6 ▲ Arrange the tomato slices over the cheese. Dot with the remaining whole basil leaves. Sprinkle with salt and pepper, Parmesan and oil. Bake for about 35 minutes. If the cheese exudes a lot of liquid during baking, tilt the pan and spoon it off to keep the pastry from becoming soggy. Serve hot or at room temperature.

Potato Pizza

Pizza di patate

This "pizza", made of mashed potatoes with a filling of anchovies, capers and tomatoes, is a speciality of Puglia.

Ingredients
1 kg/2 lb potatoes, scrubbed
100 ml/4 fl oz/$^1/_2$ cup extra-virgin olive oil
salt and freshly ground black pepper
2 cloves garlic, finely chopped
350 g/12 oz tomatoes, diced
3 anchovy fillets, chopped
30 ml/2 tbsp capers, rinsed
serves 4

1 ▲ Boil the potatoes in their skins until tender. Peel and mash or pass through a food mill. Beat in 45 ml/3 tbsp of the oil, and season.

2 Heat another 45 ml/3 tbsp of the oil in a medium saucepan. Add the garlic and the chopped tomatoes, and cook over moderate heat until the tomatoes soften and begin to dry out, 12–15 minutes. Meanwhile, preheat the oven to 200°C/400°F/gas 6.

3 ▲ Oil a shallow baking dish. Spread half the mashed potatoes into the dish in an even layer. Cover with the tomatoes, and dot with the chopped anchovies and the capers.

4 ▲ Spread the rest of the potatoes in a layer on top of the filling. Brush the top with the remaining oil. Bake in the preheated oven for 20–25 minutes, or until the top is golden brown. Serve hot, directly from the baking dish.

Bruschetta with Tomato

Bruschetta con pomodoro

Bruschetta is toasted or grilled bread, rubbed with garlic and sprinkled with olive oil or chopped fresh tomatoes. It is eaten as an appetizer or accompaniment.

Ingredients
3–4 medium tomatoes, chopped
salt and freshly ground black pepper
a few leaves fresh basil, torn
8 slices crusty white bread
2 or 3 cloves garlic, peeled and cut in half
90 ml/6 tbsp extra-virgin olive oil
serves 4

1 Place the chopped tomatoes with their juice in a small bowl. Season with salt and pepper, and stir in the basil. Allow to stand for 10 minutes.

2 ▲ Toast or grill the bread until it is crisp on both sides. Rub one side of each piece of toast with the cut garlic.

3 ▲ Arrange on a platter. Sprinkle with the olive oil. Spoon on the chopped tomatoes, and serve at once.

Fish and Shellfish

Garlic, herbs and olive oil transform both sea and freshwater fish, giving them a true Mediterranean taste. Succulent shellfish, enhanced with aromatic seasonings, evoke the summer pleasures of sea and sun.

Stewed Mussels and Clams

Zuppa di cozze e vongole

Casseroles of mixed shellfish are very popular on the Ligurian coast.

Ingredients

750 g/1 1/2lb fresh mussels, in their shells
750 g/1 1/2lb fresh clams, in their shells
75 ml/5 tbsp olive oil
3 cloves garlic, peeled and crushed
300 ml/1/2 pint/1 1/4 cups dry white wine
75 ml/5 tbsp chopped fresh parsley
freshly ground black pepper
rounds of crusty bread, toasted, to serve

serves 4

1 Cut off the "beards" from the mussels. Scrub and rinse the mussels and clams in cold water. Discard any with broken shells.

2 Heat the oil in a large saucepan with the garlic. As soon as this is golden, add the mussels, clams and the wine. Cover, and steam until all the shells have opened, about 5–8 minutes. (Discard any that do not open.)

3 Lift the clams and mussels out, pouring any liquid in the shells back into the saucepan. Place in a warmed serving bowl. Discard the garlic.

4 ▲ Strain the liquid in the saucepan through a layer of paper towels held in a sieve, pouring it over the clams and mussels in the bowl. Sprinkle with parsley and black pepper.

5 ▲ To serve, place rounds of toasted bread in the bottom of individual soup bowls, and ladle in the mussels and clams with some of the hot liquid.

Broiled Prawns with Herbs

Gamberi con erbe aromatiche

Large prawns are delicious marinated with fresh herbs, lemon and garlic. They can be grilled or cooked on a barbecue.

Ingredients

24 large raw prawns, in their shells
3 cloves garlic, finely chopped
45 ml/3 tbsp finely chopped fresh basil
15 ml/1 tbsp fresh thyme leaves
30 ml/2 tbsp finely chopped fresh parsley
15 ml/1 tbsp coarsely crushed black pepper
juice of 1 lemon
60 ml/4 tbsp olive oil
8 bay leaves
50 g/2 oz/1/4 cup salt pork or pancetta, cut into 8 small squares

serves 4

1 Shell the prawns and devein them either by using a deveiner, or by making a shallow incision with a small sharp knife down the center of the back to disclose the long black vein. Remove and discard this.

2 ▲ Place the prawns in a bowl with the garlic, chopped herbs, pepper, lemon juice and olive oil. Mix well, cover, and leave to marinate in the refrigerator for at least 6 hours, or preferably overnight.

3 ▲ Preheat the grill. Arrange 6 prawns on each of 4 skewers so that they lie flat, threading a bay leaf and a square of salt pork between every 2 shrimp. Brush with the remaining marinade. Place in one layer under the grill or on a barbecue. Cook for about 3 minutes. Turn, and cook for 3 minutes more.

Baked Mussels and Potatoes

Cozze in tortiera con patate

This dish originates from Puglia, noted for its imaginative baked casseroles.

Ingredients

750 g/1 $^{1}/_{2}$lb large mussels, in their shells
225 g/8oz potatoes, unpeeled
75 ml/5 tbsp olive oil
2 cloves garlic, finely chopped
8 leaves fresh basil, torn
225 g/8oz tomatoes, peeled and thinly sliced
45 ml/3 tbsp plain breadcrumbs
freshly ground black pepper
serves 2–3

1 Cut off the "beards" from the mussels. Scrub and soak in several changes of cold water. Discard any with broken shells. Place the mussels with a cupful of water in a large saucepan over moderate heat. As soon as they open, lift them out. Remove and discard the empty half shells, leaving the mussels in the other half. (Discard any mussels that do not open.) Strain any liquid in the pan through a layer of paper towels, and reserve.

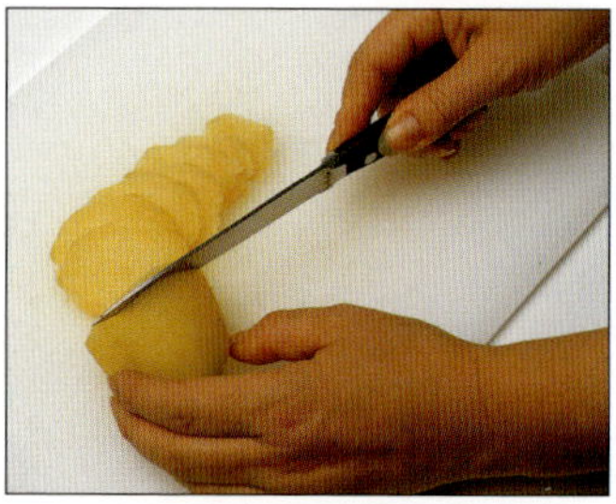

2 ▲ Boil the potatoes. Remove them from the water when they are still quite firm and peel and slice them.

3 ▲ Preheat the oven to 180°C/350°F/ gas 4. Spread 30 ml/2 tbsp of the olive oil in the bottom of a shallow ovenproof dish. Cover with the potato slices in one layer. Add the mussels in their half shells in one layer. Sprinkle with garlic and pieces of basil.

4 ▲ Cover with a layer of the tomato slices. Sprinkle with breadcrumbs and black pepper, the filtered mussel liquid and the remaining olive oil. Bake for about 20 minutes, or until the tomatoes are soft and the breadcrumbs golden. Serve directly from the baking dish.

Prawns in Spicy Tomato Sauce

Gamberi alla marinara

The tomato sauce base can be sharpened up by adding hot chillies.

Ingredients

90 ml/6 tbsp olive oil
1 medium onion, finely chopped
1 stick celery, finely chopped
1 small red pepper, seeded and chopped
100 ml/4 fl oz/$^{1}/_{2}$ cup red wine
15 ml/1 tbsp wine vinegar
1 x 400 g/14 oz can plum tomatoes, chopped, with their juice
salt and freshly ground black pepper
1 kg/2 lb fresh prawns, in their shells
2–3 cloves garlic, finely chopped
45 ml/3 tbsp finely chopped fresh parsley
1 piece dried chilli, crumbled or chopped (optional)

serves 6

1 In a heavy saucepan, heat half of the oil. Add the chopped onion, and cook over low heat until soft. Stir in the celery and pepper, and cook gently for 5 minutes more. Raise the heat to medium high, and add the wine, vinegar and tomatoes. Season with salt and pepper. Bring to a boil and cook for about 5 minutes.

2 ▲ Lower the heat, cover the pan, and simmer until the vegetables are soft, about 30 minutes. Purée the sauce through a food mill.

3 Shell the prawns and devein them, either by using a deveiner or by making a shallow incision with a small sharp knife down the centre of the back to disclose the long black vein. Remove and discard.

4 ▲ Heat the remaining oil in a clean heavy saucepan. Stir in the garlic, parsley and chilli, if using. Cook over moderate heat, stirring constantly, until the garlic is golden. Do not let it brown. Add the tomato sauce and bring to the boil. Taste for seasoning.

5 ▲ Stir in the prawns. Bring the sauce back to a boil. Reduce the heat slightly and simmer until the prawns are pink and stiff, 6–8 minutes, depending on their size. Remove from the heat and serve.

Grilled Fresh Sardines

Sarde alla griglia

Fresh sardines are flavourful and firm-fleshed, and quite different in taste and consistency from those canned in oil. They are excellent simply grilled and served with lemon.

Ingredients

1 kg/2 lb very fresh sardines, gutted and with heads removed
olive oil, for brushing
salt and freshly ground black pepper
45 ml/3 tbsp chopped fresh parsley, to serve
lemon wedges, to garnish

serves 4–6

1 Preheat the grill. Rinse the sardines in water. Pat dry with paper towels.

2 ▲ Brush the sardines lightly with olive oil and sprinkle generously with salt and pepper. Place the sardines in one layer on the grill pan. Grill for about 3–4 minutes.

3 ▲ Turn, and cook for 3–4 minutes more, or until the skin begins to brown. Serve immediately, sprinkled with parsley and garnished with lemon wedges.

Baked Aromatic Sea Bass

Branzino aromatizzato al forno

Sea bass is a firm white-fleshed fish which benefits from simple cooking. Use fresh herbs for this recipe, if possible.

Ingredients

1 large sea bass, about 1.5 kg/3 lb
4 bay leaves
few sprigs fresh thyme
8–10 sprigs fresh parsley
few sprigs fresh fennel, tarragon or basil
15 ml/1 tbsp peppercorns
135 ml/9 tbsp extra-virgin olive oil
salt and freshly ground black pepper
flour, for coating
lemon wedges, to garnish

serves 5–6

1 Gut the fish, leaving the head on. Wash carefully in cold water. Pat dry with paper towels. Place half the herbs and peppercorns in the bottom of a shallow platter, and lay the fish on top. Arrange the remaining herbs on top of the fish and in its cavity. Sprinkle with 45 ml/3 tbsp of the oil. Cover lightly with foil, and refrigerate for 2 hours.

2 ▲ Preheat the oven to 205°C/400°F/gas 6. Remove and discard all the herbs from around the fish, and pat it dry with paper towels. Spread a little flour in a platter and season it with salt and pepper. Roll the fish in the flour, then shake off the excess.

3 ▲ Heat the remaining olive oil in a flameproof dish just large enough to hold the fish comfortably. When the oil is hot, add the fish, and brown it quickly on both sides. Transfer the dish to the oven, and bake for 25–40 minutes, depending on the size of the fish. The fish is cooked when the dorsal fin (in the middle of the backbone) comes out easily when pulled. Serve garnished with sprigs of herbs or lemon wedges.

Stuffed Squid

Calamari ripieni

Squid are popular in all the coastal regions of Italy. They are very tender and easy to cook.

Ingredients
900 g/2 lb fresh squid (about 16 medium)
juice of $^1/_2$ lemon
2 anchovy fillets, chopped
2 cloves garlic, finely chopped
3 medium tomatoes, peeled, seeded and finely chopped
30 ml/2 tbsp chopped fresh parsley
50 g/2 oz/$^1/_2$ cup plain breadcrumbs
1 egg
salt and freshly ground black pepper
30 ml/2 tbsp olive oil
100 ml/4 fl oz/$^1/_2$ cup dry white wine
few sprigs fresh parsley, to garnish
serves 4

1 Working near the sink, clean the squid by first peeling off the thin skin from the body section. Rinse well. Pull the head and tentacles away from the body sac. Some of the intestines will come away with the head. Remove and discard the translucent quill and any remaining insides from the sac. Sever the tentacles from the head. Discard the head and intestines.

2 Remove and discard the small hard beak from the base of the tentacles. Place the tentacles in a bowl of water with the lemon juice. Rinse the sacs well under cold running water. Pat the insides dry with paper towels.

3 ▲ Preheat the oven to 180°C/350°F/ gas 4. Drain the tentacles. Chop them coarsely and place in a mixing bowl. Stir in the next 6 ingredients and season. Use this mixture to loosely stuff the squid sacs. Close the opening to the sacs with wooden toothpicks.

4 ▲ Oil a shallow baking dish large enough to accommodate the squid in one layer. Arrange the squid sacs in the dish. Pour over the oil and wine. Bake uncovered for 35–45 minutes, or until tender. Remove the toothpicks and serve garnished with parsley.

~ COOK'S TIP ~

Do not overstuff the squid sacs or they may burst during cooking.

Deep-fried Prawns and Squid

Fritto misto

The Italian name of this recipe means "mixed fry". Any mixture of seafood can be used.

Ingredients
vegetable oil, for deep-frying
600 g/1 lb 5 oz medium-sized fresh prawns, shelled and deveined
600 g/1 lb 5 oz squid (about 12 medium) cleaned and cut into bite-size pieces
115 g/1 cup flour
lemon wedges, to serve
For the batter
2 egg whites
30 ml/2 tbsp olive oil
15 ml/1 tbsp white wine vinegar
100 g/3$^1/_2$ oz/scant 1 cup flour
10 ml/2 tsp baking soda
75 g/3 oz/$^1/_3$ cup cornflour
salt and freshly ground black pepper
250 ml/8 fl oz/1 cup water
serves 6

1 Make the batter in a large bowl by beating the egg whites, olive oil and vinegar together lightly with a wire whisk. Beat in the dry ingredients, and whisk until well blended. Beat in the water, a little at a time. Cover the bowl, and allow to stand 15 minutes.

2 Heat the oil for deep-frying until a small piece of bread sizzles as soon as it is dropped in (about 185°C/360°F).

3 Dredge the prawns and squid pieces in the flour, shaking off any excess. Dip them quickly into the batter. Fry in small batches for about 1 minute, stirring with a slotted spoon to keep them from sticking to each other.

4 ▲ Remove and drain on paper towels. Allow the oil to come back up to the correct temperature between batches. Sprinkle lightly with salt, and serve hot with lemon wedges.

Seafood Stew

Zuppa di pesce

"Soups" - really stews - of mixed fish and shellfish are specialities of the Mediterranean.

Ingredients

45 ml/3 tbsp olive oil
1 medium onion, sliced
1 carrot, sliced
$^1/_2$ stick celery, sliced
2 cloves garlic, chopped
1 x 400 g/14 oz can plum tomatoes, chopped, with their juice
225 g/8 oz fresh prawns, peeled and deveined (reserve the shells)
450 g/1 lb white fish bones and heads, gills removed
1 bay leaf
1 sprig fresh thyme, or $^1/_4$ tsp dried thyme leaves
a few peppercorns
salt and freshly ground black pepper
750 g/1$^1/_2$ lb fresh mussels, in their shells, scrubbed and rinsed
500 g/1 lb fresh small clams, in their shells, scrubbed and rinsed
250 ml/8 fl oz/1 cup white wine
1 kg/2 lb mixed fish fillets, such as cod, monkfish, red snapper or hake, bones removed and cut into chunks
45 ml/3 tbsp finely chopped fresh parsley
rounds of French bread, toasted, to serve

serves 6–8

1 ▲ Heat the olive oil in a medium saucepan. Add the sliced onion, and cook slowly until soft. Stir in the carrot and celery, and cook gently for 5 minutes more. Add the chopped garlic, the tomatoes and their juice, and 250 ml/8 fl oz/1 cup of water. Cook over moderate heat until the vegetables are soft, about 15 minutes. Purée in a food processor or pass through a food mill. Set aside.

2 ▲ Place the prawn shells in a large pan with the fish bones and heads. Add the herbs and peppercorns, and pour in 700 ml/1$^1/_4$ pints/3 cups of water. Bring to the boil, reduce the heat, and simmer for 25 minutes, skimming off any scum that rises to the surface. Strain and pour into a pan with the tomato sauce. Season.

3 Place the mussels and clams in a saucepan with the wine. Cover, and steam until all the shells have opened. (Discard any that do not open.)

4 Lift the clams and mussels out and set aside. Filter the cooking liquid through a layer of paper towel and add it to the stock and tomato sauce. Check the seasoning.

5 ▲ Bring the sauce to a boil. Add the fish, and boil for 5 minutes. Add the prawns and boil for 3–4 minutes. Stir in the mussels and clams and cook for 2–3 minutes more. Transfer the stew to a warmed casserole. Sprinkle with parsley, and serve with the toasted rounds of French bread.

Trout Baked in Paper with Olives

Trota in cartoccio con olive

Baking fish in paper packets keeps in all the flavour and moisture.

Ingredients

- 4 medium trout, about 275 g/10 oz each, gutted
- 75 ml/5 tbsp olive oil
- 4 bay leaves
- salt and freshly ground black pepper
- 4 slices pancetta or bacon
- 60 ml/4 tbsp chopped shallots
- 60 ml/4 tbsp chopped fresh parsley
- 100 ml/4 fl oz/$^{1}/_{2}$ cup dry white wine
- 24 green olives, stoned

serves 4

1 ▲ Preheat the oven to 200°C/400°F/ gas 6. Wash the trout well in cold running water. Drain. Pat dry with paper towels.

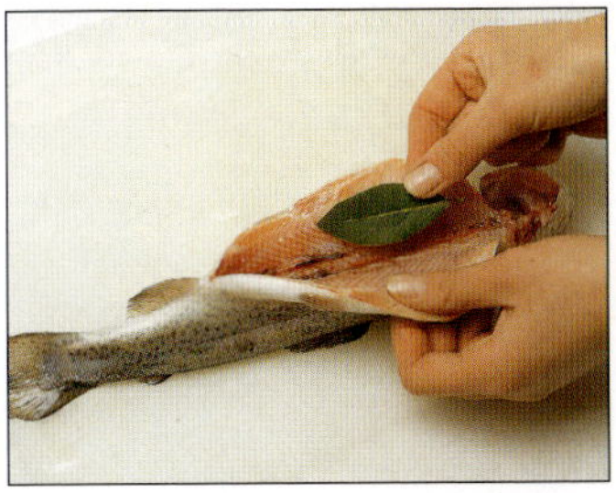

2 ▲ Lightly brush oil onto 4 pieces of baking parchment each large enough to enclose one fish. Lay one fish on each piece of oiled paper. Place a bay leaf in each cavity, and sprinkle with salt and pepper.

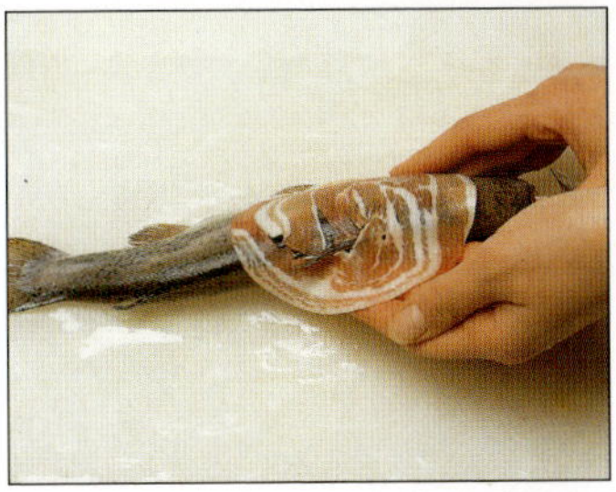

3 ▲ Wrap a slice of pancetta or bacon around each fish. Sprinkle with 15 ml/ 1 tbsp each of chopped shallots and parsley. Drizzle each fish with 15 ml/ 1 tbsp of oil and 30 ml/2 tbsp of white wine. Add 6 olives to each packet.

4 ▲ Close the paper loosely around the fish, rolling the edges together to seal them completely. Bake for 25 minutes. Place each packet on an individual plate and open at the table.

Grilled Salmon Steaks with Fennel

Salmone alla griglia

Fennel grows wild all over the south of Italy. Its mild aniseed flavour goes well with fish.

Ingredients

juice of 1 lemon
45 g/3 tbsp chopped fresh fennel herb, or the green fronds from the top of a fennel bulb
5 ml/1 tsp fennel seeds
45 ml/3 tbsp olive oil
4 salmon steaks of the same thickness, about 700 g/$1^1/_2$ lb total
salt and freshly ground black pepper
lemon slices, to garnish
serves 4

1 Combine the lemon juice, chopped fennel and fennel seeds with the olive oil in a bowl. Add the salmon steaks, turning them to coat them with the marinade. Sprinkle with salt and pepper. Cover and place in the refrigerator. Allow to stand for 2 hours.

2 ▲ Preheat the grill. Arrange the fish in one layer on a grill pan or baking tray. Grill about 10 cm/4 in from the heat source for 3–4 minutes.

3 ▲ Turn. Spoon on the remaining marinade and grill for 3–4 minutes on the other side, or until the edges begin to brown. Serve hot, garnished with lemon slices.

Octopus with Lemon and Garlic

Polpo con limone e aglio

Octopus is widely appreciated in Italy. Dressed with oil and lemon it is delicious.

Ingredients

1 kg/2 lb octopus (young and small if possible)
30 ml/2 tbsp capers
2 cloves garlic, very finely chopped
60 ml/4 tbsp extra-virgin olive oil
45 ml/3 tbsp fresh lemon juice
freshly ground black pepper
serves 3–4

1 Beat the octopus repeatedly against a strong table or marble surface. Clean, removing the eyes, beak and sacs. (Or ask your fishmonger to do this.) Wash carefully under cold running water.

2 Place the octopus in a large pan with cold water to cover. Bring to the boil, cover the pan tightly, and simmer gently until tender, 45 minutes for small octopus and up to 2 hours for larger ones. Skim off any scum which rises to the surface.

3 ▲ Remove from the pan, and allow to cool slightly. Rub the octopus lightly with a clean cloth to remove any loose dark skin. Slice the warm octopus into rounds $1^1/_2$ cm/$^3/_4$ inch wide.

~ COOK'S TIP ~

In Italy, a wine cork is placed in the pan with the octopus to reduce the scum.

4 ▲ Place the octopus pieces in a serving bowl. Toss with the parsley, garlic, olive oil and lemon juice. Sprinkle with pepper. Mix well. Allow to stand for at least 20 minutes before serving at room temperature.

Baked Cod with Garlic Mayonnaise

Merluzzo al forno

Because cod is not native to the Mediterranean, a similar species is used for this dish.

Ingredients
4 anchovy fillets
45 ml/3 tbsp finely chopped fresh parsley
coarsely ground black pepper
90 ml/6 tbsp olive oil
4 cod fillets, about 750 g/1 $^{1}/_{2}$ lb total, skinned
40 g/1 $^{1}/_{2}$ oz/ $^{1}/_{3}$ cup plain breadcrumbs
For the mayonnaise
2 cloves garlic, finely chopped
1 egg yolk
5 ml/1 tsp Dijon mustard
175 ml/6 fl oz/ $^{3}/_{4}$ cup vegetable oil
salt and freshly ground black pepper
serves 4

1 Make the mayonnaise. first put the garlic in a mortar or small bowl. Mash it to a paste. Beat in the egg yolk and mustard. Add the oil in a thin stream while whisking vigorously with a small wire whisk. When the mixture is thick and smooth, season with salt and pepper. Cover the bowl and keep cool.

2 ▲ Preheat the oven to 200°C/400°F/ gas 6. Chop the anchovy fillets with the parsley very finely. Place in a small bowl, and add pepper and 45 ml/3 tbsp of the oil. Stir to a paste.

3 ▲ Place the cod fillets in one layer in an oiled baking dish. Spread the anchovy paste on the top of the cod fillets. Sprinkle with the breadcrumbs and the remaining oil. Bake for 20–25 minutes, or until the breadcrumbs are golden. Serve hot with the garlic mayonnaise.

Monkfish Medallions with Thyme

Pescatrice con timo

Monkfish has a sweet flesh that combines well with Mediterranean flavours.

Ingredients
600 g/1 $^{1}/_{4}$ lb monkfish fillet, preferably in one piece
45 ml/3 tbsp extra-virgin olive oil
75 g/3 oz/ $^{1}/_{2}$ cup small black olives, preferably from the Riviera, stoned
1 large or 2 small tomatoes, seeded and diced
1 sprig fresh thyme, or 1 tsp dried thyme leaves
salt and freshly ground black pepper
15 ml/1 tbsp very finely chopped fresh parsley, to serve
serves 4

1 Preheat the oven to 200°C/400°F/ gas 6. Remove the grey membrane from the monkfish, if necessary. Cut the fish into slices 1 cm/ $^{1}/_{2}$ in thick.

2 Heat a non-stick frying pan quite hot, without oil. Sear the fish quickly on both sides. Remove to a side dish.

3 ▲ Spread 15 ml/1 tbsp of the olive oil in the bottom of a shallow baking dish. Arrange the fish in one layer. Distribute the olives and diced tomato on top of the fish.

4 Sprinkle the fish with thyme, salt and pepper, and the remaining oil. Bake for 10–12 minutes.

5 ▲ To serve, divide the medallions between 4 warmed plates. Spoon on the vegetables and any cooking juices. Sprinkle with the chopped parsley.

Stuffed Swordfish Rolls

Involtini di pesce spada

Swordfish is abundant around Sicily and it features in many dishes.

Ingredients

4 slices fresh swordfish, about 1 cm/$^1/_2$ in thick
90 ml/6 tbsp olive oil
1 clove garlic, finely chopped (optional)
50 g/2 oz/$^1/_2$ cup plain breadcrumbs
30 ml/2 tbsp capers, rinsed, drained and chopped
10 leaves fresh basil, chopped, plus a few whole leaves, to garnish
60 ml/4 tbsp fresh lemon juice
salt and freshly ground black pepper

For the tomato sauce

30 ml/2 tbsp olive oil
1 clove garlic, peeled and crushed
1 small onion, finely chopped
450 g/1 lb tomatoes, peeled
100 ml/4 fl oz/$^1/_2$ cup dry white wine
salt and freshly ground black pepper

serves 4

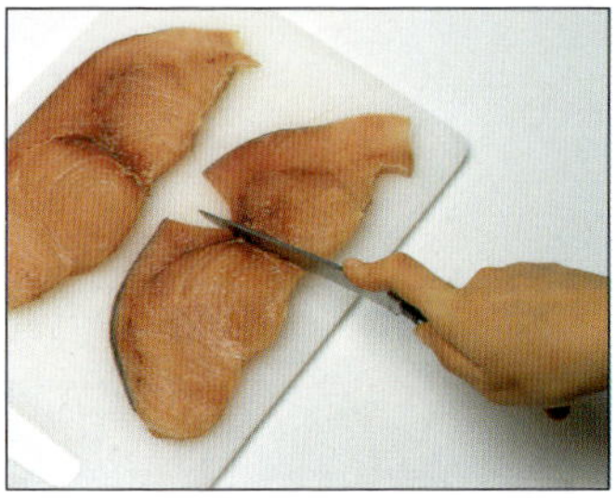

1 ▲ Cut the swordfish slices in half, removing any bones. Brush with 30 ml/2 tbsp of the oil, and refrigerate until needed.

2 Make the tomato sauce by heating the oil in a medium heavy saucepan. Add the garlic, and cook until golden. Discard the garlic. Add the onion, and cook over low heat until soft. Stir in the tomatoes and wine. Season with salt and pepper. Cover the pan, and cook over moderate heat for 15 minutes. Pass the sauce through a food mill or purée in a food processor. Season, and keep warm while you prepare the fish. Preheat the oven to 200°C/400°F/gas 6.

3 In a small bowl combine 30 ml/2 tbsp of olive oil with the garlic, if using, breadcrumbs, capers, basil and lemon juice. Season with salt and pepper and mix to a paste.

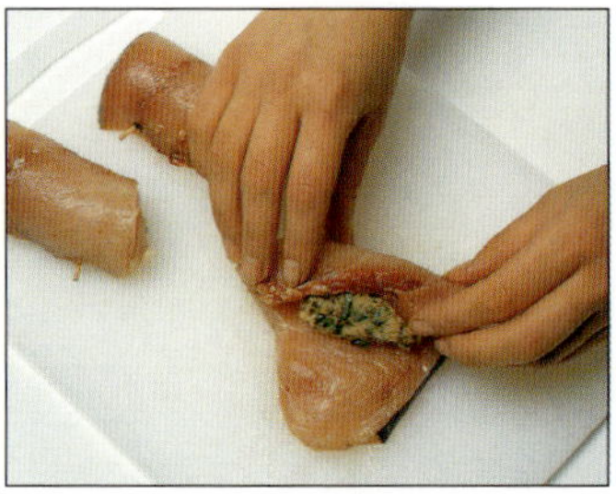

4 ▲ Lay the swordfish slices out flat on a board. Divide the stuffing between the slices and spread it over the center of each. Roll the slices and secure with wooden toothpicks.

5 ▲ Heat the remaining oil in a flameproof dish. Add the swordfish rolls and brown them quickly over high heat, turning them once or twice. After 3–4 minutes pour in the tomato sauce. Place the dish in the oven, and bake for 15 minutes, basting occasionally. Serve warm.

Red Mullet with Tomatoes

Triglie con pomodoro

Red mullet is a popular fish in Italy, and this recipe accentuates both its flavour and colour.

Ingredients

4 red mullet or red snapper, about 175–200 g/6–7oz each
450 g/1 lb tomatoes, peeled, or
1 x 400 g/14 oz can plum tomatoes
60 ml/4 tbsp olive oil
60 ml/4 tbsp finely chopped fresh parsley
2 cloves garlic, finely chopped
salt and freshly ground black pepper
100 ml/4 fl oz/$^{1}/_{2}$ cup white wine
4 thin lemon slices, cut in half

serves 4

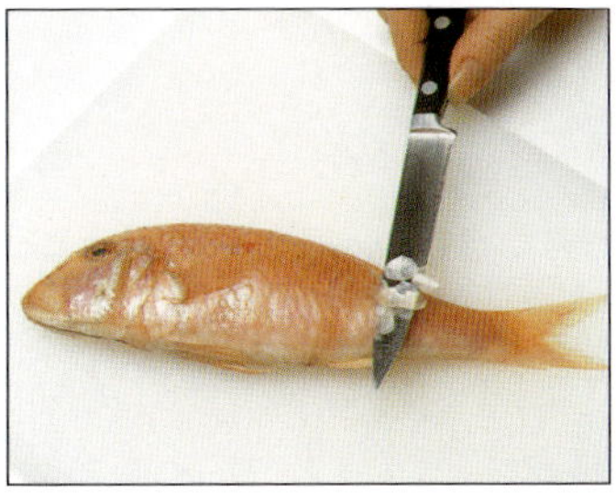

1 ▲ Scale and clean the fish without removing the liver. Wash and pat dry with paper towels.

2 ▲ Chop the tomatoes into small pieces. Heat the oil in a pan large enough to hold the fish in one layer. Add the parsley and garlic, and sauté for 1 minute. Stir in the tomatoes and cook over moderate heat for 15–20 minutes. Season with salt and pepper.

3 ▲ Add the fish to the tomato sauce and cook over moderate to high heat for 5 minutes. Add the wine and the lemon slices. Bring the sauce back to the boil, and cook for about 5 minutes more. Turn the fish over, and cook for 4–5 minutes more, until tender. Remove the fish to a warmed serving platter and keep warm until needed.

4 ▲ Boil the sauce for 3–4 minutes to reduce it slightly. Spoon it over the fish, and serve.

~ VARIATION ~

Small sea bass may be substituted.

Sole with Sweet and Sour Sauce

Sfogi in saor

This Venetian dish should be prepared 1–2 days before it is to be eaten.

Ingredients

3–4 fillets of sole, about 500 g/1 $^{1}/_{4}$ lb total, divided in half
60 ml/4 tbsp flour
salt and freshly ground black pepper
pinch of ground cloves
90–120 ml/6–8 tbsp olive oil
35 g/1 $^{1}/_{2}$ oz/generous $^{1}/_{4}$ cup pine nuts
3 bay leaves
pinch of ground cinnamon
pinch of grated nutmeg
4 cloves
1 small onion, very finely sliced
50 ml/2 fl oz/$^{1}/_{4}$ cup dry white wine
50 ml/2 fl oz/$^{1}/_{4}$ cup white wine vinegar
50 g/2 oz/$^{1}/_{3}$ cup sultanas
serves 4

1 Dredge the sole fillets in the flour seasoned with salt and pepper and the ground cloves.

2 Heat 45 ml/3 tbsp of the oil in a heavy frying pan or skillet. Cook the sole fillets a few at a time until golden, about 3 minutes on each side. Add more oil as necessary.

3 ▲ Remove with a slotted spatula to a large shallow serving dish. Sprinkle with the pine nuts, bay leaves, cinnamon, nutmeg and whole cloves.

4 ▲ Heat the remaining oil in a pan. Add the onion, and cook over low heat until golden. Add the wine, vinegar and sultanas, and boil for 4–5 minutes. Pour over the fish. Cover the dish with foil, and leave in a cool place for 24–48 hours. Remove 2 hours before serving. This dish is traditionally eaten at room temperature.

Salt Cod with Parsley and Garlic

Baccalà alla bolognese

Salt cod is very popular all over Italy. For centuries it has been imported from Scandinavia. The very salty fish must be soaked for 24 hours in water to reduce its salt content.

Ingredients

750 g/1 $^{1}/_{2}$ lb boneless and skinless salt cod, preferably in one piece
flour seasoned with freshly ground black pepper, for dredging
30 ml/2 tbsp extra-virgin olive oil
45 ml/3 tbsp finely chopped fresh parsley
2 cloves garlic, finely chopped
25 g/1 oz/2 tbsp butter, cut into small pieces
serves 4–5

1 Cut the salt cod into 5 cm/2in squares. Place them in a large bowl and cover with cold water. Allow to stand for at least 24 hours, changing the water several times.

2 ▲ Preheat the oven to 190°C/375°F/ gas 5. Drain the fish, shaking out the excess moisture. Remove any remaining bones or skin. Dredge lightly in the seasoned flour.

3 Spread 15 ml/1 tbsp of the oil over the bottom of a baking dish large enough to hold the fish in one layer.

4 ▲ Place the fish in the dish. Combine the chopped parsley and garlic, and sprinkle evenly over the fish. Sprinkle with the remaining oil, and dot with butter. Bake for 15 minutes. Turn the fish, and bake for 15–20 minutes more, or until tender. Serve at once, with the lemon wedges.

Meat, Poultry and Game

From the Florentine simplicity of Chicken Breasts Cooked in Butter to the more complex flavours of Lamb Stewed with Tomatoes and Garlic, this chapter presents the highlights of classic Italian cuisine.

Chicken with Peppers

Pollo con peperoni

This colourful dish comes from the south of Italy, where sweet peppers are plentiful.

Ingredients

1.5 kg/3 lb chicken, cut into serving pieces
3 large peppers, red, yellow, or green
90 ml/6 tbsp olive oil
2 medium red onions, finely sliced
2 cloves garlic, finely chopped
small piece of dried chilli, crumbled (optional)
100 ml/4 fl oz/$^1/_2$ cup white wine
salt and freshly ground black pepper
2 tomatoes, fresh or canned, peeled and chopped
45 g/3 tbsp chopped fresh parsley
serves 4

1 Trim any fat off the chicken, and remove all excess skin. Wash the peppers. Prepare by cutting them in half, scooping out the seeds, and cutting away the stem. Slice into strips.

2 ▲ Heat half the oil in a large heavy saucepan or casserole. Add the onion, and cook over low heat until soft. Remove to a side dish. Add the remaining oil to the pan, raise the heat to moderate, add the chicken and brown on all sides, 6–8 minutes. Return the onions to the pan, and add the garlic and dried chilli, if using.

3 ▲ Pour in the wine, and cook until it has reduced by half. Add the peppers. Season. After 3–4 minutes, stir in the tomatoes. Lower the heat, cover the pan and cook until the peppers are soft, and the chicken is cooked, about 25–30 minutes. Stir occasionally. Stir in the parsley and serve.

Chicken Breasts Cooked in Butter

Petti di pollo alla fiorentina

This simple and delicious way of cooking chicken brings out all of its delicacy.

Ingredients

4 small chicken breasts, skinned and boned
flour seasoned with salt and freshly ground black pepper, for dredging
75 g/3 oz/$^1/_3$ cup butter
1 sprig fresh parsley, to garnish
serves 4

1 Separate the two fillets of each breast. They come apart very easily; one is large, the other small. Pound the large fillets lightly to flatten them. Dredge the chicken in the seasoned flour, shaking off any excess.

~ COOK'S TIP ~

This chicken dish should be accompanied by delicately flavoured vegetables so that its subtle taste is not overpowered.

2 ▲ Heat the butter in a large heavy frying pan until it bubbles. Place all the chicken fillets in the pan, in one layer if possible. Cook over moderate to high heat for 3–4 minutes until they are golden brown.

3 ▲ Turn the chicken over. Reduce the heat to low to moderate, and continue cooking until the fillets are cooked through but still springy to the touch, about 9–12 minutes in all. If the chicken begins to brown too much, cover the pan for the final minutes of cooking. Serve immediately, garnished with a little parsley.

Roast Chicken with Fennel

Pollo con finocchio

In Italy this dish is prepared with wild fennel. Cultivated fennel bulb works just as well.

Ingredients
1.8 kg/3$^1/_2$ lb roasting chicken
salt and freshly ground black pepper
1 onion, quartered
100 ml/4 fl oz/$^1/_2$ cup olive oil
2 medium fennel bulbs
1 clove garlic, peeled
pinch of grated nutmeg
3–4 thin slices pancetta or bacon
100 ml/4 fl oz/$^1/_2$ cup dry white wine
serves 4–5

1 Preheat the oven to 180°C/350°F/ gas 4. Rinse the chicken in cold water. Pat it dry inside and out with paper towels. Sprinkle the cavity with salt and pepper. Place the onion quarters in the cavity. Rub the chicken with about 45 ml/3 tbsp of the olive oil. Place in a roasting pan.

2 Cut the green fronds from the tops of the fennel bulbs. Chop the fronds with the garlic. Place in a small bowl and mix with the nutmeg. Season with salt and pepper.

3 ▲ Sprinkle the fennel mixture over the chicken, pressing it onto the oiled skin. Cover the breast with the slices of pancetta or bacon. Sprinkle with 30 ml/2 tbsp of oil. Place in the oven and roast for 30 minutes.

4 Meanwhile, boil or steam the fennel bulbs until barely tender. Remove from the heat and cut into quarters or sixths lengthwise. After the chicken has been cooking for 30 minutes, remove the pan from the oven. Baste the chicken with any oils in the pan.

5 Arrange the fennel pieces around the chicken. Sprinkle the fennel with the remaining oil. Pour about half the wine over the chicken, and return the pan to the oven.

6 ▲ After 30 minutes more, baste the chicken again. Pour on the remaining wine. Cook for 15–20 minutes more. To test, prick the thigh with a fork. If the juices run clear, the chicken is cooked. Transfer the chicken to a serving platter, and arrange the fennel around it.

Chicken with Ham and Cheese

Petti di pollo alla bolognese

This tasty combination comes from Emilia-Romagna, where it is also prepared with veal.

Ingredients
4 small chicken breasts, skinned and boned
flour seasoned with salt and freshly ground black pepper, for dredging
50 g/2 oz/$^1/_4$ cup butter
3–4 leaves fresh sage
4 thin slices prosciutto crudo, or cooked ham, cut in half
50 g/2 oz/$^1/_2$ cup freshly grated Parmesan cheese
serves 4

1 Cut each chicken breast in half lengthwise to make two flat fillets of approximately the same thickness. Dredge the chicken in the seasoned flour, and shake off the excess.

2 ▲ Preheat the grill. Heat the butter in a large heavy frying pan or skillet with the sage leaves. Add the chicken in one layer, and cook over low to moderate heat until golden brown on both sides, turning as necessary. This will take about 15 minutes.

3 ▲ Remove the chicken from the heat, and arrange on a flameproof serving dish or grill pan. Place one piece of ham on each chicken fillet, and top with the grated Parmesan. Grill for 3–4 minutes, or until the cheese has melted. Serve at once.

Mediterranean Turkey Skewers

Spiedini di tacchino

These skewers are delicious, and can be cooked on a grill or on a charcoal barbecue.

Ingredients
90 ml/6 tbsp olive oil
45 ml/3 tbsp fresh lemon juice
1 clove garlic, finely chopped
30 ml/2 tbsp chopped fresh basil
salt and freshly ground black pepper
2 medium courgettes
1 long thin aubergine
300 g/11oz boneless turkey, cut into 5 cm/2in cubes
12–16 pickled onions
1 pepper, red or yellow, cut into 5 cm/2in squares
serves 4

1 ▲ In a small bowl mix the oil with the lemon juice, garlic and basil. Season with salt and pepper.

2 ▲ Slice the courgettes and aubergine lengthwise into strips 5mm/$^1/_4$ inch thick. Cut them crosswise about two-thirds of the way along their length. Discard the shorter length. Wrap half the turkey pieces with the courgette slices, and the other half with the aubergine slices.

3 ▲ Prepare the skewers by alternating the turkey, onions, and pepper pieces. Lay the prepared skewers on a platter, and sprinkle with the flavored oil. Leave to marinate for at least 30 minutes. Preheat the grill, or prepare a barbecue.

4 ▲Grill for about 10 minutes, or until the vegetables are tender, turning the skewers occasionally. Serve hot.

Turkey Cutlets with Olives

Petto di tacchino con olive

This quick and tasty dish makes a good light main course.

Ingredients
90 ml/6 tbsp olive oil
1 clove garlic, peeled and lightly crushed
1 dried chilli, lightly crushed
500 g/1 1/4 lb boneless turkey breast, cut into 5 mm/ 1/4 in slices
salt and freshly ground black pepper
100 ml/4 fl oz/1/2 cup dry white wine
4 tomatoes, peeled and seeded, cut into thin strips
about 24 black olives
6–8 leaves fresh basil, torn into pieces
serves 4

1 ▲ Heat 60 ml/4 tbsp of the olive oil in a large frying pan. Add the garlic and dried chilli, and cook over low heat until the garlic is golden.

2 ▲ Raise the heat to moderate. Place the turkey slices in the pan, and brown them lightly on both sides. Season with salt and pepper. The turkey will be cooked after about 2 minutes. Remove the turkey to a heated dish.

3 ▲ Discard the garlic and chilli. Add the wine, tomato strips and olives. Cook over moderate heat for 3–4 minutes, scraping up any meat residue from the bottom of the pan.

4 ▲ Return the turkey to the pan. Sprinkle with the basil. Heat for about 30 seconds, and serve.

Stuffed Turkey Breast with Lemon

Petto di tacchino ripieno

This elegant dish of rolled turkey breast makes an impressive but economical main course.

Ingredients

750 g/1$^1/_2$ lb turkey breast, in one piece
1 carrot, cut into matchsticks
1 medium courgette, cut into matchsticks
75 g/3 oz/$^1/_3$ cup ham, cut into matchsticks
115 g/4 oz/2 thick slices white bread, crusts removed, softened in a little milk
10 green olives, stoned and finely chopped
1 large clove garlic, finely chopped
60 ml/4 tbsp chopped fresh parsley
60 ml/4 tbsp finely chopped fresh basil
1 egg
$^1/_8$ tsp grated lemon zest
30 ml/2 tbsp freshly grated Parmesan cheese
salt and freshly ground black pepper
60 ml/4 tbsp olive oil
250 ml/8 fl oz/1 cup chicken broth or stock, warmed
$^1/_2$ lemon, cut into thin wedges
25 g/1 oz/2 tbsp butter
serves 4–5

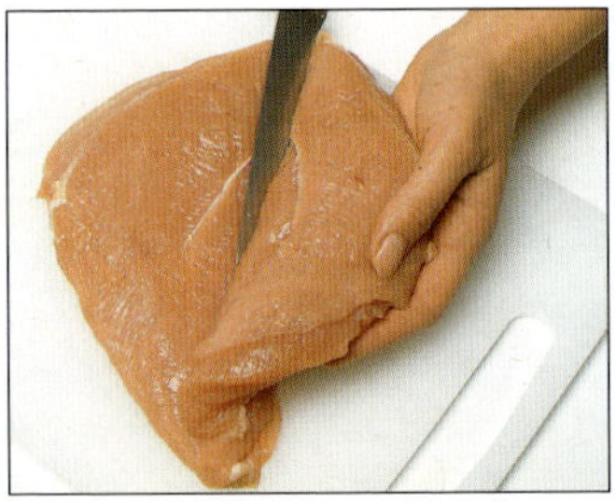

1 ▲ Remove any bones, skin or fat from the turkey. Using a sharp knife, cut part of the way through the turkey breast and open the two halves out like a book.

~ VARIATION ~

Substitute 75 g/3 oz sliced mushrooms sautéed lightly in 45 g/1$^1/_2$ oz/3 tbsp butter for the ham in step 3. Omit the lemon wedges during cooking.

2 ▲ Pound the meat with a mallet to obtain one large piece of meat of as even a thickness as possible.

3 ▲ Preheat the oven to 200°C/400°F/gas 6. Blanch the carrot and courgette pieces in a small saucepan of boiling water for 2 minutes. Drain. Combine with the matchsticks of ham.

4 ▲ Squeeze the bread, and place in a mixing bowl, breaking it into small pieces with a fork. Stir in the olives, garlic and herbs, and the egg. Add the lemon zest and grated Parmesan. Season with salt and pepper.

5 ▲ Spread the bread mixture in one layer over the meat, leaving a small border all around. Cover with the ham and vegetable mixture. Roll the turkey up. Tie the roll in several places with string.

6 ▲ Heat the oil in a ovenproof casserole. When the oil is hot, brown the meat on all sides. Remove from the heat, add the broth or stock, and arrange the lemon wedges around the meat. Cover and place in the oven.

7 After 15 minutes remove the cover, discard the lemon and baste the meat. Continue cooking, uncovered, for a further 25-30 minutes, basting occasionally. Allow the roll to stand for at least 10 minutes before slicing.

8 Strain the sauce. Stir in the butter and taste for seasoning. Serve the sliced roll warm with the sauce. If you wish to serve it cold, slice the roll just before serving and omit the sauce.

Pan-Fried Marinated Poussin

Galletti marinati in padella

These small birds are full of flavour when marinated for several hours before cooking.

Ingredients
2 poussins, about 450 g/1 lb each
5–6 leaves fresh mint, torn into pieces
1 leek, sliced into thin rings
1 clove garlic, finely chopped
salt and coarsely ground black pepper
60 ml/4 tbsp olive oil
30 ml/2 tbsp fresh lemon juice
50 ml/2 fl oz/1/4 cup dry white wine
mint leaves, to garnish
serves 3–4

1 Cut the poussins in half down the backbone, dividing the breast. Flatten the 4 halves with a mallet. Place them in a bowl with the mint, leek, garlic and pepper. Sprinkle with oil and half the lemon juice, cover, and allow to stand in a cool place for 6 hours.

2 ▲ Heat a large heavy frying pan or skillet. Place the poussins and their marinade in the pan. Cover and cook over moderate heat for about 45 minutes, turning occasionally. Season with salt during the cooking. Remove to a warm serving platter.

3 ▲ Tilt the pan and spoon off any fat on the surface. Pour in the wine and remaining lemon juice, and cook until the sauce reduces. Strain the sauce, pressing the vegetables to extract all the juices. Place the poussins on individual dishes, and spoon over the sauce. Sprinkle with mint, and serve.

Quail with Grapes

Quaglie con uva

Small birds often feature in Italian recipes. Use the most flavourful grapes for this dish.

Ingredients
6–8 fresh quail, gutted
salt and freshly ground black pepper
60 ml/4 tbsp olive oil
50 g/2 oz/1/4 cup pancetta or bacon, cut into small dice
250 ml/8 fl oz/1 cup dry white wine
250 ml/8 fl oz/1 cup chicken broth, warmed
350 g/12 oz green grapes
serves 4

1 Wash the quail carefully inside and out with cold water. Pat dry with paper towels. Sprinkle salt and pepper into the cavities.

2 Heat the oil in a heavy sauté pan or casserole large enough to accommodate all the quail in one layer. Add the pancetta or bacon, and cook over low heat for 5 minutes.

3 ▲ Raise the heat to moderate to high, and place the quail in the pan. Brown them evenly on all sides. Pour in the wine, and cook over moderate heat until it reduces by about half. Turn the quail over. Cover the pan, and cook for about 10–15 minutes. Add the stock, turn the quail again, cover, and cook for 15–20 minutes more, or until the birds are tender. Remove to a warmed serving platter and keep warm while the sauce is being finished.

4 ▲ Meanwhile drop the grapes into a pan of boiling water, and blanch for about 3 minutes. Drain and reserve.

5 Strain the pan juices into a small cup. If bacon has been used, allow the fat to separate and rise to the top. Spoon off the fat and discard. Pour the strained gravy into a small saucepan. Add the grapes and warm them gently for 2–3 minutes. Spoon around the quail and serve.

Duck with Chestnut Sauce

Petti di anatra con salsa di castagne

This autumnal dish makes use of the sweet chestnuts that are gathered in Italian woods.

Ingredients
1 sprig fresh rosemary
1 clove garlic, thinly sliced
30 ml/2 tbsp olive oil
4 duck breasts, boned and fat removed
For the sauce
450 g/1 lb chestnuts
5 ml/1 tsp oil
350 ml/12 fl oz/1 $^{1}/_{2}$ cups milk
1 small onion, finely chopped
1 carrot, finely chopped
1 small bay leaf
salt and freshly ground black pepper
30 ml/2 tbsp cream, warmed
serves 4–5

1 ▲ Pull the leaves from the sprig of rosemary. Combine them with the garlic and oil in a shallow bowl. Pat the duck breasts dry with paper towels. Brush the duck breasts with the marinade. Allow to stand for at least 2 hours before cooking.

2 Preheat the oven to 180°C/350°F/ gas 4. Cut a cross in the flat side of each chestnut with a sharp knife.

3 ▲ Place the chestnuts in a baking pan with the oil, and shake the pan until the nuts are coated with the oil. Bake for about 20 minutes, then peel.

4 Place the peeled chestnuts in a heavy pan with the milk, onion, carrot and bay leaf. Cook slowly for about 10–15 minutes until the chestnuts are very tender. Season with salt and pepper. Discard the bay leaf. Press the mixture through a strainer.

5 Return the sauce to the saucepan. Heat gently while the duck is cooking. Just before serving, stir in the cream. If the sauce is too thick, add a little more cream. Preheat the grill, or prepare a barbecue.

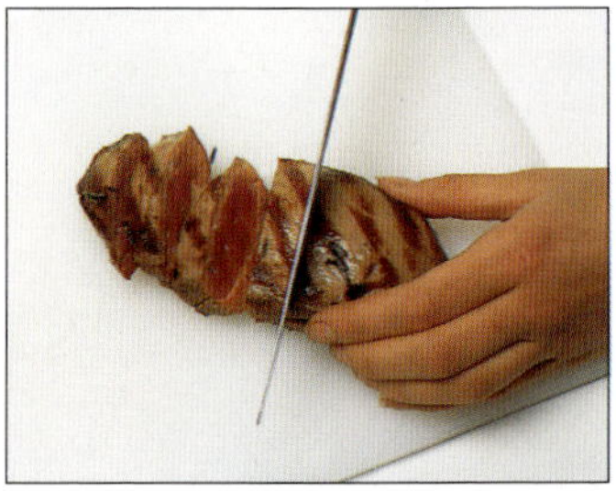

6 ▲ Grill the duck breasts until medium rare, about 6–8 minutes. The meat should be pink when sliced. Slice into rounds and arrange on warm plates. Serve with the heated sauce.

~ COOK'S TIP ~

The chestnut sauce may be prepared in advance and kept in the refrigerator for up to 2 days, or it may be made when chestnuts are in season and frozen. Allow to thaw to room temperature before re-heating.

Roast Pheasant with Juniper Berries

Fagiano arrosto

Sage and juniper are often used in Italian cooking to flavour pheasant and other game.

Ingredients

1.2-1.4 kg/$2^1/_2$-3 lb pheasant with liver, finely chopped (optional)
45 ml/3 tbsp olive oil
2 sprigs fresh sage
3 shallots, chopped
1 bay leaf
2 lemon quarters, plus 5 ml/1 tsp juice
30 g/2 tbsp juniper berries, lightly crushed
salt and freshly ground black pepper
4 thin slices pancetta or bacon
90 ml/6 tbsp dry white wine
250 ml/8 fl oz/1 cup fresh chicken broth or stock, heated
25 g/1 oz/2 tbsp butter, at room temperature
30 ml/2 tbsp flour
30 ml/2 tbsp brandy

serves 3–4

1 ▲ Wash the pheasant under cool water. Drain well, and pat dry with paper towels. Rub with 15 ml/1 tbsp of the olive oil. Place the remaining oil, sage leaves, shallots, and bay leaf in a shallow bowl. Add the lemon juice and juniper berries. Place the pheasant and lemon quarters in the bowl with the marinade, and spoon it over the bird. Allow to stand for several hours in a cool place, turning the pheasant occasionally. Remove the lemon.

2 Preheat the oven to 180°C/350°F/ gas 4. Place the pheasant in a roasting pan, reserving the marinade. Sprinkle the cavity with salt and pepper, and place the lemon quarters and bay leaf inside.

3 Arrange some of the sage leaves on the breast of the pheasant, and lay the pancetta or bacon over the top. Secure with string.

4 ▲ Spoon the remaining marinade on top of the pheasant, and roast until tender, about 30 minutes per 450 g/1 lb. Baste frequently with the pan juices and with the white wine. Transfer the pheasant to a warmed serving platter, discarding the string and pancetta.

5 Tilt the baking pan and skim off any surface fat. Pour in the stock. Stir over moderate heat, scraping up any meat residues from the bottom of the pan. Add the pheasant liver, if using. Bring to a boil and cook for 2–3 minutes Strain into a saucepan.

6 ▲ Blend the butter to a paste with the flour. Stir into the gravy a little at a time. Boil for 2–3 minutes, stirring to smooth out any lumps. Remove from the heat, stir in the brandy, and serve.

Veal Escalopes with Marsala

Scaloppine di vitello con Marsala

This quick and delicious dish enlivens the mild flavour of veal with the sweetness of Marsala.

Ingredients

450 g/1 lb veal escalopes, preferably cut across the grain, about 5 mm/ $^1/_4$ in thick
50 g/2 oz/$^1/_2$ cup flour seasoned with salt and freshly ground black pepper, for dredging
50 g/2 oz/$^1/_4$ cup butter
75 ml/5 tbsp Marsala
75 ml/5 tbsp stock or water
serves 4

1 Pound the escalopes flat to a thickness of about 4 mm/$^1/_4$in. If they have not been cut across the grain or from one muscle, cut small notches around the edges to stop them from curling during cooking.

2 ▲ Spread the flour out on a plate. Heat the butter in a large frying pan. Lightly dredge the veal slices in the flour, shaking off any excess. As soon as the foam from the butter subsides, put the veal into the pan in one layer, and brown the slices quickly on both sides, in two batches if necessary. Remove to a warmed serving plate.

3 ▲ Pour in the Marsala and the stock. Cook over moderate to high heat for 3–4 minutes, scraping up any meat residues from the bottom of the pan. Pour the sauce over the meat, and serve at once.

Ham and Cheese Veal Escalopes

Scaloppine alla bolognese

This dish from Bologna can be made with Parmesan or Gruyère cheese.

Ingredients

8 veal escalopes, about 450 g/1 lb total, preferably cut across the grain
50 g/2 oz/$^1/_2$ cup flour seasoned with salt and freshly ground black pepper, for dredging
25 ml/1 oz/2 tbsp butter
30 ml/2 tbsp olive oil
45 ml/3 tbsp dry white wine
8 thin slices ham
50 g/2 oz/$^1/_2$ cup freshly grated Parmesan cheese, or 8 small slices Gruyère cheese
serves 4

1 Preheat the oven to 200°C/400°F/ gas 6. Pound the escalopes flat. If they have not been cut across the grain or from one muscle, cut small notches around the edges to prevent them from curling during cooking. Spread the seasoned flour over a plate.

2 ▲ Heat the butter with the oil in a large frying pan. Lightly dredge the veal slices in the flour, shaking off any excess. As soon as the foam from the butter subsides, put the veal into the pan in one layer, and brown the slices quickly on both sides. Remove to a shallow oven dish. Add the wine to the pan and cook for 1–2 minutes, scraping up the brown residue from the bottom of the pan with a wooden spoon. Pour over the escalopes.

3 ▲ Place one slice of ham on top of each escalope. Sprinkle with one tablespoon of Parmesan, or top with one slice of Gruyère. Place in the oven and cook until the cheese melts, 5–7 minutes. Serve hot.

Cold Veal with Tuna Sauce

Vitello tonnato

This classic summer dish is best when prepared in advance and refrigerated for a few hours before serving. The dish can be kept for up to 3 days in the refrigerator.

Ingredients

800 g/1¾ lb boneless roasting veal, in one piece
1 carrot, peeled
1 stick celery
1 small onion, peeled and quartered
1 bay leaf
1 clove
5 ml/1 tsp whole peppercorns

For the tuna sauce

400 g/14 oz canned tuna, preferably in olive oil
4 anchovy fillets
10 ml/2 tsp capers, rinsed and drained
45 ml/3 tbsp fresh lemon juice
300 ml/½ pint/1¼ cups mayonnaise
salt and freshly ground black pepper
capers and pickled gherkins, to garnish

serves 6–8

1 ▲ Place the veal, vegetables and flavourings in a medium saucepan (not aluminium or copper). Cover with water. Bring to a boil and simmer for 50–60 minutes. Skim off any scum that rises to the surface. Do not overcook, or the veal will fall apart when sliced. Allow it to cool in its cooking liquid for several hours, or overnight.

2 Drain the tuna. Place it in a food processor or blender, and add the anchovies, capers and lemon juice. Process to a creamy paste. If it seems too thick, add 30–45 ml/2–3 tbsp of the cool veal broth and process again.

3 ▲ Scrape the tuna purée into a bowl. Fold in the mayonnaise. Check the seasoning and adjust as necessary.

4 Slice the veal as thinly as possible. Spread a little of the tuna sauce over the bottom of a serving platter.

5 ▲ Arrange a layer of the veal slices on top of the sauce. Cover with a thin layer of sauce. Make another layer or two of veal slices and sauce, ending with the sauce. Garnish with capers and gherkins. Cover with plastic wrap and refrigerate until needed.

Milanese Stewed Shin of Veal

Ossobuco alla milanese

"Ossobuco" means "hollow bone", and this dish calls for shin of veal cut into sections across the bone. Each bone should have its centre of marrow, which is considered a great delicacy.

Ingredients

50 g/2 oz/$^1/_4$ cup butter
1 clove garlic, peeled and crushed
4 pieces of shin of veal, each about 5 cm/2in thick
flour, for dredging
salt and freshly ground black pepper
250 ml/8 fl oz/1 cup dry white wine
300 ml/$^1/_2$ pint/1 $^1/_4$ cups meat or chicken broth
1 bay leaf
1 sprig fresh thyme, or $^1/_4$ tsp dried thyme

For the gremolada

1 small clove garlic
30 ml/2 tbsp chopped fresh parsley
5 ml/1 tsp chopped lemon zest
$^1/_2$ anchovy fillet (optional)

serves 4

1 Preheat the oven to 160°C/325°F/gas 3. Heat the butter with the crushed garlic clove in a heavy casserole large enough to accommodate all the meat lying flat in one layer. Dredge the veal lightly in the flour. Add it to the pan and brown it first on one side, and then on the other. Season with salt and pepper. Discard the garlic.

2 ▲ Add the wine, and cook over moderate to high heat for 3–4 minutes, turning the veal over several times. Pour in the broth, add the bay leaf and thyme, and bring to the boil. Cover the casserole and place it in the centre of the oven. Bake for 2 hours.

3 ▲ In the meantime, prepare the gremolada by placing the garlic, parsley, lemon rind and anchovy, if using, on a board and chopping them together very finely.

4 ▲ After 2 hours, remove the casserole from the oven. Taste the sauce for seasoning. Sprinkle in the gremolada, and mix it well into the sauce. Return the casserole to the oven for 10 more minutes, and serve.

Milanese Veal Chops

Costolette alla milanese

This famous dish depends on the chops being cooked carefully in butter.

πIngredients
2 veal chops or cutlets, on the bone
1 egg
salt and freshly ground black pepper
90–120 ml/ 6–8 tbsp plain breadcrumbs
50 g/2 oz/¼ cup butter
15 ml/1 tbsp vegetable oil
lemon wedges, to serve
serves 2

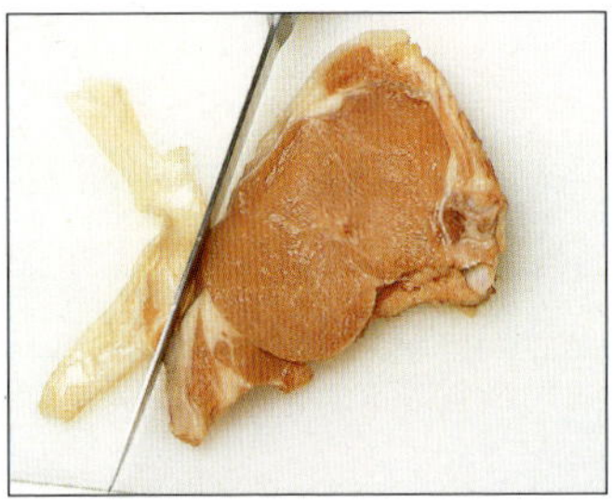

1 ▲ Trim any gristle or thick fat from the chops. Cut along the rib bone, if necessary, to free the meat on one side. Pound the meat slightly to flatten.

2 ▲ Beat the egg in a shallow bowl and season it with salt and pepper. Spread the breadcrumbs over a plate. Dip the chops into the egg, and then into the breadcrumbs. Pat the breadcrumbs to help them to stick.

~ COOK'S TIP ~

Milanese cooks sometimes soak the chops in milk for about an hour to soften the meat.

3 ▲ Heat the butter with the oil in a heavy frying pan large enough to hold both chops side by side. Do not let it brown. Add the chops to the pan, and cook them slowly over low to moderate heat until the breadcrumbs are golden and the meat is cooked through. The timing will depend on the thickness of the chops. The important thing is not to overcook the breadcrumb coating while undercooking the meat. Serve hot with lemon wedges.

Veal Rolls with Sage and Ham

Saltimbocca

These rolls are so good that, as their Italian name implies, they "jump into your mouth".

Ingredients
8 small veal escalopes
8 small slices prosciutto
8 leaves fresh sage
salt and freshly ground black pepper
40 g/1½ oz/3 tbsp butter
100 ml/4 fl oz/½ cup meat broth or stock, warmed
serves 3-4

1 Gently pound the veal slices with a mallet until thin. Lay a piece of prosciutto over each slice. Top with a sage leaf, and season with salt and pepper. Roll the escalopes around the filling and secure each roll with a wooden toothpick.

2 ▲ Heat half the butter in a frying pan just large enough to hold the rolls in one layer. When the butter is bubbling add the veal, turning the rolls to brown them on all sides. Cook for about 7–10 minutes, or until the veal is cooked. Remove to a warmed plate.

3 ▲ Add the remaining butter and the hot broth or stock to the frying pan, and bring to the boil, scraping up the brown residue on the bottom of the pan with a wooden spoon. Pour the sauce over the veal rolls, and serve.

Pizzaiola Steak

Bistecchine alla pizzaiola

This dish comes from Naples, where tomato sauces are used in all kinds of dishes.

Ingredients

450 g/1 lb beef steaks, preferably rump or chuck, thinly sliced
45 ml/3 tbsp flour, for dredging
45 ml/3 tbsp olive oil
3 cloves garlic, peeled and crushed
400 g/14 oz can plum tomatoes, with their juice, passed through a food mill
30 ml/2 tbsp chopped fresh basil
salt and freshly ground black pepper
serves 4

1 Trim any excess fat from the steaks, and notch the edges slightly with a sharp knife to prevent them from curling during cooking. Pat the steaks dry with paper towels, and dredge lightly in the flour.

2 ▲ In a large heavy frying pan or skillet, heat 30 ml/2 tbsp of the oil with the garlic cloves. As soon as they are golden, raise the heat, push them to the side of the pan, and add the steaks. Brown quickly on both sides. Remove the meat to a dish.

3 ▲ Add the tomatoes, the remaining oil, and the herbs to the pan. Season with salt and pepper. Cook over moderate heat for about 15 minutes. Discard the garlic cloves. Return the steaks to the pan, stir to cover them with the sauce, and cook for 4–5 minutes more.

Herbed Burgers

Polpette

Dress up minced beef with fresh herbs and a tasty tomato sauce.

Ingredients

750 g/1$^1/_2$ lb lean minced beef
1 clove garlic, finely chopped
1 spring onion, very finely chopped
45 ml/3 tbsp chopped fresh basil
45 ml/2 tbsp chopped fresh parsley
salt and freshly ground black pepper
40 g/1$^1/_2$ oz/3 tbsp butter

For the tomato sauce

45 ml/3 tbsp olive oil
1 medium onion, finely chopped
300 g/11oz tomatoes, chopped
a few leaves fresh basil
45–60 ml/3–4 tbsp water
5 ml/1 tsp sugar
15 ml/1 tbsp white wine vinegar
salt and freshly ground black pepper
serves 4

1 To make the tomato sauce, heat the oil in a large pan and sauté the onion gently until translucent. Add the tomatoes and cook for 2–3 minutes. Add the basil, cover the pan, and cook for 7–8 minutes over moderate heat.

2 Add the water, sugar and vinegar, and cook for 2–3 minutes more. Season with salt and pepper. Remove from the heat, allow to cool slightly, and pass the sauce through a food mill or strainer. Check the seasoning.

3 ▲ Combine the meat with the garlic, spring onion and herbs in a mixing bowl. Season with salt and pepper. Form into 4 burgers, patting the meat as lightly as possible.

4 ▲ Heat the butter in a frying pan. When the foam subsides add the burgers, and cook over moderate heat until brown on the underside. Turn the burgers over, and continue cooking until done. Remove to a warmed plate.

5 Tilt the frying pan, and spoon off any surface fat. Pour in the sauce, raise the heat and bring to a boil, scraping up the meat residue from the bottom of the pan. Serve with the burgers.

Meatballs

Polpettine

These meatballs are delicious served hot with pasta or rice. They are also good cold.

Ingredients

7.5 g/$^1/_4$ oz/2 tbsp dried porcini mushrooms
150 ml/$^1/_4$ pint/$^2/_3$ cup warm water
450 g/1 lb lean ground beef
2 cloves garlic, finely chopped
60 ml/4 tbsp chopped fresh parsley
45 ml/3 tbsp chopped fresh basil
1 egg
4 tbsp/6 tbsp plain breadcrumbs
30 ml/2 tbsp freshly grated Parmesan cheese
salt and freshly ground black pepper
60 ml/4 tbsp olive oil
1 medium onion, very finely chopped
50 ml/2 fl oz/$^1/_4$ cup dry white wine
chopped fresh parsley, to garnish

serves 3–4

1 Soak the dried mushrooms in the warm water for 15 minutes. Lift them out of the water and chop finely. Filter the soaking water through paper towels and reserve.

2 ▲ In a mixing bowl, combine the meat with the chopped mushrooms, garlic and herbs. Stir in the egg. Add the breadcrumbs and Parmesan, and season with salt and pepper. Form the mixture into small balls 3.5 cm/1$^1/_2$ inches in diameter.

3 ▲ In a large heavy frying pan or skillet, heat the oil. Add the onion and cook over low heat until soft. Raise the heat and add the meatballs, rolling them often to brown them evenly on all sides. After about 5 minutes add the filtered mushroom soaking water. Cook for 5–8 minutes more, or until the meatballs are cooked through.

4 ▲ Remove the meatballs to a heated serving plate with a slotted spoon or spatula. Add the wine to the pan, and cook for 1–2 minutes, stirring to scrape up any residues on the bottom of the pan. Pour the sauce over the meatballs. Sprinkle with parsley, and serve at once.

Beef Stew with Red Wine

Spezzatino di manzo con vino rosso

This rich, hearty dish should be served with mashed potatoes or polenta.

Ingredients

75 ml/5 tbsp olive oil
1.2 kg/$2^1/_2$ lb boneless beef chuck, cut into 3 cm/$1^1/_2$ in cubes
1 medium onion, very finely sliced
2 carrots, chopped
45 ml/3 tbsp finely chopped fresh parsley
1 clove garlic, chopped
1 bay leaf
a few sprigs fresh thyme, or pinch of dried thyme leaves
pinch of grated nutmeg
250 ml/8 fl oz/1 cup red wine
400 g/14 oz can plum tomatoes, chopped, with their juice
100 ml/4 fl oz/$^1/_2$ cup beef or chicken broth
about 15 black olives, stoned and halved
salt and freshly ground black pepper
1 large red sweet pepper, cut into strips

serves 6

1 ▲ Preheat the oven to 180°C/350°F/gas 4. Heat 45 ml/3 tbsp of the oil in a large, heavy casserole. Brown the meat a little at a time, turning it to colour on all sides. Remove to a side plate while the remaining meat is being browned.

2 When all the meat has been browned and removed, add the remaining oil, the onion and carrots. Cook over low heat until the onion softens. Add the parsley and garlic, and cook for 3–4 minutes more.

3 ▲ Return the meat to the pan, raise the heat, and stir well to mix the vegetables with the meat. Stir in the bay leaf, thyme and nutmeg. Add the wine, bring to a boil and cook, stirring, for 4–5 minutes. Stir in the tomatoes, stock and olives, and mix well. Season with salt and pepper, and return to the boil. Cover the casserole, and place in the centre of the preheated oven. Bake for $1^1/_2$ hours.

4 ▲ Remove the casserole from the oven. Stir in the strips of pepper. Return the casserole to the oven and cook, uncovered, for 30 minutes more, or until the beef is tender.

Roast Lamb with Herbs

Arrosto d'agnello con erbe e aglio

This dish originates from southern Italy, where lamb is roasted with garlic and wild herbs.

Ingredients

1.5 kg/3 lb leg of lamb
45–60 ml/3–4 tbsp olive oil
4 cloves garlic, peeled and halved
2 sprigs fresh sage, or pinch of dried sage leaves
2 sprigs fresh rosemary, or 5 ml/1 tsp dried rosemary leaves
2 bay leaves
2 sprigs fresh thyme, or $^1/_2$ tsp dried
salt and freshly ground black pepper
175 ml/6 fl oz/$^3/_4$ cup dry white wine
serves 4–6

1 Cut any excess fat from the lamb. Rub with olive oil. Using a sharp knife, make small cuts just under the skin all around the meat. Insert the garlic pieces in some of the cuts, and a few of the fresh herbs in the others. (If using dried herbs, sprinkle them over the surface of the meat.)

2 Rub the remaining fresh herbs all over the lamb, and allow it to stand in a cool place for at least 2 hours before cooking. Preheat the oven to 190°C/375°F/gas 5.

3 ▲ Place the lamb in a baking pan, surrounded by the herbs. Pour on 30 ml/2 tbsp of the oil. Season. Place in the oven and roast for 35 minutes, basting occasionally.

4 ▲ Pour the wine over the lamb. Roast for 15 minutes more, or until the meat is cooked. Remove the lamb to a heated serving dish. Tilt the pan, spooning off any fat on the surface. Strain the pan juices into a gravy boat. Slice the meat, and serve with the sauce handed separately.

Lamb Stewed with Tomatoes and Garlic

Spezzatino d'agnello

This rustic stew comes from the plateau of Puglia, where sheep graze alongside vineyards.

Ingredients

2 large cloves garlic
1 sprig fresh rosemary, or 45 ml/3 tbsp chopped fresh parsley if fresh rosemary is not available
90 ml/6 tbsp olive oil
1.3 kg/2$^1/_2$ lb stewing lamb, trimmed of fat and gristle and cut into chunks
flour seasoned with freshly ground black pepper, for dredging
175 ml/6 fl oz/$^3/_4$ cup dry white wine
10 ml/2 tsp salt
450 g/1 lb fresh tomatoes, chopped, or 1 x 400g/14oz can tomatoes, chopped
100 ml/$^1/_2$ cup beef stock, heated
serves 5–6

1 Preheat the oven to 180°C/350°F/gas 4. Chop the garlic with the parsley, if using. Heat 60 ml/4 tbsp of the oil in a wide casserole.

2 Add the garlic and rosemary or parsley and cook over moderate heat, until the garlic is golden.

3 ▲ Dredge the lamb in the flour. Add a batch of lamb chunks to the pan in one layer, turning to brown them evenly. When brown, remove them to a side plate. Add a little more oil, and brown the remaining lamb.

4 ▲ When all the lamb has been browned, return it to the casserole with the wine. Raise the heat and bring to the boil, scraping up any residues from the bottom. Sprinkle with the salt. Stir in the tomatoes and the stock. Stir well. Cover the casserole, and place in the centre of the oven. Bake for 1$^3/_4$–2 hours, or until the meat is tender.

Pork Braised in Milk with Carrots

Lonza al latte con carote

This method of slowly cooking a joint of pork produces a deliciously creamy gravy. It is a speciality of the Veneto region.

Ingredients

750 g/1½ lb lean loin of pork
45 ml/3 tbsp olive oil
25 g/2 tbsp butter
1 small onion, finely chopped
1 stick celery, finely chopped
8 carrots, cut into 5 cm/2 in strips
2 bay leaves
15 ml/1 tbsp peppercorns
salt, to taste
500 ml/2 cups milk, scalded
serves 4–5

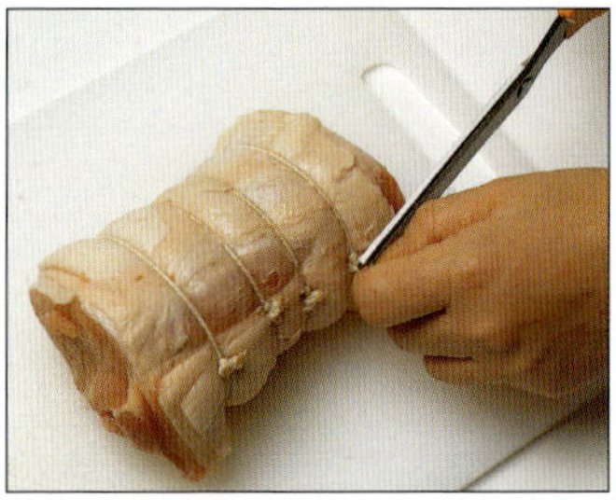

1 ▲ Trim any excess fat from the pork, and tie it into a roll with string.

2 ▲ Preheat the oven to 180°C/350°F/gas 4. Heat the oil and butter in a large casserole. Add the vegetables, and cook over low heat until they soften, 8–10 minutes. Raise the heat, push the vegetables to one side and add the pork, browning it on all sides. Add the bay leaves and peppercorns, and season with salt.

3 ▲ Pour in the hot milk. Cover the casserole and place it in the centre of the oven. Bake for about 90 minutes, turning and basting the pork with the sauce about once every 20 minutes. Remove the cover for the last 20 minutes of baking.

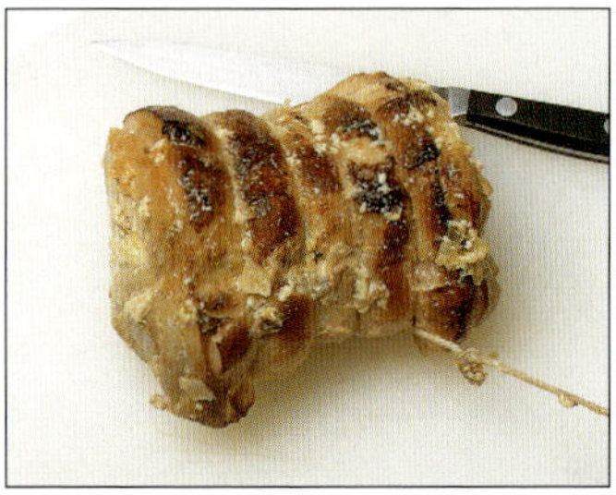

4 ▲ Remove the meat from the casserole, and cut off the string. Place the meat on a warmed serving platter and cut into slices.

~ VARIATION ~

This dish can also be made using a joint of veal. Substitute a piece of boneless veal and proceed as in the recipe. This dish is delicious served hot or cold.

5 ▲ Discard the bay leaves. Press about one-third of the carrots and all the liquids in the pan through a strainer. Arrange the remaining carrots around the meat.

6 ▲ Place the sauce in a small saucepan, taste for seasoning, and bring to the boil. If it seems too thin, boil it for a few minutes to reduce it slightly. Serve the sliced meat with the carrots, and pass the hot sauce separately.

Pork Fillet with Caper Sauce

Fettine di maiale con salsa di capperi

The caper sauce can be made in advance and reheated while the pork is sautéed.

Ingredients
450 g/1 lb pork fillet, cut into thin slices
flour seasoned with freshly ground black pepper, for dredging
25 g/1 oz/2 tbsp butter
30 ml/2 tbsp olive oil
For the caper sauce
30 ml/2 tbsp olive oil
50 g/2 oz/$^1/_4$ cup butter
$^1/_2$ small onion, very finely chopped
1 anchovy fillet, rinsed and chopped
15 ml/1 tbsp flour
30 ml/2 tbsp capers, rinsed
15 ml/1 tbsp finely chopped fresh parsley
60 ml/4 tbsp wine vinegar
60 ml/4 tbsp water
60 ml/4 tbsp balsamic vinegar
serves 4–5

1 Make the sauce by heating the oil and 25 g/1 oz/2 tbsp of the butter in a small saucepan (not aluminium) and slowly cooking the onion. When it is soft, add the anchovy, mashing it into the onion with a wooden spoon.

2 ▲ Stir in the flour and, when it is well amalgamated, the capers and parsley. Add the wine vinegar and water, stirring constantly over low heat to thicken the sauce. Just before serving stir in another 25 g/1 oz/2 tbsp of butter, and the balsamic vinegar.

3 Meanwhile, flatten the pork fillets with a meat pounder until thin. Dredge lightly in the seasoned flour, shaking off any excess.

4 ▲ Heat 25 g/ 1 oz/2 tbsp of butter and the oil in a large frying pan, and when hot add some of the pork slices in one layer. Brown the meat on both sides, cooking it for a total of 5–6 minutes. Remove to a heated serving dish, and repeat with the remaining pork slices. Serve hot, with the sauce.

Pork Chops with Mushrooms

Costolette di maiale con funghi

The addition of dried porcini mushrooms gives fresh cultivated mushrooms a richer flavour.

Ingredients
15 g/$^1/_2$ oz/3 tbsp dried porcini mushrooms, soaked in 250 ml/8 fl oz/ 1 cup warm water and drained (reserve the soaking water)
75 g/3 oz/$^1/_3$ cup butter
2 cloves garlic, peeled and crushed
300 g/11oz fresh cultivated mushrooms, thinly sliced
salt and freshly ground black pepper
15 ml/1 tbsp olive oil
4 pork chops, trimmed of excess fat
$^1/_2$ tsp fresh thyme leaves, or $^1/_4$ tsp dried
100 ml/$^1/_2$ cup dry white wine
75 ml/$^1/_3$ cup light cream
serves 4

1 Filter the mushroom soaking water through a layer of paper towels and reserve. Melt two-thirds of the butter in a large frying pan. Add the garlic. When the foam subsides, stir in all the mushrooms. Season and cook over moderate heat until the mushrooms give up their liquid, 8–10 minutes.

2 Remove the mushrooms to a side dish. Add the remaining butter and the oil to the frying pan. When hot, add the pork in one layer and sprinkle with thyme. Cook over moderate to high heat for about 3 minutes per side to seal. Reduce the heat, and cook for 15–20 minutes more. Remove to a warmed plate.

4 ▲ Spoon off any fat in the pan. Pour in the wine and the mushroom water. Cook over high heat until reduced by about half, stirring to scrape up the residues at the bottom. Add the mushrooms and the cream, and cook for 4–5 minutes more. Serve the sauce poured over the chops.

Liver with Onions

Fegato alla veneziana

This classic Venetian dish is very good served with grilled polenta. Allow enough time for the onions to cook very slowly, to produce a sweet flavour.

Ingredients
75 g/3 oz/$^1/_3$ cup butter
45 ml/3 tbsp olive oil
750 g/1$^1/_2$ lb onions, very finely sliced
salt and freshly ground black pepper
800 g/1$^3/_4$ lb calf's liver, sliced thinly
45 ml/3 tbsp finely chopped fresh parsley, to garnish
grilled polenta wedges, to serve (optional)
serves 6

1 ▲ Heat two-thirds of the butter with the oil in a large heavy frying pan. Add the onions, and cook over low heat until soft and tender, about 40–50 minutes, stirring often. Season with salt and pepper. Remove to a side dish.

2 ▲ Heat the remaining butter in the pan over moderate to high heat. When it has stopped bubbling add the liver, and brown it on both sides. Cook for about 5 minutes, or until done. Remove to a warmed side dish.

3 ▲ Return the onions to the pan. Raise the heat slightly, and stir the onions to mix them into the liver cooking juices.

4 ▲ When the onions are hot, turn them out onto a heated serving platter. Arrange the liver on top, and sprinkle with parsley. Serve with grilled polenta wedges, if desired.

Rabbit with Tomatoes

Coniglio con pomodori

Rabbit is very popular in Italy, and is prepared in many ways. This is a hearty dish with strong and robust flavours.

Ingredients

750 g/1 $^{1}/_{2}$lb boned rabbit, cut into chunks
2 cloves garlic, thinly sliced
115 g/4 oz/$^{1}/_{2}$ cup thinly sliced pancetta or bacon
750 g/1 $^{1}/_{2}$ lb tomatoes, peeled, seeded and roughly chopped
45 ml/3 tbsp chopped fresh basil
salt and freshly ground black pepper
60 ml/4 tbsp olive oil

serves 4–5

1 ▲ Preheat the oven to 200°C/400°F/gas 6. Pat the rabbit pieces dry with paper towels. Place a thin slice of garlic on each piece. Wrap a slice of pancetta or bacon around it, making sure the garlic is held in place.

2 ▲ Place the tomatoes in a non-stick pan, and cook them for a few minutes until they give up some of their liquid and begin to dry out. Stir in the basil, and season with salt and pepper.

3 ▲ Place the tomatoes in a layer in the bottom of a baking dish. Arrange the rabbit pieces on top of the tomatoes. Sprinkle with olive oil and place, uncovered, in the oven. Roast for 40–50 minutes.

4 ▲ Baste the rabbit occasionally with any fat in the dish. After the rabbit has cooked for about 25 minutes the dish may be covered with foil for the remaining time if the sauce seems to be too dry.

DESSERTS

This delectable sampler of Italy's most popular family desserts is drawn from many regions and includes scrumptious tarts and creamy puddings, nutty biscuits, baked fruits and refreshing summer ices.

Italian Coffee Dessert

Tiramisù

"Tiramisù" means "Pick me up", and this rich egg and coffee dessert does just that!

Ingredients
500 g/1lb 2oz mascarpone cheese
5 eggs, separated, at room temperature
100 g/3½ oz/scant ½ cup caster sugar
pinch of salt
savoyard or sponge biscuits, to line dish(es)
100 ml/4 fl oz/½ cup strong espresso coffee
60 ml/4 tbsp brandy or rum (optional)
unsweetened cocoa powder, to sprinkle
serves 6–8

1 Beat the mascarpone in a small bowl until soft. In a separate bowl beat the egg yolks with the sugar (reserving 15 ml/1 tbsp) until the mixture is pale yellow and fluffy. Gradually beat in the softened mascarpone.

2 ▲ Using an electric beater or wire whisk, beat the egg whites with the salt until they form stiff peaks. Fold the egg whites into the mascarpone mixture.

3 Line one large or several individual serving dishes with the biscuits. Add the reserved sugar to the coffee, and stir in the liqueur, if using.

4 ▲ Sprinkle some of the coffee over the biscuits. They should be moist but not saturated. Cover with half of the egg mixture. Make another layer of biscuits moistened with coffee, and cover with the remaining egg mixture. Sprinkle with cocoa powder. Refrigerate for at least 1 hour, and preferably more, before serving.

Italian Custard

Zabaione

This airy egg custard fortified with sweet wine is most often eaten warm with cookies or fruit.

Ingredients
3 egg yolks
45 ml/3 tbsp caster sugar
75 ml/5 tbsp Marsala or white dessert wine
pinch of grated orange zest
serves 3–4

1 ▲ In the top half of a double boiler, or in a bowl, away from the heat, whisk the egg yolks with the sugar until pale yellow. Beat in the Marsala or wine.

2 ▲ Place the pan or bowl over a pan of simmering water, and continue whisking until the custard is a frothy, light mass and evenly coats the back of a spoon, 6–8 minutes. Do not let the upper container touch the hot water, or the zabaione may curdle.

3 ▲ Stir in the orange zest. Serve immediately.

~ COOKS TIP ~

A small teaspoon of ground cinnamon may be added.

Italian Trifle

Zuppa inglese

Known in Italy as "English Soup", this is a kind of trifle that has little to do with England!

Ingredients
500 ml/16 fl oz/2 cups milk
grated zest of 1/2 lemon
4 egg yolks
75 g/3 oz/1/3 cup superfine sugar
50 g/2 oz/1/2 cup flour, sifted
15 ml/1 tbsp rum or brandy
25 g/1 oz/2 tbsp butter
200 g/7 oz savoyard bicuits or 300 g/ 11oz sponge cake, sliced into 1 cm/ 1/2 in slices
75 ml/3 fl oz/1/3 cup Alchermes liqueur or cherry brandy
75 ml/3 fl oz/1/3 cup Strega liqueur
45 ml/3 tbsp apricot jam
fresh whipped cream, to garnish
chopped toasted nuts, to garnish
serves 6–8

1 Heat the milk with the lemon zest in a small saucepan. Remove from the heat as soon as small bubbles form on the surface.

2 ▲ Beat the egg yolks with a wire whisk. Gradually incorporate the sugar, and continue beating until pale yellow. Beat in the flour. Stir in the milk very gradually, pouring it in through a strainer to remove the lemon. When all the milk has been added, pour the mixture into a heavy saucepan. Bring to a boil stirring constantly with a whisk. Simmer for 5-6 minutes, stirring constantly. Remove from the heat and stir in the rum or brandy. Beat in the butter. Allow to cool to room temperature, stirring to prevent a skin from forming.

3 ▲ Brush the biscuits or cake slices with the Alchermes liqueur or cherry brandy on one side, and the Strega liqueur on the other. Spread a thin layer of the custard over the bottom of a serving dish. Line the dish with a layer of biscuits or cake slices. Cover with some of the custard. Add another layer of cookies which have been brushed with liqueur.

4 ▲ Heat the jam in a small saucepan with 30 ml/2 tbsp water. When it is hot, pour or brush it evenly over the biscuits. Continue with layers of custard and liqueur-brushed biscuits until the ingredients have been used up. End with custard. Cover with plastic wrap or foil, and refrigerate for at least 2-3 hours. To serve, decorate the top of the trifle with whipped cream and garnish with chopped nuts.

Chestnut Pudding

Budino di castagne

Sweet chestnuts are found in the mountainous regions of Italy in October and November.

Ingredients
450 g/1lb fresh sweet chestnuts
300 ml/½ pint/1¼ cups milk
115 g/4 oz/½ cup caster sugar
2 eggs, separated, at room temperature
25 g/1 oz/¼ cup unsweetened cocoa powder
½ tsp pure vanilla extract
50 g/2 oz/⅓ cup icing sugar, sifted
butter, for the mould(s)
fresh whipped cream, to garnish
marrons glacés, to garnish
serves 4–5

1 Cut a cross in the side of the chestnuts, and drop them into a pan of boiling water. Cook for 5–6 minutes. Remove with a slotted spoon, and peel while still warm.

2 ▲ Place the peeled chestnuts in a heavy or non-stick saucepan with the milk and half of the caster sugar. Cook over low heat, stirring occasionally, until soft. Remove from the heat and allow to cool. Press the contents of the pan through a strainer.

3 Preheat the oven to 180°C/350°F/ gas 4. Beat the egg yolks with the remaining caster sugar until the mixture is pale yellow and fluffy. Beat in the cocoa powder and the vanilla.

4 ▲ In a separate bowl, whisk the egg whites with a wire whisk or electric beater until they form soft peaks. Gradually beat in the sifted icing sugar and continue beating until the mixture forms stiff peaks.

5 ▲ Fold the chestnut and egg yolk mixtures together. Fold in the egg whites. Turn the mixture into one large or several individual buttered pudding moulds. Place on a baking sheet, and bake in the oven until firm, 12–20 minutes depending on the size. Remove from the oven, and allow to cool for 10 minutes before unmolding. Serve garnished with whipped cream and marrons glacés.

Fruit Salad

Macedonia

A really good fruit salad is always refreshing, and in Italy it comes bathed in fresh orange and lemon juices. Use any mixture of fresh seasonal fruits.

Ingredients

juice of 3 large sweet oranges
juice of 1 lemon
1 banana
1–2 apples
1 ripe pear
2 peaches or nectarines
4–5 apricots or plums
115 g/4 oz/$^2/_3$ cup black or green grapes
115 g/4 oz/$^2/_3$ cup berries (strawberries, raspberries etc)
any other fruits in season
sugar, to taste (optional)
30–45 ml/2–3 tbsp Kirsch, maraschino or other liqueur (optional)
serves 4–6

1 Place the fresh orange and lemon juices in a large serving bowl.

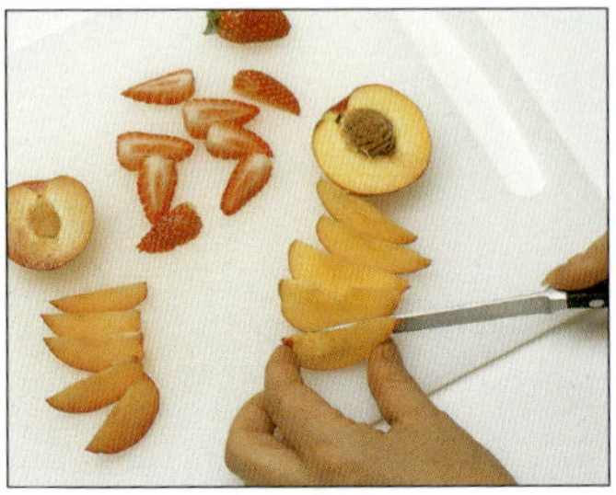

2 ▲ Prepare all the fruits by washing or peeling them as necessary. Cut them into bite-size pieces. Halve the grapes and remove any seeds. Core and slice the apples. Stone and slice soft fruits and leave small berries whole. As soon as each fruit is prepared, put it into the bowl with the juices.

3 ▲ Taste the salad, adding sugar if using. A few tablespoons of liqueur may also be added. Cover the bowl and refrigerate for at least 2 hours. Mix well before serving. In Italy, fruit salad is eaten alone, with vanilla ice cream or with zabaione. It is not usually served with cream.

Baked Apples with Red Wine

Mele al forno

Italian baked apples include a delicious filling of sultanas soaked in spiced red wine.

Ingredients

65 g/ 2$^1/_2$ oz/scant $^1/_2$ cup sultanas
350 ml/12 fl oz/1$^1/_2$ cups red wine
pinch of grated nutmeg
pinch of ground cinnamon
60 g/4 tbsp granulated sugar
pinch of grated lemon zest
6 tart apples of even size
35 g/1$^1/_2$ oz/3 tbsp butter
serves 6

1 In a small bowl, combine the sultanas with the wine. Stir in the spices, sugar and lemon zest. Allow to stand for 1 hour.

2 Preheat the oven to 190°C/375°F/gas 5. Wash the apples. Use a corer or small, sharp knife to remove the central cores without cutting through to the bottom of the apples.

3 ▲ Divide the filling mixture between the 6 apples, spooning it into the hollow cores. Spoon in a little of the spiced wine.

4 ▲ Arrange the apples in a buttered baking dish. Pour the remaining wine around the apples. Top each core hole with a knob of butter. Bake for 40–50 minutes, or until the apples are soft but not mushy. Serve hot or at room temperature.

Lemon Ricotta Cake

Torta di limone e ricotta

This lemony cake from Sardinia is quite different from a traditional cheesecake.

Ingredients
75 g/3 oz/1/3 tbsp butter
170 g/6 oz/3/4 cup granulated sugar
75 g/3 oz/generous 1/3 cup ricotta
3 eggs, separated
175 g/6 oz/1 1/2 cups flour
1 1/2 tsp baking powder
grated zest of 1 lemon
45 ml/3 tbsp fresh lemon juice
icing sugar, for dusting
serves 6–8

1 Grease a 22 cm/9in round cake or springform pan. Line the bottom with baking parchment or waxed paper. Grease the paper. Dust with flour. Set aside. Preheat the oven to 180°C/350°F/ gas 4.

2 Cream the butter and sugar together until smooth. Beat in the ricotta.

3 Beat in the egg yolks, one at a time. Add 30 ml/2 tbsp of the flour, and the lemon zest and juice. Sift the baking powder into the remaining flour and beat into the batter until well blended only.

4 ▲ Beat the egg whites until they form stiff peaks. Fold them carefully into the batter.

5 ▲ Turn the mixture into the prepared pan. Bake for 45 minutes, or until a cake tester inserted in the center of the cake comes out clean. Allow the cake to cool for 10 minutes before turning it out onto a rack to cool. Dust the cake generously with icing sugar before serving.

Peaches with Amaretti Stuffing

Pesche alla piemontese

Peaches are plentiful all over Italy. They are sometimes prepared hot, as in this classic dish.

Ingredients
4 ripe fresh peaches
juice of 1/2 lemon
65 g/2 1/2 oz/2/3 cup crushed amaretti biscuits, or 90 g/31/2 oz/1 cup home-made amaretti (see recipe)
30 ml/2 tbsp Marsala, brandy or peach brandy
25 g/1 oz/2 tbsp butter, at room temperature
1/2 tsp vanilla extract
30 ml/2 tbsp granulated sugar
1 egg yolk
serves 4

1 Preheat the oven to 180°C/350°F/ gas 4. Wash the peaches. Cut them in half and remove the stones. Enlarge the hollow left by the pits by scooping out some of the peach with a small spoon. Sprinkle the peach halves with the lemon juice.

2 ▲ Soften the amaretti crumbs in the Marsala or brandy for a few minutes. Beat the butter until soft, and then stir in the amaretti mixture and all remaining ingredients.

3 ▲ Arrange the peach halves in a baking dish in one layer, hollow side upwards. Divide the amaretti mixture into 8 parts, and fill the hollows, mounding the stuffing up in the centre. Bake for 35-40 minutes, until browned and bubbling. These peaches are delicious served hot or cold.

Choux Pastries with Two Custards

Bigné alle due creme

Italian pastry shops are filled with displays of sweetly scented pastries such as these.

Ingredients

200 ml/ 7 fl oz/scant 1 cup water
115 g/4 oz/$^1/_2$ cup butter
2 cm/1 in piece vanilla pod
pinch of salt
150 g/5 oz/1$^1/_4$ cups flour
5 eggs

For the custard fillings

50 g/2 oz cooking chocolate
300 ml/$^1/_2$ pint/1$^1/_4$ cups milk
4 egg yolks
65 g/2$^1/_2$ oz/scant $^1/_3$ cup granulated sugar
40 g/ 1$^1/_2$ oz/generous $^1/_3$ cup flour
5 ml/1 tsp pure vanilla extract
300 ml/$^1/_2$ pint/1$^1/_4$ cups whipping cream
unsweetened cocoa powder and icing (confectioners') sugar, to garnish

makes about 48

1 ▲ Preheat the oven to 190°C/375°F/gas 5. Heat the water with the butter, vanilla and salt. When the butter has melted, beat in the flour. Cook over low heat, stirring constantly, for about 8 minutes. Remove from the heat.

2 ▲ Mix in the eggs one at a time. Remove the vanilla pod.

3 ▲ Butter a flat baking tray. Using a pastry bag fitted with a round nozzle, squeeze the mixture out onto the tray in balls the size of small walnuts, leaving space between the rows. Bake for 20–25 minutes, or until the pastries are golden brown. Remove from the oven and allow to cool before filling.

4 ▲ Meanwhile, prepare the custard fillings. Melt the chocolate in the top half of a double boiler, or in a bowl set over a pan of simmering water. Heat the milk in a small saucepan, taking care not to let it boil.

~ VARIATION ~

The choux pastries may be filled with fresh whipped cream flavoured with 5 ml/1 tsp vanilla extract or 30–45 ml/2–3 tbsp spirit such as brandy or rum. Mix well, spoon the cream into a piping bag and proceed as in Step 6.

5 ▲ Beat the egg yolks with a wire whisk or electric beater. Gradually incorporate the sugar, and continue beating until the mixture is pale yellow. Beat in the flour. Beat in the hot milk very gradually, pouring it in through a strainer. When all the milk has been added, pour the mixture into a heavy medium pan, and bring to a boil. Simmer for 5–6 minutes, stirring constantly. Remove from the heat and divide the custard between two bowls. Add the melted chocolate to one, and stir the vanilla extract into the other. Allow to cool completely.

6 ▲ Whip the cream. Fold half of it carefully into each of the custards. Fill two pastry bags fitted with round nozzles with the custards. Fill half of the choux pastries with the chocolate custard, and the rest with the vanilla custard, making a little hole and piping the filling in through the side of each pastry. Dust the tops of the chocolate-filled pastries with cocoa powder, and the rest with icing sugar. Serve immediately after filling.

Sultana Cornmeal Biscuits

Gialletti

These little yellow biscuits come from the Veneto region.

Ingredients
75 g/3 oz/$^1/_2$ cup sultanas
115 g/4 oz/$^3/_4$ cup finely ground yellow cornmeal
175 g/6 oz/1$^1/_2$ cups plain flour
7 ml/1$^1/_2$ tsp baking powder
$^1/_2$ tsp of salt
225 g/8 oz/1 cup butter
225 g/8 oz/1 cup granulated sugar
2 eggs
15 ml/1 tbsp marsala or 5 ml/1 tsp vanilla extract
makes about 48

1 Soak the sultanas in a small bowl of warm water for 15 minutes. Drain. Preheat the oven to 180°C/350°F/ gas 4.

2 Sift the cornmeal and flour, the baking powder and the salt together into a bowl.

3 Cream the butter and sugar together until light and fluffy. Beat in the eggs, one at a time. Beat in the marsala or vanilla extract.

4 ▲ Add the dry ingredients to the batter, beating until well blended. Stir in the sultanas.

5 ▲ Drop heaped teaspoons of batter onto a greased baking sheet in rows about 5 cm/2 in apart. Bake for 7–8 minutes, or until the cookies are golden brown at the edges. Remove to a rack to cool.

Amaretti

Amaretti

If bitter almonds are not available, make up the weight with sweet almonds.

Ingredients
150 g/5 oz/1$^3/_4$ cups sweet almonds
50 g/2 oz/$^1/_2$ cup bitter almonds
225 g/8 oz/1 cup caster sugar
2 egg whites
2.5 ml/$^1/_2$ tsp almond extract or 5 ml/1 tsp vanilla extract
icing (confectioners') sugar, for dusting
makes about 36

1 Preheat the oven to 160°C/325°F/ gas 3. Peel the almonds by dropping them into a pan of boiling water for 1–2 minutes. Drain. Rub the almonds in a cloth to remove the skins.

2 Place the almonds on a baking tray and let them dry out in the oven for 10–15 minutes without browning. Remove from the oven and allow to cool. Turn the oven off.

3 Finely grind the almonds with half of the sugar in a food processor.

4 ▲ Use an electric beater or wire whisk to beat the egg whites until they form soft peaks. Sprinkle half of the remaining sugar over them and continue beating until stiff peaks are formed. Gently fold in the remaining sugar, the vanilla and the almonds.

5 Spoon the almond mixture into a pastry bag with a smooth nozzle. Line a flat baking sheet with baking parchment. Dust this with flour.

6 ▲ Pipe out the mixture in rounds the size of a walnut. Sprinkle lightly with the icing sugar, and allow to stand for 2 hours. Near the end of this time, turn the oven on again and preheat to 180°C/350°F/ gas 4.

7 Bake the amaretti for 15 minutes, or until pale gold. Remove from the oven and cool on a rack. When completely cool, the biscuits may be stored in an airtight container.

Jam Tart

Crostata di marmellata di frutta

Jam tarts are popular in northern Italy, traditionally decorated with pastry strips.

Ingredients
200 g/7 oz/$1^3/_4$ cups flour
pinch of salt
50 g/2 oz/$^1/_4$ cup granulated sugar
115 g/4 oz/$^1/_2$ cup butter or margarine, chilled
1 egg
$^1/_4$ tsp grated lemon zest
350 g/12 oz/$1^1/_4$ cups fruit jam, such as raspberry, apricot or strawberry
1 egg, lightly beaten with 30 ml/2 tbsp whipping cream, for glazing
serves 6–8

1 ▲ Make the pastry by placing the flour, salt and sugar in a mixing bowl. Using a pastry blender or two knives, cut the butter or margarine into the dry ingredients as quickly as possible until the mixture resembles coarse meal. Beat the egg with the lemon zest in a cup, and pour it over the flour mixture. Combine with a fork until the dough holds together. If it is too crumbly, mix in 15–30 ml/1–2 tbsp of water.

2 Gather the dough into 2 balls, one slightly larger than the other, and flatten into discs. Wrap in greaseproof or waxed paper, and refrigerate for at least 40 minutes.

3 Lightly grease a shallow 23 cm/9 in tart or pie pan, preferably with a removable bottom. Roll out the larger disc of pastry on a lightly floured surface to a thickness of about 3 mm/$^1/_8$ inch.

4 Roll the pastry around the rolling pin and transfer to the prepared pan. Trim the edges evenly with a small knife. Prick the bottom with a fork. Refrigerate for at least 30 minutes.

5 ▲ Preheat the oven to 190°C/375°F/ gas 5. Spread the jam evenly over the base of the pastry. Roll out the remaining pastry.

6 ▲ Cut the pastry into strips about 1 cm/$^1/_2$ inch wide using a ruler as a guide. Arrange them over the jam in a lattice pattern. Trim the edges of the strips even with the edge of the pan, pressing them lightly onto the pastry shell. Brush the pastry with the egg and cream glaze. Bake for about 35 minutes, or until the crust is golden brown. Allow to cool before serving.

Chocolate Nut Tart

Crostata di cioccolata con nocciole

This is a luxurious relative of the simple tart in the previous recipe.

Ingredients
200 g/7 oz/$1^{3}/_{4}$ cups flour
50 g/2 oz/$^{1}/_{4}$ cup granulated sugar
pinch of salt
115 g/4 oz/$^{1}/_{2}$ cup butter or margarine, chilled
1 egg
15 ml/1 tbsp Marsala
$^{1}/_{4}$ tsp grated lemon zest

For the filling
200 g/7 oz/$1^{3}/_{4}$ cups dry amaretti biscuits or 300 g/11 oz/2 cups home-made amaretti (see recipe)
100 g/31/2 oz/$^{3}/_{4}$ cup blanched almonds
50 g/2 oz/$^{1}/_{2}$ cup blanched hazelnuts
45 ml/3 tbsp sugar
200 g/7 oz plain cooking chocolate
45 ml/3 tbsp milk
50 g/2 oz/$^{1}/_{4}$ cup butter
3 tbsp liqueur, such as amaretto, or brandy
30 ml/2 tbsp single cream

serves 6–8

1 ▲ Make the pastry as for the Jam Tart, beating the Marsala with the egg and lemon zest, and mixing into the dry ingredients.

2 Lightly grease a shallow 26 cm/10 inch tart or pie pan, preferably with a removable bottom. Roll out the pastry on a lightly floured surface to a thickness of about 3mm/$^{1}/_{8}$ inch. Roll the pastry around the rolling pin and transfer to the prepared pan. Trim the edges evenly with a small knife. Prick the bottom with a fork. Refrigerate for at least 30 minutes.

3 Grind the amaretti to crumbs in a food processor. Remove to a mixing bowl. Set 8 whole almonds aside, and place the rest in the food processor bowl with the hazelnuts and sugar. Grind to a medium texture. Add the nuts to the amaretti, and mix well.

4 ▲ Preheat the oven to 190°C/375°F/gas 5. In a bowl set over a pan of simmering water, melt the chocolate with the milk and butter. Stir until smooth.

5 Pour the chocolate mixture into the ground amaretti and nuts, and mix well. Add the liqueur and cream.

6 ▲ Spread the chocolate and nut filling evenly in the pastry shell. Bake for about 35 minutes, or until the crust is golden brown and the filling has puffed up and is beginning to darken. Allow to cool to room temperature. Split the remaining almonds in half, and use them to decorate the tart.

Coffee Granita

Granita di caffè

A granita is a cross between a frozen drink and a flavoured ice. The consistency should be slushy, not solid. They can be made at home with the help of a food processor.

Ingredients
500 ml/16 fl oz/2 cups water
115 g/4 oz/$^1/_2$ cup granulated sugar
250 ml/8 fl oz/1 cup very strong espresso coffee, cooled
whipped cream, to garnish (optional)
serves 4–5

1 ▲ Heat the water and sugar together over low heat until the sugar dissolves. Bring to the boil. Remove from the heat and allow to cool.

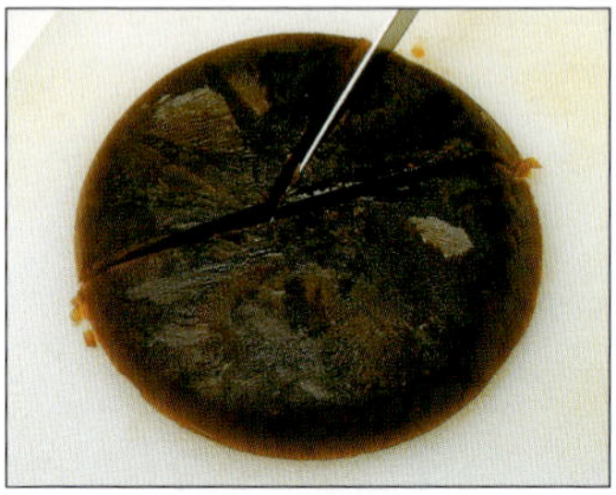

2 ▲ Combine the coffee with the sugar syrup. Place in a shallow container or freezer tray, and freeze until solid. Plunge the bottom of the frozen container or tray in very hot water for a few seconds. Turn the frozen mixture out, and chop it into large chunks.

3 ▲ Place the mixture in a food processor fitted with metal blades, and process until it forms small crystals. Spoon into serving glasses and top with whipped cream, if desired. If you do not want to serve the granita immediately, pour the processed mixture back into a shallow container or ice tray and freeze until serving time. Allow to thaw for a few minutes before serving, or process again.

Lemon Granita

Granita di limone

Nothing is more refreshing on a hot summer's day than a fresh lemon granita.

Ingredients
500 ml/16 fl oz/2 cups water
115 g/4 oz/$^1/_2$ cup granulated sugar
grated zest of 1 lemon, scrubbed before grating
juice of 2 large lemons
serves 4–5

1 Heat the water and sugar together over low heat until the sugar dissolves. Bring to the boil. Remove from the heat, and allow to cool.

2 Combine the lemon zest and juice with the sugar syrup. Place in a shallow container or freezer tray, and freeze until solid.

3 ▲ Plunge the bottom of the frozen container or tray in very hot water for a few seconds. Turn the frozen mixture out, and chop it into chunks.

4 ▲ Place the mixture in a food processor fitted with metal blades, and process until it forms small crystals. Spoon into serving glasses.

Custard Ice Cream

Gelato di crema

Italian ice creams are soft in consistency, and should not be over-sweet.

Ingredients
750 ml/24 fl oz/3½ cups milk
½ tsp grated lemon zest
6 egg yolks
150 g/5 oz/½ cup granulated sugar
makes about 850 ml/1½ pints/3¾ cups

1 To make the custard, heat the milk with the lemon zest in a small saucepan. Remove from the heat as soon as small bubbles start to form on the surface. Do not let it boil.

2 Beat the egg yolks with a wire whisk or electric beater. Gradually incorporate the sugar, and continue beating for about 5 minutes until the mixture is pale yellow. Strain the milk. Slowly beat it into the egg mixture drop by drop.

3 ▲ When all the milk has been added, pour the mixture into the top of a double boiler, or into a bowl placed over a pan of simmering water. Stir over moderate heat until the water in the pan is boiling, and the custard thickens enough to lightly coat the back of a spoon. Remove from the heat and allow to cool.

4 Freeze in an ice cream maker, following the manufacturer's instructions. The ice cream is ready when it is firm but still soft.

5 ▲ If you do not have an ice cream maker, pour the mixture into a metal or plastic freezer container and freeze until set, about 3 hours. Remove from the container and chop roughly into 7 cm/3in pieces. Place in the bowl of a food processor and process until smooth. Return to the freezer container, and freeze again until firm. Repeat the freezing-chopping process 2 or 3 times, until a smooth consistency is reached.

Chocolate Ice Cream

Gelato al cioccolato

Use good quality plain or cooking chocolate for the best flavour.

Ingredients
750 ml/ 24 fl oz/3½ cups milk
10 cm/4in piece of vanilla pod
225 g/8oz cooking chocolate, melted
4 egg yolks
150 g/5 oz/½ cup granulated sugar
makes about 850 ml/1½ pints/3¾ cups

1 Make the custard as for Custard Ice Cream, replacing the lemon with the vanilla.

2 Beat the egg yolks with a wire whisk or electric beater. Gradually incorporate the sugar, and continue beating for about 5 minutes until the mixture is pale yellow. Strain the milk. Slowly add it to the egg mixture drop by drop.

3 ▲ Pour the mixture into a double boiler with the melted chocolate. Stir over moderate heat until the water in the pan is boiling, and the custard thickens enough to lightly coat the back of a spoon. Remove from the heat and allow to cool.

4 ▲ Freeze in an ice cream maker, or follow step 5 of Custard Ice Cream, freezing and processing until a smooth consistency has been reached.

Hazelnut Ice Cream

Gelato di nocciola

This popular flavour goes very well with the chocolate and custard ice creams.

Ingredients

75 g/3 oz/$^1/_2$ cup hazelnuts
500 ml/16 fl oz/2 cups milk
10 cm/4 in piece vanilla bean
4 egg yolks
75 g/3 oz/6 tbsp granulated sugar
serves 4–6

1 Spread the hazelnuts out on a baking tray, and place under a grill for about 5 minutes, shaking the pan frequently to turn the nuts over. Remove from the heat and allow to cool slightly. Place the nuts on a clean dish towel, and rub them with the cloth to remove their dark outer skin. Chop very finely, or grind in a food processor with 30 ml/2 tbsp of the sugar.

2 Make the custard. Heat the milk with the vanilla pod in a small saucepan. Remove from the heat as soon as small bubbles start to form on the surface. Do not let it boil.

3 ▲ Beat the egg yolks with a wire whisk or electric beater. Gradually incorporate the sugar, and continue beating for about 5 minutes until the mixture is pale yellow. Add the milk very gradually, pouring it in through a strainer and discarding the vanilla pod. Stir constantly until all the milk has been added.

4 ▲ Pour the mixture into the top of a double boiler, or into a bowl placed over a pan of simmering water. Add the chopped nuts. Stir over moderate heat until the water in the pan is boiling, and the custard thickens enough to lightly coat the back of a spoon. Remove from the heat and allow to cool.

5 ▲ Freeze in an ice cream maker, or follow step 5 of Custard Ice Cream, freezing and processing until a smooth consistency has been reached.

INDEX

amaretti 244
peaches with amaretti stuffing 240
anchovies:
pizza with mozzarella and 156
potato pizza 178
apples:
baked with red wine 238
artichokes:
salad with eggs 70
stewed 46
stuffed 44
asparagus:
risotto with 127
sauce 114
with eggs 45
aubergine:
aubergine Parmesan 48
sweet and sour 48

bacon:
spaghetti with eggs and 91
spaghetti with onions and 92
baked beans 74
balsamic vinegar 9
barley and vegetable soup 36
basil:
mozzarella, tomato and basil salad 150
tomato and basil tart 177
beans 9
green beans with tomatoes 46
pasta and dried bean soup 38
and tuna salad 25
Tuscan baked 74
white bean soup 34
béchamel sauce 112
beef:
baked lasagne with meat sauce 112
Bolognese meat sauce 85
cannelloni stuffed with meat 120
carpaccio with rocket 26
herbed burgers 220
meat-stuffed cabbage rolls 52
meatballs 222
pizzaiola steak 220
stew with red wine 223
biscuits:
amaretti 244
sultana cornmeal 244
Bolognese meat sauce 85
borlotti beans:
and pasta soup 38
tuna pasta salad 25
and tuna salad 106
bread:
focaccia 170–2
grissini 174
tomato and bread salad 68
tomato and bread soup 32
with grapes 176
bread with grapes 176
broad beans:
purée with ham 54
and rice soup 36
broccoli:
with oil and garlic 50
and orecchiette 90
soup 32
bruschetta with tomato 178

cabbage:
meat-stuffed cabbage rolls 52
cakes:
lemon ricotta 240
calzones 168
cannellini beans:
baked 74
and pasta soup 38
tuna pasta salad 106
and tuna salad 25
white bean soup 34
cannelloni stuffed with meat 120
capers:
and olive sauce 94
pork fillet with caper sauce 228
carpaccio with rocket 26
carrots:
with Marsala 50
pork braised in milk with 226
cauliflower:
deep-fried 54
pasta with 92
caviar and vodka sauce 100
celery:
stuffed with Gorgonzola 16
cheese 10
aubergine Parmesan 48
baked eggs with 146
baked fennel with Parmesan 56
baked macaroni with 99
celery stuffed with Gorgonzola 16
cheese and tomato pizza 156
chicken with ham and 204
with crostini 18
egg and cheese soup 29
fried mozzarella 149
fried rice balls stuffed with 133
grilled cheese sandwiches 150
grilled polenta with Gorgonzola 132
ham and cheese veal escalops 214
pizza with four cheeses 160
pizza with mozzarella and anchovies 156
polenta baked with 133
risotto with Parmesan 124
stuffed pasta half-moons 119
tuna and mozzarella sauce 100
chestnuts:
pudding 237
sauce 212
chicken:
breasts cooked in butter 202
with ham and cheese 204
pasta salad 106
with peppers 202
roast with fennel 204
chickpeas:
and pasta soup 40
salad 72
chilli:
turkey cutlets with olives and 207
chocolate:
choux pastries with two custards 242
ice cream 250
nut tart 247
choux pastries with two custards 242
clam and tomato sauce 95
clams:
with crostini 19
seafood salad 20
seafood stew 190
stewed mussels and 182
cod:
baked with garlic mayonnaise 194
salt cod with parsley and garlic 198
coffee dessert 234
coffee granita 248
cold veal with tuna sauce 216
courgette:
grilled with radicchio 64
crostini:
with cheese 18
with mussels and clams 19
custard 242
ice cream 250
Italian 234

dips:
fonduta 148
olive oil 16
dried goods 9

duck:
- with chestnut sauce 212

eggs:
- artichoke salad with 70
- with asparagus 45
- baked with cheese 146
- baked with tomatoes 146
- and cheese soup 29
- egg noodles 78–9
- egg pasta 80–1
- frittata of leftover pasta 142
- frittata with onions 142
- frittata with spinach and ham 144
- frittata with sun-dried tomatoes 141
- Italian custard 234
- sliced frittata salad 145
- spaghetti with 91
- with tuna sauce 24

fennel:
- baked with Parmesan cheese 56
- grilled salmon steaks with 192
- and orange salad 71
- roast chicken with 204

fettuccine with ham and cream 110
figs with prosciutto 22
fish soup 35
focaccia 170
- with olives 172
- with onions 171
- with rosemary 172

folded pizza 168
fonduta with steamed vegetables 148
four seasons pizza 158
fresh sardines:
- fresh sardine sauce 98
- grilled 186

fried mozzarella 149
fried rice balls stuffed with cheese 136
frittata 141–5
- of leftover pasta 142
- with onions 142
- sliced frittata salad 145
- with spinach and ham 144
- with sun-dried tomatoes 141

fruit:
- salad 238
- *see also* apples, oranges etc

fusilli with peppers and onions 88

garlic:
- baked cod with garlic mayonnaise 194
- octopus with lemon and 192
- salt cod with parsley and 198

gnocchi:
- potato 137
- potato and spinach 138
- semolina 140

Gorgonzola cheese 10, 16, 132
granita:
- coffee 248
- lemon 248

grapes:
- bread with 176
- quail with 210

green beans with tomatoes 46
grissini 174

ham 10
- with broad bean purée 54
- and cheese veal escalops 214
- chicken with ham and cheese 204
- fettucine with ham and cream 110
- frittata with spinach and 144
- prosciutto with figs 22
- prosciutto with melon 23
- sautéed with peas 60
- stuffed onions 59
- timballo of rice with peas 134
- veal rolls with sage and 218

hand-made pasta 78–9
hazelnut ice cream 252
herbs 8
- focaccia with rosemary 172
- grilled prawns with 166
- grilled salmon steaks with fennel 192
- herbed burgers 220
- monkfish medallions with thyme 194
- pizza with 166
- roast lamb with 224
- salt cod with parsley and garlic 198
- veal rolls with sage and ham 218

ice cream:
- chocolate 250
- custard 250
- hazelnut 252

Italian custard 234
Italian trifle 236

jam tart 246
juniper berries:
- with roast pheasant 213

kitchen cupboard ingredients 9
kitchen equipment 11

lamb:
- roast with herbs 224
- stewed with tomatoes and garlic 224

lasagne:
- baked with meat sauce 112
- baked vegetable 116

lemon:
- granita 248
- octopus with lemon and garlic 192
- ricotta cake 240

lentils:
- and pasta soup 39
- stewed 75

linguine:
- with clam and tomato sauce 95
- with pesto sauce 84

liver:
- with onions 230

macaroni:
- baked with cheese 99

machine-made pasta 80
mascarpone cheese 10
mayonnaise:
- garlic 194

meat 10
- baked lasagne with meat sauce 112
- meat-stuffed cabbage rolls 52
- meat-stuffed cannelloni 120
- meatballs 222

Mediterranean pizza 162
Mediterranean turkey skewers 206
melon:
- with prosciutto 23

Milanese stewed shin of veal 217
Milanese veal chops 218
monkfish:
- medallions with thyme 194

mozzarella cheese 10
- mozzarella, tomato and basil salad 150
- pizza with mozzarella and anchovies 156
- and tuna sauce 100

mullet:
- red mullet with tomatoes and white wine 197

mushrooms:
- aromatic stewed 60
- polenta with 130
- porcini 9
- pork chops with 228
- risotto with 126
- roast mushroom caps 56

mussels:
- baked mussels and potatoes 184
- baked seafood spaghetti 104
- with crostini 19
- pizza with seafood 164
- seafood salad 20

seafood stew 190
with spaghetti 96
stewed mussels and clams 182
stuffed 28

nuts:
amaretti 244
chocolate nut tart 247
hazelnut ice cream 252
walnut sauce 86

octopus:
with lemon and garlic 192
olive oil 9
olive oil dip 16
olives 9
focaccia with 172
olive and caper sauce 94
pasta salad with 109
pizza with onions and 162
trout baked in paper with 191
turkey cutlets with olives and chilli 207
onions:
focaccia with 172
frittata with 142
liver with 230
pizza with olives and 162
spaghetti with bacon and 92
stuffed 59
oranges:
fennel and orange salad 71
orecchiette with broccoli 90

pancetta:
sautéed peas with ham 60
Parmesan cheese 10, 124
pasta 78–81
bows with prawns and peas 102
and chickpea soup 40
and dried bean soup 38
with fresh sardine sauce 98
and lentil soup 39
salad with olives 109
short pasta with cauliflower 92
short pasta with spring vegetables 102
stuffed half-moons 119
stuffing 67
types 12–13
verde 80
pastries:
chocolate nut tart 247
choux with two custards 242
jam tart 246
peaches:
baked with amaretti stuffing 240
peas:
pasta bows with shrimp and 102
sautéed with ham 60
timballo of rice with 134
Pecorino cheese 10
penne with tuna and mozzarella 100
peppers:
chicken with 202
with fusilli 88
grilled pepper salad 68
stewed 64
stuffed 62
tuna in rolled red peppers 26
pesto:
minestrone with pesto 30
pesto sauce with linguine 84
with tomatoes 22
pheasant:
roast with juniper berries 213
pizza:
cheese and tomato 156
dough 154–5
with four cheeses 160
four seasons 158
with fresh vegetables 159
with herbs 166
Mediterranean 162
with mozzarella and anchovies 156
with onions and olives 162
pizza pies 166
potato 178
with sausage 160
with seafood 164
pizzaiolo steak 220
polenta 128
baked with cheese 133
fried 128
grilled with Gorgonzola 132
with mushrooms 130
porcini 9
polenta with mushrooms 130
risotto with mushrooms 126
roast mushroom caps 56
pork:
braised in milk with carrots 226
chops with mushrooms 228
fillet with caper sauce 228
potatoes:
baked mussels and 184
baked with tomatoes 66
gnocchi 137
pizza 178
salad 72
and spinach gnocchi 138
poussin:
pan-fried marinated 210
prosciutto:
with figs 22
with melon 23
pumpkins:
soup 30
tortelli with pumpkin stuffing 118
prawns:
baked seafood spaghetti 104
deep-fried prawns and squid 188
grilled with herbs 182
pasta bows with 102
risotto with 124
seafood salad 20
seafood stew 190
in spicy tomato sauce 185

quail:
with grapes 210

rabbit:
with tomatoes 232
radicchio:
grilled with courgette 64
ravioli:
with ricotta and spinach 115
red mullet with tomatoes and white wine 197
rice 9
and broad bean soup 36
fried rice balls 136
timballo with peas 134
ricotta:
lemon ricotta cake 240
ravioli with spinach and 115
risotto:
with asparagus 127
with cheese 124
with mushrooms 126
with prawns 124
rocket:
carpaccio with 26
rosemary:
focaccia with 172

sage:
veal rolls with sage and ham 218
salads:
artichoke with eggs 70
chicken pasta 106
chickpea 72
fennel and orange 71
fruit salad 238
grilled pepper 68
mozzarella, tomato and basil 150
pasta with olives 109
potato 72
seafood 20
sliced frittata 145
tomato and bread 68
tuna and bean 25
tuna pasta 106
wholewheat pasta 108

salmon:
- grilled salmon steaks with fennel 192
- tagliatelle with smoked salmon 110

salt cod with parsley and garlic 198
sardines:
- fresh sardine sauce 98
- grilled fresh 186

sauces:
- asparagus 114
- bacon and onion 92
- béchamel 112
- Bolognese 85
- caper 228
- caviar and vodka 100
- cheese 148
- chestnut 212
- clam and tomato 95
- fish 35
- fonduta 148
- ham and cream 110
- meat 85, 112
- olive and caper 94
- pesto 84
- sardine 98
- sweet and sour 198
- tomato 82, 119, 145, 185, 196, 197, 220
- tuna 24, 216
- tuna and mozzarella 100
- walnut 86

sausages 10
- pizza with 160

scamorza cheese 10
sea bass:
- baked aromatic 186

seafood:
- baked seafood spaghetti 104
- pizza with 164
- salad 20
- stew 190

semolina gnocchi 140
Sicilian closed pizza 166
smoked salmon:
- with tagliatelle 110

sole:
- with sweet and sour sauce 198

soup:
- barley and vegetable 36
- broccoli 32
- egg and cheese 29
- fish 35
- minestrone with pesto 30
- pasta and chickpea 40
- pasta and dried bean 38
- pasta and lentil 39
- pumpkin 30
- rice and broad bean 36
- tomato and bread 32
- white bean 34

spaghetti:
- with bacon and onion 92
- baked with seafood 104
- with eggs and bacon 91
- with garlic and oil 86
- with mussels 96
- with olives and capers 94
- with walnut sauce 86

spaghettini with vodka and caviar 100
spicy tomato sauce 185
spinach:
- frittata with spinach and ham 144
- potato and spinach gnocchi 138
- ravioli with ricotta and 115

squid:
- deep-fried prawn and 188
- pizza with seafood 164
- seafood salad 20
- stuffed 188

stuffing:
- amaretti 240
- cheese 136
- pumpkin 118

sultana cornmeal cookies 244
sun-dried tomatoes:
- with courgettes 58
- frittata with 141
- Mediterranean pizza 162

sweet and sour aubergine 48
swordfish:
- stuffed swordfish rolls 196

tagliatelle with smoked salmon 110
tagliolini with asparagus 114
thyme:
- monkfish medallions with 194

timballo of rice with peas 134
tiramisù 234
tomato sauce 82, 95, 119, 145, 185, 196, 197, 220
tomatoes:
- and basil tart 177
- baked eggs with 146
- and bread salad 68
- and bread soup 32
- bruschetta with 178
- cheese and tomato pizza 156
- courgette with sun-dried 58
- frittata with sun-dried 141
- with green beans 46
- lamb stewed with 224
- Mediterranean pizza 162
- mozzarella, tomato and basil salad 150
- with pasta stuffing 67
- with pesto 22
- potatoes baked with 66
- rabbit with 232
- red mullet with 197

tortelli with pumpkin stuffing 118
trifle 236
trout:
- baked in paper with olives 191

tuna:
- and bean salad 25
- pasta salad 106
- in rolled red peppers 26

tuna sauce:
- cold veal with 216
- with eggs 24
- with mozzarella 100

turkey:
- cutlets with olives and chilli 207
- Mediterranean turkey skewers 206
- stuffed with lemon 208

Tuscan baked beans 74

veal:
- cold with tuna sauce 216
- escalops with Marsala 214
- ham and cheese escalops 214
- Milanese stewed shin of 217
- Milanese veal chops 218
- rolls with sage and ham 218

vegetables 8
- barley and vegetable soup 36
- fonduta with steamed 148
- lasagne 116
- with olive oil dip 16
- pizza with fresh 159
- sauce 102
- minestrone with pesto 30
- short pasta with 102
- wholewheat pasta salad 108

vodka and caviar sauce 100

walnut sauce 86
white bean soup 34
wholewheat pasta salad 108
wholewheat pizza dough 155

Notes

NOTES

Notes

NOTES

Notes

Notes

Notes

Notes